THE COMPLETE IDIOT'S GUIDE® TO

Sex on the Net

by James Anders, Ph.D.
Rachel Anders

que®

A Division of Macmillan Computer Publishing
201 W. 103rd Street, Indianapolis, IN 46290

The Complete Idiot's Guide to Sex on the Net

Copyright © *1999* by *Que*

International Standard Book Number: 0-7897-1798-0

Library of Congress Catalog Card Number: 98-86229

Printed in the United States of America

First Printing: *December 1998*

00 99 4 3 2 1

Trademarks

Executive Editor
Angela Wethington

Acquisitions Editor
Stephanie J. McComb

Development Editor
Robert Bogue

Managing Editor
Thomas F. Hayes

Project Editor
Tom Stevens

Copy Editor
Keith Cline

Technical Editor
Bill Bruns

Reviewer
Chip Rowe

Illustrator
Judd Winick

Indexer
Larry Sweazy

Proofreader
Megan Wade

Layout Technician
Christy M. Lemasters

Contents at a Glance

11. Amateur Sites
   Just what you've always dreamed about. Here's the girl next door—naked.

12. Of Interest to Women
   Believe it or not (we do), sex isn't just for men. These sites are designed with women in mind, but men will want to visit them, too.

13. Women with Women
   These photo and discussion sites feature women with women—a little something for the voyeur in all of us.

14. Fetishes: Sexual Special Interest Groups
   If there's one thing that turns you on more than anything else, look for it here. The Web and newsgroups are filled with what we refer to as "sexual special interest groups" for spanking, BD/SM, voyeurism, celebrity sex, and more.

15. Cartoons and Anime
   Ever wonder what Jessica Rabbit looks like naked? You're not alone.

16. Just for Laughs
   Under the right circumstances, sex can be a laugh riot. Here are dozens of funny, sexy Web sites for you to visit.

17. Special Interest Sites
   Check here to find out where you can get those bedroom photos developed; download sexy wallpaper, screen savers, and games; and send your lover an erotic (and usually free) electronic greeting card.

18. Multimedia: Lights, Camera, Action!
   Sex is often visual. Find out where you can download sexy video and audio clips, experience streaming video and audio, and participate in live sex sessions.

19. Erotica
   Erotica is sex with class, sex that sparks your imagination. Take a peek at some of the world's best erotic photography sites and erotic stories.

20. Spice Up Your Love Life
   Visit these commercial sites to buy sex toys, lotions, and potions.

21. Let's Play Dress Up
   Clothes make the man (or, in this case, the woman). Shop these Web sites for some of the world's sexiest lingerie, corsets, and fantasy wear.

Contents

Part 2: A Resource Guide to Sex Sites and Newsgroups

20 Spice Up Your Love Life   213

Foreword

As the advice columnist for *Playboy* magazine, I receive hundreds of letters and email messages from readers each month asking about all varieties of sexual topics. Many of these letters are from men, women, and couples who want to know more about how to find the sexiest material online, including erotic stories, hot chat, explicit Web sites, and live sex. I do my best to provide guidance, but as anyone who has surfed for sex knows, it's difficult to distinguish the good from the bad and ugly in the vast expanse of cyberspace.

This book is a step in the right direction. Its authors spent hours searching for sexy sites and chat areas and then, without much prodding, returned to ferret out more. No guide to the Internet can be complete, simply because the digital world moves so quickly. But the chapters that follow provide the basics to get you started, including the software you'll need, simple instructions to exchange information and navigate online, and tips on protecting your privacy and shielding children from adult material. Most of the sites that the authors bookmarked and reviewed are designed to appeal to men, but many chapters include pointers and information that will be of interest to women and couples, as well.

As you probably know, online sex has been under attack. Some parents and politicians believe it should be tightly regulated. Others argue that laws to restrict adult material online violate the First Amendment. As you will see, attempting to control sexual expression, especially in cyberspace, is impractical. Never before has sex been so openly discussed and exposed, which is a good thing. The Internet has done wonders to educate and bring people together. Look no further than the tantilizing lists of sites at directories such as Yahoo! Adults who enjoy erotic stories, naughty fantasies, slow sex, fast sex, upside-down sex—these are the everyday folks who come online to upload their secrets. People who find themselves attracted to feet, belly buttons, or inflatable pool toys use the Net to find each another, to commune, to assure themselves that the rest of us are oddballs with our mass-market desire for the missionary position after the late news. Perhaps they're right. We all have sexual peccadilloes; most of us just haven't discovered them yet. Rest assured, if more than one person shares your fetish, someday a Web page will exist to celebrate it (perhaps you'll create it).

Sex online brings people together, but more important, it gives them a stage on which to share their experiences. In writing my column, I find that my readers are often the best teachers. Many times someone will respond to a letter we've printed and say, "Here's what happened to me." People exchange recipes, gossip, jokes, handyman tips, computer game cheats, and all sorts of life skills—why not what they've learned about sex? The Internet allows for that, both by letting people communicate instantly from great distances and by providing anonymity. The most common question I receive is a simple one, "Am I normal?" In a few short years, the Net has created a way for millions of people to respond with a resounding "Yes!" Many adults are just now, because of cyberspace, starting to explore their fantasies and boundaries without judgment. Where else can a woman so easily and safely take control of sex as in a chat room of submissive men? In what other venue can a man discover that a redhead wearing blue overalls drenched in yellow mustard zaps his Id just the right way? An entire shopping mall's worth of sex shops provide discreet online ordering, allowing couples to buy kinky toys, books, and videos that aren't readily available in many communities. That alone makes the Net worthwhile. Better sex through technology!

Before you jump in to learn more about sex online, keep in mind what you won't find. No matter what sort of "you-are-there" gizmos they invent in the next millennium, the Internet will never reproduce the skin-against-skin contact that makes us human and keeps us horny. Heed the words of the online pioneer j@sin, who compiled a list of things he refuses to do in cyberspace. One is sex. "I want to feel the moisture and the sweat, I want to hear the squishes, I want to smell that funky odor," he writes. "When the deed is done, I want it to be because I ran out of steam, not because the batteries are getting low." Sex online is no substitute for the real thing, but it can point you in the right direction. Use it as a tool to explore and expand your sexuality. Just don't allow that pulsating monitor to become the whole of your sex life, or your life.

Chip Rowe, The *Playboy* Advisor

About the Authors

James Anders, Ph.D., is a psychologist and the author of several dozen computer books. He has been an Internet fanatic for many years and regularly visits chat sites. Sex has always been a special interest of James's, but his interest is personal, not professional.

Rachel Anders provides the woman's perspective on Internet sex. When you come across sites in this book that don't make you go "Ewwwww...," it is probably one that she found. Her well-honed Web research skills are responsible for the huge number of classy—yet sexy—sites in these pages.

Note: Neither of the authors are sex professionals nor are they in any way allied with the sex field—proving conclusively that this *is* something you can try at home.

Acknowledgments

Of all the books I have written, this one required more preparation and research than any other. In addition to the hundreds of Web sites we chose (culled from the thousands we visited), several of our chat friends made suggestions:

➤ Kayleen, Lee Ann, and Candi kept me entertained and focused on the task at hand.

➤ Jen contributed several sexual humor sites—inadvertently. She didn't *know* she was making a contribution when she sent them.

➤ Scott, Richard, and Michael provided useful URLs, company, and amusement.

A special thanks to *Playboy* Advisor, Chip Rowe, for writing the foreword and reviewing the manuscript, and to Richard Burry, Miss Antoinette, and all the other kind souls for providing us with an insider's view of the Internet sex industry.

We also want to thank the many Web site owners who graciously allowed us to publish pictures from their sites, as well as to those who kindly gave us complimentary subscriptions so that we could see and describe exactly what their sites had to offer.

Last—but certainly not least—we are extremely grateful to Matt Wagner of Waterside Productions for giving us the opportunity to do this title, to Stephanie McComb (Macmillan Computer Publishing), and Robert Bogue (Thor Projects) for their gentle, yet skillful, editorial direction.

Tell Us What You Think!

As the reader of this book, *you* are our most important critic and commentator. We value your opinion and want to know what we're doing right, what we could do better, what areas you'd like to see us publish in, and any other words of wisdom you're willing to pass our way.

As the Executive Editor for the General Desktop Applications team at Macmillan Computer Publishing, I welcome your comments. You can fax, email, or write me directly to let me know what you did or didn't like about this book—as well as what we can do to make our books stronger.

Please note that I cannot help you with technical problems related to the topic of this book, and that due to the high volume of mail I receive, I might not be able to reply to every message.

When you write, please be sure to include this book's title and authors as well as your name and phone or fax number. I will carefully review your comments and share them with the authors and editors who worked on the book.

Fax: 317-581-4663

Email: **internet@mcp.com**

Mail: Angela Wethington
          Executive Editor
          General Desktop Applications
          Macmillan Computer Publishing
          201 West 103rd Street
          Indianapolis, IN 46290 USA

Introduction

I have always wanted to write a computer book with nudity in it. Somehow, however, my editors failed to grasp what breasts had to do with a Quicken book. Therefore, writing *The Complete Idiot's Guide to Sex on the Net* has enabled me to fulfill a long-held dream—a twisted one in some people's eyes, but a dream nonetheless.
—James Anders, Ph.D.

Anything for a buck. —Rachel Anders

About This Book

Every person has different personality traits, physical characteristics, skills, aptitudes, and interests. The majority of us do have one thing in common, however: We all love *sex*!

In the "good old days," we fed our sexual appetites by renting movies and buying glossy magazines—frequently with considerable embarrassment, although we shouldn't feel embarrassed by our natural interest in sex. Today, the Internet has changed all that. With an Internet account now costing less than a cable TV subscription, we can get an infinite amount of sexual information and stimulation in the privacy of our homes.

The purpose of this book is to help you find the most interesting sexual content on the Internet in all its forms, whether your interest is in pictures, video clips, audio clips, sexual techniques and safer sex information, or flirtatious or explicit chat sites. With the help of this book, you can experience the wild world of Internet sex.

If you'd like to contact the authors with suggestions or comments, you can reach them at **cigsex@hotmail.com**.

How Is This Book Organized?

The book is divided into three parts. Part 1, "Essential Tools," tells you about the hardware (computer and accessories) and software (computer programs and Web browser plug-ins) that you will need to experience sex on the Net. Not surprisingly, these same tools are essential for experiencing *anything* on the Internet, so they will come in handy. Those of you who have some experience on the Net will find the information about the latest technologies particularly useful.

When you are ready to start surfing for sex, turn to Part 2, "A Resource Guide to Sex Sites and Newsgroups," for our recommendations. Part 2 has descriptions and addresses (URLs) for many, many sex Web sites and newsgroups.

Over a period of several months, the vivacious Rachel and I handpicked sites that contain the best pictures, video, and audio on the Internet. (As you can imagine, we had a lot of fun putting this book together.) Although commercial sex sites overwhelmingly outnumber free ones, you will find that many of our select sites have excellent samples or provide free trial accounts.

Uniform Compliance

"When authorities warn you of the sinfulness of sex, there is an important lesson to be learned. Do not have sex with the authorities."

—Matt Groening, from "Basic Sex Facts for Today's Youngfolk," *Life in Hell*

Part 3, "Chat," is a guide to chat (one-on-one or group discussions that occur in real-time, like a phone call). Read these chapters to find out how the process of chat works, what you can expect to find there, and the software that you will need.

The book concludes with a glossary that explains the meaning of the Internet, computer, and sexual terms used in this book that may not be familiar to you.

So How Do I Use the Book?

Far be it from us to tell you how to read this or any other book. On the other hand, a little gentle guidance never hurt, right?

The Good, the Bad, and the Ugly

"Documentation is like sex: When it is good, it is very, very good; and when it is bad, it is better than nothing."

—Dick Brandon

Unless you have purchased this book just for its Web site recommendations, you should start by reading Chapter 1. In it, you learn about the hardware and software necessary to connect to the Internet, the types of sexual content you can find, and the software tools you need to view, save, and otherwise deal with this stuff. Because the Internet's main source of sexual goodies is the World Wide Web, you should also read Chapter 2 to learn how to use a Web browser. (Even if you are already familiar with a browser, you'll find several browsing tips and tricks that can come in handy.)

Chapters 3–5 can be read on an as-needed basis. When you want to learn about sending and receiving pictures through your email program, for example, you can turn to Chapter 4 for instructions.

Chapters 6–8 are not essential reading, but you'll find them helpful when searching for new sex sites (Chapter 6), trying to prevent your minors from viewing sex sites, protecting your privacy (Chapter 7), and learning the differences between free and commercial sex sites (Chapter 8).

When you are ready to explore the Web sites or newsgroups, flip to Part 2. Because the chapters are arranged according to sexual topic, you can jump right to any topic that piques your interest or curiosity. Each chapter highlights dozens of Web sites.

Finally, when the time comes to dive into the world of chat, you can rely on Part 3 for everything you need to know. Chapters 17 and 18 deal with the process of chat (the mechanics of using a chat program, what actually happens in chat, how to chat "correctly," and some dangers you should know about). Chapters 19–21 discuss specific chat programs and environments that you might want to try out.

Conventions Used in This Book

As you're reading this book you'll notice a few special conventions used throughout this book. Anything that is typed, pressed, selected, or chosen appears in **bold**. You'll also notice the following types of special note boxes:

Techno Talk

These are technical notes. They tell you things that you don't need to know to find sex on the Internet but might want to know.

Check This Out

These are special tips and tricks, or a special way of finding things.

Sex Quote

In this box, you'll find quotes from famous or infamous people about sex.

Some Important Warnings

Just so you don't think this is all fun and games (even if most of it *is*), consider the following important points while surfing for sex on the Internet.

➤ **Web page addresses may change** The Internet is constantly evolving. Between the time this paragraph was written and this moment, millions of Web sites have appeared, and others have disappeared. This may include some sites mentioned in this book. If you type an address into your Web browser and get an error message (such as 404 not found. The requested URL was not found on this server.), try the following things before you give up:

  ➤ Check the spelling and capitalization of the address, and make sure that you are typing forward slashes (/) rather than backslashes (\). A single mistake in a Web page address is equivalent to dialing a wrong digit in a phone number. It won't work.

  ➤ If a server is busy, you will occasionally get an error message. Wait a couple of minutes, and then try the same address again. (With the address shown in the browser's Address or Location box, press Return or Enter to retry the address.)

  ➤ In some cases, a Web page may have been renamed. Back up to the parent directory by stripping off everything to the right of the final slash in the address. Keep stripping until you find a partial address that works. Suppose, for example, that the address is **http://www.sexsite.com/chat/list.html**. Try typing **http://www.sexsite.com/chat/** or **http://www.sexsite.com**. If either of these partial addresses works, you may find a new link from there to the desired page.

  ➤ If a page or graphic partially loads and then stops, click the browser's Refresh or Reload button. (If that fails, try holding down the Ctrl key on your keyboard as you click the Refresh or Reload button.)

➤ **This book has something for everyone** Sexual tastes vary widely. Although some of the material in the sites chosen for this book does not appeal to Rachel or me personally, we assume that it *will* appeal to some of our readers.

➤ **A little nudity goes a long way** To give you some idea of the types of images you can find on the Web, many chapters are illustrated with R-rated images, borrowed (with permission) from sex sites. These photos do not represent all the photos that appear on the site; most sex sites offer explicit X-rated photos of, well, people having sex. This book and the sites discussed in it are for adults only.

Part 1
Essential Tools

These introductory chapters tell you all about the types of sexual content and activities available to Internet users, as well as the software tools you need to access or participate in them—a Web browser, email program, newsgroup reader, chat programs, picture viewers and editors, and archive creation and extraction utilities.

You also find helpful instructions on using search engines to find topics of interest on the World Wide Web and in newsgroups, software and methods for protecting your privacy and keeping your children safe on the Internet, a discussion of free versus membership sex sites, and basic information and instructions for America Online users.

Chapter 1

Sexual Content on the Net: What's out There, Where Can I Find It, and What Software Do I Need?

> **In This Chapter**
>
> ➤ Getting connected to the Internet
>
> ➤ Obtaining and learning about essential Internet programs
>
> ➤ Finding and dealing with sexual content on the Net

This chapter introduces you to the hardware and software you need to get at all the sex that the Internet has to offer. The end of this chapter ("Dealing with Content on the Internet: Different Strokes for Different Folks") explains where on the Internet you can find the different types of content and the software you need.

Getting Connected: Recommended Hardware and Software

If you just bought your computer, it probably came with much of the hardware and software necessary to connect to the Internet. As part of the system software (Windows 95 or 98 for a PC, OS 8.1 for a Macintosh), new computers typically include a dialer utility, a Web browser for viewing pages on the World Wide Web, and an electronic mail program for sending and receiving messages (*email*). It may also have a hardware device called a *modem* that enables your computer to communicate with other computers over ordinary telephone lines. At a minimum, you need the appropriate software and a modem to connect to the Internet.

This chapter discusses the hardware and software you need (or want) to make your Internet experience as erotic as possible. Note, however, that the software coverage in this chapter is meant only as an introduction. Chapters 2–7 and 25–27 contain detailed discussions of these programs.

Keep It Private

"It doesn't make any difference what you do in the bedroom as long as you don't do it in the street and frighten the horses."

—Mrs. Patrick Campbell

Essential Hardware

The only equipment you absolutely *must* have is a computer and a means of connecting to the Internet. Although you might be using a UNIX workstation, we will assume that most of you have either a Windows PC or a Macintosh—or are currently contemplating the purchase of one or the other.

Connecting from a Network

If you are connecting at work or college, a word of caution: Many employers and schools have Internet usage policies that preclude the use of their computers to surf for sexually explicit material. (They own the computers; they can dictate how they're used.) Some companies monitor their employees' use of the Internet or email without letting them know. It's better to surf for adult material from the privacy of your own home computer.

In addition to a computer, you must have a modem and an account with an *Internet service provider* (ISP) or an online service, such as America Online.

A *modem* is a hardware device that enables your computer to send and receive data. Modems can be *external* (a small box that sits on your desk and is connected to your computer's serial port) or *internal* (a card installed inside your computer). Either type is fine. Most modems transmit and receive data over a telephone line. Your modem may connect over the same coaxial cable that brings cable television into your house, however. And if you are on a company or university network, your computer may not even *have* a modem, yet you still may have Internet access via the network. Check with your network administrator for connection details.

Need for Speed

When deciding what type of modem to buy (if you don't already have one), just keep one simple fact in mind. Where the Internet is concerned, faster is better. Speed is good! Although your old 2400bps modem may have been great in its day, it will never do for the Internet. And although you might get away with using an old 9600 or 14400bps modem, it will be agonizingly slow for Web surfing, video chat, or audio chat. Today, your best bet is a 33.6Kbps or 56Kbps modem. Be sure to contact your ISP to find out the highest speed they support. (If you can afford it, a cable modem is even better.)

Even if you already have a modem, you also need some way to connect to the Internet—that is, you need an account with an ISP or an online service. Although you can use other methods, the most common connection methods are as follows:

➤ An account with a local or nationwide ISP. (Some long-distance carriers and local phone companies also offer Internet access.)

➤ An account with an information service, such as America Online.

➤ An account through your university or place of employment.

After your Internet account has been set up (Windows and Macintosh OS 8.1 include a "wizard" program that walks you through the process) and the dialer software on your computer is properly configured—Dial-Up Networking (PC) and PPP or FreePPP (Macintosh) are common dialers—you are ready to roam the Internet.

At the start of each session, you use the dialer program to connect to your ISP, information service, or network. After the logon process finishes, you can run any (or all) of your Internet applications. If your computer has sufficient memory, for example, you can open your email program, run a browser session, and chat—all at the same time. (You may not want to try this without the proper safety gear.)

Optional Hardware

If you intend to stick primarily to Web surfing, reading newsgroups, and text chat, you don't need to add any new hardware to your system. For video and audio chats, however, you might want to consider buying these optional components:

America Online Is Different

America Online (AOL) has its own dialer program that you use to connect to it and to the Internet. See Chapter 9, "Sex and America Online," for more information about AOL.

➤ **Microphone** PC microphones are an inexpensive addition, usually costing less than $20. If you want to have private conversations, consider buying a headset that combines both microphone and speakers.

➤ **Desktop video camera** With a desktop video camera (or a camera and video capture card), you can engage in one-on-one or group video chats. Although you don't need a camera to just watch others on the Internet or to view video, you do need one if you want to join in. Many desktop video cameras can now be purchased for around $100. (Although you can still *watch* video chats, if you aren't broadcasting video of your own, you are referred to as a *lurker*. Lurkers are forbidden—or at least frowned on—in many video chats.) If you don't play, you can't stay.

Mac Mics

Most Macintosh computers require a special microphone—unless its manual says otherwise. They use a *PlainTalk microphone*, which is somewhat more costly than your run-of-the-mill PC mic ($30–$35). If you can't find a PlainTalk microphone at your local computer store, try a Macintosh mail-order company, such as MacConnection (800-800-2222) or MacMall (800-222-2808).

Which Is Better: PC or Macintosh?

For most Internet activities, the choice between systems is a toss up. Web browsing, downloading pictures, and reading newsgroups can easily be done with either type of computer. The only areas in which I have noticed a major difference between the systems are in the availability of chat software and ISP support.

The Availability of Chat Software

Many of the better server-based chat programs are for Windows only. And *IRC* (Internet Relay Chat) applications for the Macintosh are crude compared to their PC counterparts. If you suspect that chat will be a major part of your Internet experience and you will be relying on separate applications to chat (instead of using the built-in chat features of America Online or visiting browser-based chat sites), be sure to find out whether the necessary chat programs also come in a Macintosh version. See Part 3 of this book for information concerning the supported platforms for many of the most popular chat programs.

Win 3.1 Doesn't Cut It

Even if you are a card-carrying member of the PC set, you may occasionally find that you are out of luck where some chat programs are concerned. Although Windows 95 and Windows 98 users can run Windows 3.1 programs, the reverse is not true. If you are a Windows 3.1 user and find yourself left out in the cold, consider upgrading to Windows 95 or 98.

ISP Support

If you live in a big city or intend to use either America Online or a national ISP to connect to the Internet, you will generally find that both PCs and Macintosh computers are supported. If you live in an area where ISPs are rare, however, you may discover that the Macintosh gets short shrift or no support at all. A similar situation may exist if you want to connect to the Net via your local cable company and a cable modem.

If you have a PC, this problem does not exist. If you own a Macintosh, you should find out the level of Macintosh support offered prior to signing up with *any* ISP.

Do It Yourself, Mac

Even if your local ISP doesn't know diddly about Macintosh computers, you can always configure your dialer program and Internet software yourself. So long as the ISP doesn't require special PC-only hardware, a modem is a modem and a computer is a computer. That is, after you have successfully dialed in, the computers at the ISP's office could care less whether you are working on a Macintosh or a PC. (If you've seen one data bit, you've seen them all.)

Internet Software

One of the great things about the Internet is that most of the software you need *for* the Internet can be downloaded for free *from* the Internet. Depending on your interests, you will probably want to try out many of the programs discussed in this chapter.

Web Browsers

You use a *browser* to view pages on the World Wide Web. Because the Web is the primary source of erotic photos, movies, audio clips, and so on, you will definitely want to install a browser. On both Macintosh computers and PCs, the most widely used browsers are Internet Explorer (**http://www.microsoft.com/ie/download**) and Netscape Navigator (**http://www.netscape.com/computing/download**). On newer computers, you will probably find that one of these browsers has already been installed for you.

Which browser you use is a matter of personal preference. Because the browser wars between Netscape and Microsoft have been in full swing for several years now, both companies have been forced into playing a constant game of catch-up, matching each other feature for feature. Unless you are already familiar with one browser (from having used it at work or school, for instance), it may be just as simple to stick with whatever browser is pre-installed on your new computer.

Freeware, Shareware, and Demos

You can download three classes of software for free from the Internet. *Freeware* refers to fully functioning programs that generally come with no strings attached. If you redistribute the program, however, it must be in exactly the same form as it was when you got it—with all supporting documentation and files.

Shareware refers to "try before you buy" software. A shareware program may have some key features disabled, such as saving or printing. If you decide to keep a shareware program, you are expected to send the author a requested fee. If the program has been "crippled," you will either receive a password to turn it into a fully functioning program or a new copy of the program.

Demos are crippled or stripped down (lite) versions of commercial programs. Their intent is to give you a taste of a program to encourage you to buy the full version—either from a computer store, the manufacturer, or over the Internet.

Note that you can also buy many common *commercial programs* over the Internet. Depending on the publisher, you may be able to download the entire program and documentation or place an order that will be shipped to you. You can also get updates of many commercial programs the same way.

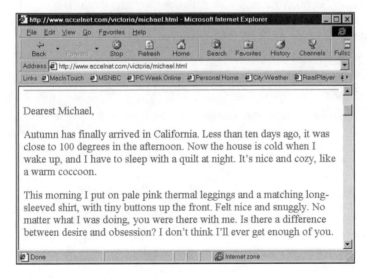

Using a browser like Internet Explorer, you can download pictures and read erotic stories from all over the world.

15

Plug-Ins and ActiveX Components

Current versions of Netscape and Internet Explorer have many built-in features that enable them to do more than just view text and graphics. Browser add-on software called *plug-ins* and *ActiveX components* enable your browser to do other tasks, such as play video and audio. You can choose from a slew of ActiveX components at **http://www.download.com/PC/Activex/** and Netscape plug-ins at **http://home.netscape.com/plugins/**.

Email Programs

An *email* (short for *electronic mail*) program enables you to exchange messages and files of any sort with anyone who has an Internet account. Although there is no direct connection with sex-related material, you can use email to exchange pictures and sound files with chat friends or to maintain a running sex dialog with a Net lover. You can also join sex-related email mailing lists, such as dirty joke lists. New material from a mailing list can be delivered automatically to you each time you fire up your email program at the start of the day.

Internet Explorer and Netscape both come with an email program (Outlook Express and Netscape Mail, respectively). You may find it easier to begin exploring the world of email using these built-in programs, because they are integrated with your browser. You can always switch later if you find an email program with a more impressive feature set or that you think will be easier to use.

Newsgroup Readers

A *newsgroup* is a message-based discussion group organized around a particular topic, such as current novels, car repair, or erotic photos. Currently, you can join more than 30,000 newsgroups (called *subscribing*, even though there is no charge to join a newsgroup).

To read messages that have been submitted to a newsgroup or to make your own contributions, you need a program called a *newsgroup reader*. Netscape and Internet Explorer both include a newsgroup reader (Netscape News and Outlook Express, respectively). Many of the current newsgroup readers enable you to view attachments to messages, such as pictures, from within the program. Older newsgroup readers often required you to run yet another program to see graphic images.

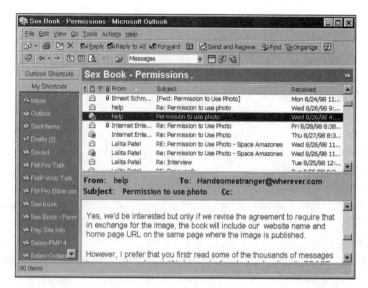

Email is an excellent medium for keeping in touch with friends and conducting business. Delivery is fast, it's relatively reliable, and you don't face nasty long-distance charges at the end of each month.

As with email programs, you can later switch to a standalone newsgroup reader if you prefer its features. Free Agent (**http://www.forteinc.com/agent/freagent.htm**) is a popular newsgroup reader for the PC, for example. If you have a Macintosh, you can use the newsgroup reader built in to Microsoft's Outlook Express (**http://www.microsoft.com/mac/ie/macoe.htm**) or Netscape Navigator (**http://www.netscape.com/download/**).

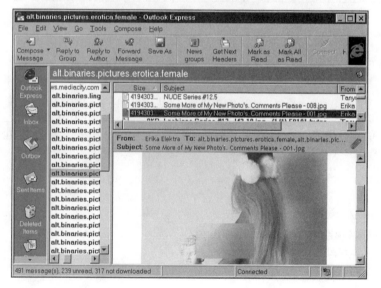

Many current newsgroup readers, such as Outlook Express, enable you to view and save image attachments without having to run a separate program.

Chat Programs

Simply put, *chat* refers to real-time one-on-one or group conversations with other people on the Internet. After typing a comment and pressing **Return** (or clicking a **Send** button), whatever you have typed is sent over the Internet and displayed on the other chatters' screens. As in any conversation, you can contribute as much or as little as you like.

The simplest way to find out about chatting is to join some Web-based chats (see Chapter 25). These chats take place inside your Web browser, so you won't need to download and set up any new software.

Later, you may also want to try out some of the dedicated chat programs (see Chapters 25–27). These programs enable you to participate in chats that you cannot join with just a Web browser. Advantages of using dedicated chat programs can include the following:

➤ More advanced features, such as audio support, video support, and the ability to represent yourself as a 3D figure or cartoon character (known as an avatar)

➤ Greater likelihood of finding friends you have talked to during previous chat sessions

➤ Improved speed over Web-based chats

Picture Viewers and Graphic Editors

Although a Web browser is fine for taking a quick look at most pictures, it lacks the features of a dedicated graphics program or picture viewer. You cannot enlarge a picture in your browser, nor can you change it in any way. For that reason, a good graphics program—enabling you to enlarge pictures, reduce the size of pictures that are larger than your monitor, and change the contrast and brightness—can be indispensable.

Regardless of whether you have a PC or a Macintosh, a lot of graphics programs will do the trick. The main criterion is that the program must be able to open JPEG and GIF files. Although Adobe Photoshop is the standard for graphic editing professionals, it's too expensive for just viewing pictures. The following are some inexpensive (or free) programs you might want to consider:

For the PC

➤ LView Pro (**http://www.lview.com**)

➤ Paint Shop Pro (**http://www.pspro.ml.org/**)

For the Macintosh

Go to **http://www.zdnet.com/mac/download.html** and search for these programs:

➤ JPEGView
➤ PICTshow
➤ ImageViewer

Unzip/Unstuff Utilities

Occasionally, you find that the files you want to download have been converted to *archives* (compressed to reduce transmission time or to enable several related files to be transmitted together). PC files are generally archived as *zip* files; the archive name ends with a .zip file extension, such as *photos.zip*. Macintosh files are typically "stuffed" with a program called StuffIt Deluxe from Aladdin Systems. In addition, they are often changed to BinHex format and are named with an .hqx extension, such as *photos.sit.hqx*. The .sit (or .sea—for *self-extracting* archive) shows that the files have been stuffed; the .hqx shows that they have been converted to BinHex format after they were stuffed.

To extract files from an archive, you need a special utility program. On a PC, you want the shareware program WinZip from Niko Mak Computing (**http://www.winzip.com**) or a similar unzipping program. If you have a Macintosh, you need StuffIt Deluxe or StuffIt Expander (**http://www.aladdinsys.com**). To learn more about these utilities, see Chapter 5.

There Are Macintosh BIN Files, Too

Because changing a file or archive to BinHex (.hqx) format can substantially increase its size, you also find smaller versions of these files and archives that end with .bin. These are Macintosh binary files, also called *MacBinary*. To convert them to normal files, you can use StuffIt Deluxe or StuffIt Expander.

Macintosh Versus PC Files

Every file that you download—whether it's a picture, text file, or word processing document—was created on a particular type of computer. Regardless of whether that computer was a Macintosh or a PC, you can open and view most file types on either platform.

To make it easy to deal with archives on both PCs and Macintosh computers, certain utilities enable you to expand the other platform's archives on your computer. To open .zip archives on a Macintosh, you can use ZipIt (**http://www.awa.com/softlock/zipit/zipit.html**) or DropStuff with Expander Enhancer (**http://www.aladdinsys.com/dropstuff/**). To open Macintosh StuffIt archives on a PC, you can use Aladdin Expander for Windows (**http://www.aladdinsys.com/expander/**).

Note, however, that *computer programs* are always platform-specific. If you intend to run a particular application on a Macintosh, you must download a version created specifically for Macintosh computers.

Dealing with Content on the Internet: Different Strokes for Different Folks

As you have undoubtedly heard (or may have witnessed), the Internet hosts a lot of sexual material. Although it can be found in many forms, it can be divided into two broad classes according to the number of people involved:

➤ **Solo** Material you can view or listen to alone, such as pictures, erotic stories, movie clips, and audio clips

➤ **Two or more participants** Situations in which you communicate with others on the Internet, such as exchanging erotic notes and pictures via email, text chat, audio chat, video chat, and live video broadcasts in which you direct the action

Regardless of the type of sexual material or interaction you are seeking, you will find three significant sources of sex on the Internet: the World Wide Web, newsgroups, and chat programs. This section covers the different types of sexual content that is available, where on the Internet you can find it, and the software that you need to access it.

Hot Pics

When asked what the phrase "Internet sex" brings to mind, most people immediately think of sexy photos (commonly referred to as *pics*). So who is appearing nude on the Net these days? You can find everyone from professional models to rank amateurs. Poses may be solo, couples, or in groups; these poses range from erotic figure studies to raw, uninhibited sex—something for everyone, regardless of your taste (or fetishes).

Where Can I Find Hot Pics?

Sexual images are readily found on Web sites and in select newsgroups, such as the 150 or so **alt.binaries.pictures.erotica** newsgroups.

Popular File Formats

Photos that you find on Web pages or that you can download from Web sites and newsgroups are generally in *JPEG* (Joint Photographic Experts Group) format. *GIF* (Graphic Interchange Format) is another popular format for Web graphics. Although the GIF format is seldom used to display photographs, you will see it used for cartoons and erotic artwork.

That's the Emperor?

"Clothes make the man. Naked people have little or no influence on society."

—Mark Twain

Necessary Software

In addition to using your browser to view and download pictures, you can use either Internet Explorer or Netscape Navigator to look at JPEG and GIF pictures that you have stored on your hard disk. To view a particular picture, choose the **Open** or **Open File** command from the File menu, and then navigate to the drive and folder where the picture was saved.

If you want to check out some of the picture-oriented newsgroups, you need a newsgroup reader, such as Netscape News, Netscape Collabra, Outlook Express, or Free Agent.

If you need to manipulate any of the pictures you have downloaded (resizing images, correcting the contrast, or changing the amount of file compression, for instance), you should obtain a graphics editing program, such as the ones discussed in this chapter. Also, because pictures are occasionally grouped together in archives (so they can all be downloaded with a single command), you should also get a copy of a program that can expand archives, changing the contents back into a series of normal files (see "Unzip/Unstuff Utilities" earlier in this chapter).

Erotic Stories to Tickle Your Fancy

Erotic stories (covered in Chapter 19) are a turn-on for many people. Because they require us to use our imagination to picture the events as they unfold, the effects of such stories can be very powerful.

Imagine That!

Joan: Oh look! Mother's diary! It's slightly torrid!

—*Mr. Blandings Builds His Dream House*, 1948

Erotic stories on the Internet run the gamut from romantic tales to stories that push the boundaries of taste and decency. Accomplished, professional writers contribute some stories; others represent real-life encounters and fantasies of ordinary folk. You can also find the full text of classic erotic books, such as *Fanny Hill* and *Lady Chatterley's Lover*.

Where Can I Find Erotic Stories?

You can find erotic stories on many free and commercial Web sites. In fact, erotic stories are frequently used as teasers or giveaways to entice new users into paying for site memberships.

A Tad Too Crude?

Depending on your sexual tastes, you may have to do quite a bit of hunting before finding stories that appeal to you. Some erotic stories focus on activities such as rough sex, group scenes, or acts that you might find distasteful. If your interests run to the softer side, begin your search at women's erotica sites. Chapter 12, "Of Interest to Women," provides some examples.

Some newsgroups devote themselves entirely to erotic stories (**alt.sex.stories**, for example). If you have never explored the newsgroups before, this may be the excuse you've been waiting for.

Popular File Formats

Most erotic stories that you find on the Web are in plain text format and designed to be read in the browser window. When you click a story link, the story automatically appears. To see text that is offscreen, you just scroll the window by clicking or dragging in the scrollbar on the right side of the screen.

Occasionally, you may find stories that have been saved as word processing documents—frequently in some version of Microsoft Word. To view these stories, download the ones that interest you (by clicking the appropriate link), and then open them in Word.

Do-It-Yourself Erotica

Perhaps you'd like to take a crack at writing your own stories. One fun approach is to find a willing chat or email partner and take turns writing lines for an erotic story.

But I Don't Have Microsoft Word!

Go to Microsoft's Web site and download Word 97 Viewer, a utility that enables you to read and print Microsoft Word documents: **http://officeupdate. microsoft.com/downloadCatalog/dldWord.htm**.

Different viewers are provided for Windows 95/98/NT users and those who are still running Windows 3.1x. Be sure to download the correct version for your system.

If you already have a *different* word processing program, you may discover that it has an Open, Import, or Insert command that you can use to read stories that were saved as Microsoft Word files.

Necessary Software

The majority of erotic stories can be found on the Web, so the main tool you need is a Web browser (see Chapter 2). Although any browser will suffice for viewing text-only stories, graphics and audio clips accompany some of these stories. For these, a high-end browser such as Internet Explorer or Netscape Navigator is recommended—that is, if you want the full impact that was intended by the author.

Saving a Story for Later

If you find a great story that you think you'll want to read again or share with a friend, you can save a copy of it on your hard disk. Choose the **Save As** command from your browser's File menu or highlight the text of the story, choose **Copy** from the Edit menu, and then paste the text into a word processing or text-editor document.

To read stories that have been posted to newsgroups, you need a newsgroup reader (see Chapter 3). As an alternative, you can also search for and read newsgroup stories with AltaVista (**http://www.altavista.com**), Lycos (**http://www.lycos.com**), or DejaNews (**http://www.dejanews.com**), three widely used Web and newsgroup search engines. See the end of Chapter 6, "Finding Sex Sites on the Web," for instructions.

To search newsgroups from AltaVista, click **Usenet** *before you enter a search string. To view any of the found messages (called posts), click its link (the underlined text).*

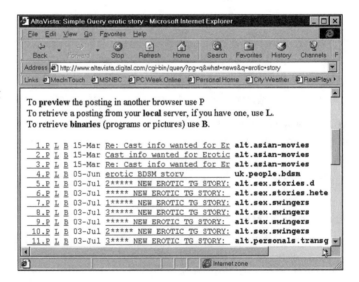

Movie Clips and Streaming Video

One of the most exciting features of the World Wide Web is the ability to view movies on Web pages. Depending on your particular browser and how the page designer set up the Web page, movie clips can be played in the browser window, played in a separate window, or downloaded and played in another program. Movie clips can vary in size from several hundred kilobytes (for a few seconds of action) to many megabytes (for clips lasting a minute or more). To play a movie clip, you begin by clicking the clip's link. (Unless it is actually a streaming video, this downloads the clip to your hard disk.) The clip opens and begins playing as soon as the download finishes.

Save 'em for a Rainy Day

Downloaded movie clips can be saved to your hard disk, so you can replay them whenever you like. Right-click the clip window or the link (on a Windows PC running Internet Explorer), right-click the link (on a Windows PC running Netscape Navigator), or click the clip window and hold down the mouse button (on a Macintosh). Then choose the **Save** command in the pop-up menu that appears.

Streaming video generally plays in your browser as part of a Web page. Unlike a video clip, which—in some formats—must be downloaded in its entirety before it can be played, streaming video plays as the download occurs. Otherwise, streaming video is very similar to a downloaded movie clip.

Saving Streaming Video

You might be dismayed to learn that you may not be able to save streaming video in the same manner as you can movie clips. To save a RealVideo or VivoActive video stream, you must shell out a few bucks for their more advanced players. The free players do not have a Save feature.

Where Can I Find Movie Clips and Streaming Video?

Free sexually explicit movie clips once were plentiful on the Web, but the situation has changed. Pay sites are now the primary source of sexual video clips and streaming video.

Popular File Formats

Downloadable clips are usually in one of three major formats: AVI, MPEG, and MOV (Apple Computer's QuickTime). In those instances when streaming video is not broadcast using your browser's Java capabilities, it is typically in RealVideo or Vivo format.

Necessary Software

To play video clips, most people use their current multimedia browser, such as Netscape Navigator or Internet Explorer. Internet Explorer's ActiveX technology currently supports both AVI and MPG movie formats. To add QuickTime (MOV) support, you can download the necessary software for Macintosh computers or PCs from **http://www.apple.com/quicktime/download/**.

To handle streaming video broadcasts, you can download RealPlayer at **http://www.real.com** and the VivoActive Player at **http://egg.real.com/vivo-player/vivodl.html**.

Another way to play virtually any type of movie—whether it is a clip or streaming video—is to install the new version of Windows Media Player, as discussed later in this chapter.

Live Video

Live video is streaming video, but the action is live rather than prerecorded. In addition to the video, live sex sites may also broadcast the accompanying audio, so you can hear the action as well as see it. They may also incorporate chat. You can type comments and directions to the performers, telling them how they should pose or what you would like them to do.

Where Can I Find Live Video?

The Web is the main source of live video sex. Although most of it occurs in pay sites, isolated free examples can be found, too.

The other source of live video is in video chat programs, such as NetMeeting, CU-SeeMe, and Connectix VideoPhone. By installing one of these programs and adding an optional desktop video camera and microphone to your system, you can participate in one-on-one or group chats that incorporate video and audio. (Whether they also incorporate sex is up to you.)

Necessary Software

To view live sex on the Web, all you normally need is a current version of Internet Explorer or Netscape Navigator. If any special video plug-ins are required, the Web site tells you where to go to download and install them.

For video chat, you can find free versions of several popular programs—such as NetMeeting, CU-SeeMe, and HoneyCom—that you can download. Other video chat programs, however, may only be available for a fee (Connectix VideoPhone, WebPhone, and Intel Internet Phone, for example).

Audio Clips and Streaming Audio

Although not as popular as video, audio clips and streaming audio have their devotees. Some of the clips and broadcasts you can find include stories ("How I Seduced My High School Gym Teacher While Maintaining a B+ Average"), recordings of lovemaking sessions, and sexual information. If you are a chat fanatic, you can search for humorous or sexy WAV files that you can play during chat encounters.

Air Supply

"One way to break up any kind of tension is good deep breathing."

—Byron Nelson, professional golfer

Where Can I Find Audio Clips and Streaming Audio?

Audio clips and streaming audio can be found on the Web and in some newsgroups.

Popular File Formats

The most popular file formats for downloadable audio clips are WAV, AU, and—for Macintosh users—AIFF. Songs— with vocals—are usually in WAV, MP3, or AIFF format. (Although you'll also find plenty of MIDI files, they are instrumental music files.) Streaming audio is typically broadcast as RealAudio.

Necessary Software

If you have a current version of Internet Explorer or Netscape Navigator, you will probably find that it can already play many of the downloadable audio clip formats, such as WAV and AU files. If you have a PC and are having difficulty playing sound files in your browser, try opening them in Media Player, a program that comes with Windows 95/98. It can be found by clicking **Start**, **Programs**, **Accessories**, **Multimedia**.

You may also find the following sound-playing utilities useful:

For the PC

➤ Beatnik Player Plug-in for Win95 (**http://www.davecentral.com/2109.html**)

➤ Maplay (**http://www.davecentral.com/93.html**)

27

New and Improved!

Windows Media Player has recently been updated, enabling it to play several new video and audio formats, including RealVideo, VivoActive, and QuickTime. You can download a free copy from

http://www.microsoft.com/windows/mediaplayer/download

For the Macintosh

➤ SoundApp (search for "SoundApp" at **http://www.zdnet.com/mac/download.html**)

See Chapter 2, "Web Browsers," for more information about adding new plug-ins and helper apps for your browser.

For streaming audio, you can download RealPlayer at **http://www.real.com**.

Chat

Chat is one of the hottest phenomena on the Internet. Using your browser or a text, audio, or video chat program, you can converse in real-time with current friends or you can use chat to meet new people. Flirting among complete strangers is extremely common in chat. And the anonymity of chat seems to bring out the sexual side of many people.

Erotic Masquerade

"One's real life is so often the life that one does not lead."

—Oscar Wilde

Where Can I Find Chat?

You can go to hundreds of Web sites to chat. Because of the increasing popularity of chat and the desire to build an online community, many of the Web search engines, such as Excite and Yahoo!, have a chat component.

Server-based chats may have their own programs that you have to buy or download (such as LOL Chat, Worlds Chat, and OnLive Traveler).

CU-SeeMe Reflectors

CU-SeeMe video chats are hosted by sites called *reflectors*. To connect to a reflector, you need a copy of the CU-SeeMe software and the reflector's address. Like Web page addresses, a reflector address identifies the reflector's location on the Internet. See Chapter 27, "Video Chat," for information on finding interesting reflectors.

Necessary Software

Many Web-based chats rely only on Java, so you can join in with nothing more than a current browser. Some chats, such as The Palace, require a browser plug-in. You can generally download these plug-ins from the chat sites.

Other chats, such as LOL Chat, Microsoft V-Chat, Powwow, Worlds Chat, ICQ, and AOL Instant Messenger, require their own software. See Chapters 25–27 for details on obtaining the necessary programs. In addition to certain text chats, audio and video chats typically require their own separate program.

There Are Many Paths to IRC, Grasshopper

To participate in Internet Relay Chat (IRC), you can use any of dozens of IRC client programs, such as MIRC, PIRCH, or Microsoft Chat.

The Least You Need to Know

➤ If you are a typical Internet user, all you need to experience the depth and breadth of sex on the Internet is a computer (PC or Macintosh), a modem, and an Internet connection—through an ISP, an online information service, or a network.

➤ An inexpensive microphone and a desktop video camera are necessary hardware additions for audio and video chats.

➤ Much of the software that you will use to roam the Internet is free and can be downloaded from the Internet. Essential programs include a Web browser (for viewing content on the World Wide Web), an email program (for exchanging messages and files with others), and a newsgroup reader (for tracking select message topics).

➤ You can participate in many chats using nothing more than your Web browser. Some chat arenas, however, require you to download or purchase additional software.

Chapter 2

Web Browsers

In This Chapter

➤ Learning the basics of using a Web browser

➤ Viewing and saving pictures found on the Web

➤ Downloading programs, picture archives, movie clips, and audio clips

➤ Using your browser to chat with others

➤ Tips for getting more out of your browser

The *World Wide Web* (or *Web*, for short) is that part of the Internet that most people assume actually *is* the Internet in its entirety. The Web contains millions upon millions of pages filled with text, pictures, animated graphics, music, and files that you can download to your computer. These pages illustrate the lives and work of individuals, companies, schools, and government agencies from all over the world. To participate in this rich multimedia experience, all you need is Internet access and a computer program called a *Web browser*.

Home Pages, Web Pages, and Web Sites

In this and other books, magazines, and the Web, you will see many references to these three terms.

A *Web page* is a page on the World Wide Web that has its own unique address, such as **http://www.mcp.com/resources** (a resource page for the publisher of this book). This address can be typed into the Address box of a Web browser to download and display that particular page.

A *Web site* is a collection of Web pages, all created, organized, and managed by the same person or company.

A *home page* is a Web site's starting or main page. (Note that a Web site can consist of as little as one page or it may contain thousands of Web pages.)

What Is a Browser?

A *Web browser* is an application that enables you to view and interact with content on the World Wide Web. Although some browsers can only display text, the most popular browsers enable you to see Web pages in all the glory that their designers intended. In addition to text, they may contain graphics, clickable buttons, sound effects, music, and forms that you can fill in. Chances are good that you already have one of the most popular browsers installed on your computer: a version of Internet Explorer, Netscape Navigator, or Netscape Communicator (a suite of Internet programs that includes Netscape Navigator as its browser).

Browsing Basics

After you connect to the Internet (either by dialing an Internet service provider or an information service or by connecting through your company's network), you can launch your browser. (Note that your browser may be configured to automatically connect to the Internet whenever you run it.)

Toolbar

Menus   Address (or location) box

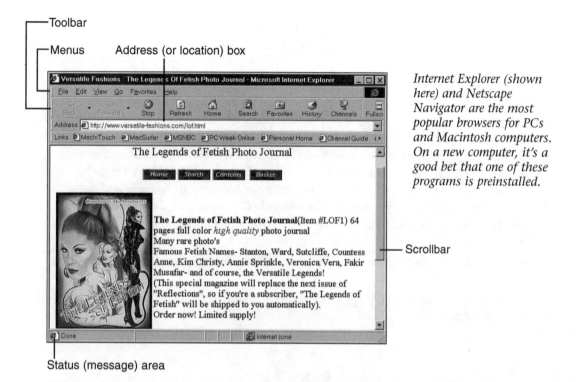

Internet Explorer (shown here) and Netscape Navigator are the most popular browsers for PCs and Macintosh computers. On a new computer, it's a good bet that one of these programs is preinstalled.

Scrollbar

Status (message) area

Both Internet Explorer and Netscape Navigator/Communicator are designed so that you can perform most tasks by just clicking buttons in the toolbar, clicking text and graphic links to other pages, and choosing favorite Web sites from a list.

Visiting Web Pages

To distinguish one Web page from another, each one has a unique *address* or *URL* (Uniform Resource Locator) beginning with **http://**, such as **http://www. intel.com/**. You can display a particular Web page by doing any of the following:

➤ Type the page's address in the Address or Location box. (In later versions of browsers, it is not necessary to type **http://**.)

➤ Copy the page's address from another document (such as an email message or word processing file), and then paste it into the Address or Location box.

➤ Choose **Open**, **Open Page**, or **Open Location** from the File menu, and then type or paste the address in the dialog box that appears.

Copying and Pasting

To copy and paste on a Windows PC, you select the text to be copied (a Web page address, in this instance), select whatever address is currently displayed in the Address/Location box of your Web browser, and then press **Ctrl+V** (Paste) to replace the current address with the one you have just copied. To copy and paste on a Macintosh, the commands are **Command+C** (Copy) and **Command+V** (**Paste**). You can also copy and paste by choosing the **Copy** and **Paste** commands from any program's Edit menu.

➤ Revisit a stored Web page by choosing its name from your browser's Favorites or Bookmarks list.

Saving Your Favorite Web Sites

You can record important or frequently visited Web sites as *favorites* (Internet Explorer) or *bookmarks* (Netscape Navigator/Communicator). To record the address of a favorite site in Internet Explorer, for example, visit the Web page and choose **Add to Favorites** from the Favorites menu.

➤ Click a text or graphic *link* (such as a banner) on the current Web page.

What's a Link?

In Internet parlance, a *link* is any text string or graphic on a Web page that you can click to make your browser do one of the following:

➤ Jump to a specific spot on the current Web page

➤ Display a different page in the same Web site

➤ Go to a Web page in a different site

The person who designs the Web page determines where the link takes you; that is, it's coded into the link.

Links are usually displayed as underlined text or a graphic image of some sort, such as the Next and Back buttons that you find at the bottom of many Web pages. Whether a link is text or a graphic is irrelevant; the purpose is always the same. You click links to navigate within and between Web sites. (Other links, when clicked, enable you to send email to a company or Web page owner; still other links enable you to download files.)

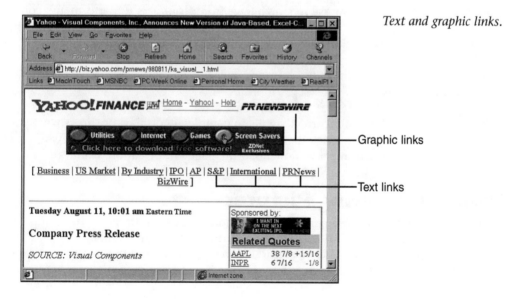

Text and graphic links.

Graphic links

Text links

Which Ones Are the Links?

Do you sometimes find that you can't tell ordinary text and graphics from click-able links? In many browsers, when you move the cursor over a link, the shape of the cursor changes. In Internet Explorer, for example, the cursor becomes a point-ing hand—indicating that you can click something beneath the cursor.

After you have viewed several Web pages during a browsing session, you can go back to previously viewed pages by clicking the browser's **Back** button.

Stopping a Page from Loading

When you're surfing or searching for information on the Web, it's common to occa-sionally pull up the wrong page or one that doesn't interest you. Nothing requires you to let a page load completely. To halt the loading process, click the **Stop** button. (This also proves useful for turning off annoying music that a page may be playing *ad nauseum* or when you don't feel like waiting for all the graphics on a page to load.)

Another technique you can use to stop a page from loading is to perform any com-mand that requests a new page or action, such as clicking a link, choosing a favorite from the Favorites or Bookmarks list, or clicking the browser's **Back** or **Forward** button.

Refreshing the Current Page

If a given Web page loads incorrectly, fails to completely display, or shows what you believe is old information, click the **Refresh** or **Reload** button in the browser's tool-bar. This instructs the browser to download the page's information again.

Viewing and Saving Pictures

Photos and pictures are a major attraction in many sex sites. In fact, when people talk about sex on the Internet, they are often referring to the wide availability of sexy pic-tures. It's a simple matter to view pictures in your browser and optionally save copies of them to your hard disk.

Viewing Pictures

Depending on how the designer placed the pictures on the Web page you're viewing, you may see any combination of the following:

➤ Full-size pictures

➤ Thumbnails (miniature representations of pictures that you can click to see the full-size picture)

➤ Text links that, when clicked, reveal a full-size picture

Worth a Thousand Words

Perfect Tommy: Pictures don't lie.

Reno: The hell they don't. I met my first wife that way.

—*The Adventures of Buckaroo Banzai Across the 8th Dimension,* 1984

Thumbnail, Text Links... What's the Diff?

There *is* no difference. Thumbnails and text links are both links; one is a graphic link and the other is text. Whether you click a text link to a picture or a thumbnail, the same thing happens. The browser displays the Web page or frame in which the full-size picture is embedded, enabling you to easily view and—if you like—save the picture. (Note, however, that if a Web site gives you the choice of viewing thumbnails or text links, the latter will appear instantly onscreen, although thumbnails may load slowly—especially when a lot of them display.)

Saving Pictures

After the full-sized picture is displayed (perhaps it's necessary to click a thumbnail or click a text link), you can use a browser command to save the picture as a graphic file on your hard disk. After a picture has been saved, you can look at it as often as you like by opening it in your favorite graphics program or in your browser (via the Open or Open File command).

The exact procedure you use to save a picture depends on whether you have a PC or Macintosh computer, and the particular browser you use.

Why Won't This Thumbnail Get Bigger?

Not all thumbnails are linked to bigger pictures. In some pay sites, *guests* (non-subscribers) can only view the thumbnails. If you want to see the pictures at their actual size, you must subscribe to the site.

On a PC

1. Move the cursor so that it's over the picture, and then click the right button on your mouse or trackball. As you hold the button down, a menu appears.

2. *If Internet Explorer 3 or 4 is your browser*, choose **Save Picture As**.

   or

   If Netscape Navigator is your browser, choose **Save Image As**.

3. In the standard file dialog box that appears, navigate to the disk and folder where you want to save the file, and then click the **Save** button. (If you want, you can give the file a different name before saving it.)

On a Macintosh Computer

1. Move the cursor so that it's over the picture, and then press and hold down the button on your mouse or trackball. As you hold down the button, a menu appears.

2. *If Internet Explorer 4 is your browser*, choose **Download Image to Disk**.

   or

   If Netscape Navigator is your browser, choose **Save this Image as**.

3. In the standard file dialog box that appears, navigate to the disk and folder where you want to save the file, and then click the **Save** button. (If you want, you can give the file a different name before saving it.)

Other PC and Mac browsers will offer similar commands and procedures for saving pictures. If the correct command isn't immediately obvious to you, check your browser's documentation or Help commands.

Downloading Files

You can also download files from Web sites, such as chat programs, games, and word processing documents. If your browser needs an add-on utility to play certain types of audio or video files, for example, you can obtain that add-on from the Internet.

To download a program or other type of file from a Web page, you just click the supplied text or graphics link. (In some cases, you may be asked to fill in an application form in your browser window and then click a button to submit the form.) Next, a Save dialog box appears, asking where you would like to save the program or file. After choosing a disk and folder and clicking **Save** (or **OK**), the download commences.

A Word About Copyright

Although it's hunky-dory to save copies of pictures from the Internet for your own viewing pleasure, keep in mind that most of this material is copyrighted. In fact, it's safer to assume that it *is all* copyrighted, because—in the United States, anyway—a copyright application is not required to protect the rights of the individual who created the picture. With this in mind, it is illegal to repost or otherwise distribute the pictures you have downloaded. Some sites will provide permission, however; check their legal or copyright notices, which are usually linked from the main page. Just because you can freely grab material from Web pages doesn't mean you own it. For more information, see "10 Big Myths About Copyright Explained" at **http://www.templetons.com/brad/copymyths.html**.

Downloading Directly to Disk

Alternatively, you can right-click any file or graphic link (Windows) or click and hold the mouse button on a file or graphic link (Macintosh), and then choose **Save Target As** or **Save Link As**.

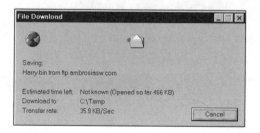

When downloading a file, most browsers display a message in the status/ message area of the browser window or put up a dialog box that indicates how the download is progressing.

39

What you do with the received file depends on whether it is an *installer* (Macintosh) or *setup* (PC) program, whether it is an *archive* (one or more compressed files that must be uncompressed or extracted before they can be used), and whether it has been encoded in some fashion. Macintosh files are frequently converted to binary (.bin) or BinHex (.hqx) format before being stored on the Internet, for example. The following information explains how to deal with these different situations.

It All Depends

After clicking the link for a file you want to download, the manner in which the download proceeds depends on your browser and the computer you have.

StuffIt Extractor Handles Most Macintosh File Types

If you work on a Macintosh, you can download files with an .hqx or .bin extension. StuffIt Extractor can interpret any of these file formats commonly found on the Internet and convert them to normal Macintosh files.

➤ **Setup/installer programs** Windows programs and documentation are often distributed as *setup programs*; Macintosh programs are often distributed as *installers*. When you double-click a setup program or installer, the program materials install in a folder of your choice. In many cases, you are stepped through the installation process in a series of dialog boxes, enabling you to choose installation and program options.

➤ **Archives** To reduce transmission time, files are often compressed and saved as archives. The most popular formats for archives are .zip (Windows) and StuffIt (Macintosh). To extract and use the contents of an archive, you need a separate utility program. Two that we recommend are WinZip (a shareware program from Nico Mak Computing at **http://winzip. com**) and StuffIt Extractor (a free program from Aladdin Systems at **http://www. aladdinsys.com**).

➤ **Encoded files** Macintosh files are typically encoded before they are stored on the Internet—either as binary or BinHex files. Frequently, they are first "stuffed" (saved as StuffIt archives) and then also encoded. StuffIt Extractor is the utility of choice for changing such encoded files into ones that you can open or run on your Mac.

Platform Problems

Some word processing documents, Adobe Acrobat files, and pictures can freely be exchanged among PC and Macintosh users. However, programs that are designed to run on one system will *not* run on the other. If you have a Macintosh, you must look for a Macintosh version of that program; the PC version will not do.

Playing and Saving Video

Video clips are the next best thing to porn flicks. Well, not really... Video clips tend to be brief and the action may be choppy, but they *are* easy to find on the Web. Video clips are generally of two types: downloadable files (in a variety of formats) and streaming video.

Downloadable Clips

Downloadable clips are usually in AVI, MPEG, or MOV (QuickTime) format. The formats that can be played in your browser depend on the *plug-ins* installed in your browser, its built-in multimedia capabilities, and the multimedia programs that have been installed in your computer. A stock copy of Internet Explorer 4, for example, can download and play most types of video clips.

If you have a PC running Windows 95 or 98, you can also play many types of video clips in MediaPlayer, a utility included with Windows 95 and 98. Click the **Start** button on the taskbar and choose **Programs**, **Accessories**, **Multimedia**, **MediaPlayer**.

An MPEG movie playing in an Internet Explorer ActiveMovie window. Click the first button to play the clip or the second button to pause or stop it. Right-click the movie and choose **Properties** *to set playback options.*

41

Downloading a movie clip is just like downloading any other type of file. Click the text or picture link for the clip, specify a location on disk in which to save the clip, and the download begins. When downloading is complete, the movie automatically plays. You can use the playback controls to replay or stop the movie.

If you want to be able to replay a movie clip whenever you like, you must save it, as follows:

Play as You Download

Some movie formats, such as MPEG and QuickTime, appear and can be played during the download process. Other formats, such as AVI, must download completely before you can play them.

➤ **On a Windows PC**   Right-click the clip and choose **Save Target As**, **Save Movie As**, or **Save Movie** from the pop-up menu that appears. (If no Save command is listed, right-click the movie's *link* and choose **Save Link As**.)

➤ *On a Mac*   Click the clip and hold down the mouse button until the pop-up menu appears. Choose **Save As** or **Save Movie As**.

New Clip-Saving Instructions for Windows MediaPlayer

If you are using Windows MediaPlayer to play movie clips, right-clicking the movie does not present you with a Save command. Instead, choose **Add to Favorites** from the Favorites menu.

Streaming Video

Streaming video plays within your Web browser. Instead of having to download an entire movie to your computer and then play it, streaming video plays as the movie data is being pulled from the Internet. Whether you can see streaming video depends on the video formats offered by the sites that you visit and the software installed on your computer. Streaming video is usually provided in one of three formats:

➤ RealVideo (requires the RealPlayer from RealNetworks, available from **http:// www.real.com/**)

➤ Vivo (requires the VivoActive Player, available from **http://www.vivo. com/products/playfree/vaplayer.html**)

➤ Java (requires any Java-enabled browser, such as Internet Explorer or Netscape Navigator)

Plug-Ins and ActiveX Components

Whether your browser can handle different types of video, audio, and pictures depends on its built-in capabilities and whether you have installed additional utilities.

Plug-ins are external programs that work in conjunction with Netscape Navigator to enable it to handle particular kinds of Web content. Navigator (and Windows) determines the content type from a file's *extension* (the three letters that follow the period in a filename). A file with an .avi extension is a type of movie file, for example. Internet Explorer's *ActiveX components* serve the same function as Navigator plug-ins.

When using your browser, you will sometimes find that you cannot view certain types of Web files, such as particular audio or video files. In those instances, you will usually be offered the option of downloading the necessary plug-in or ActiveX component.

In addition, you can manually download and install browser add-ins. If you're looking for Netscape Navigator plug-ins, try **http://home.netscape.com/ plugins/**. For Internet Explorer ActiveX components, check out **http://www. download.com/PC/Activex/**.

Before you rush out and download RealPlayer, VivoActive Player, or a newer version of your browser, do a trial run with your current browser. You may discover that you can already view some types of streaming video with your present setup. Another way to test your system is to go to the RealNetworks and Vivo sites, and try playing the test files you find there.

MediaPlayer

The newest version of Microsoft's MediaPlayer can play streaming video in the following formats: RealPlayer, VivoActive, or Windows Media (formerly known as NetShow). It can also play RealAudio, WAV, QuickTime, and AVI files. If you have Windows 95, 98, or NT 4.0, you can download a free copy of MediaPlayer from **http://www.microsoft.com/windows/mediaplayer/download**.

It's Free!

Many of the better managed sex sites will provide the video software you need (or offer a link to another site where you can get the software).

Well, It's Not *All* Free

Both the RealPlayer and VivoActive Player come in two versions. The free version enables you to play, but not save, videos. For a fee, you can buy the commercial version and take advantage of its additional features (such as saving videos to disk).

Playing and Saving Audio

Would you like to hear someone describing his or her first sexual experience or thrill to the sounds of a simultaneous orgasm? A few Web sites have sexy audio clips that you can download, play, and save to disk. The primary formats for audio of this type are WAV files and streaming audio (RealAudio).

WAV Files

WAV files are standard Windows audio files, commonly used to record voices, sound effects, and music. Many people collect WAVs and exchange them with friends via email or chat programs, such as LOL Chat and IRC.

Before you can listen to a WAV file, you must first download it by clicking a text or graphic link on a Web page. In Internet Explorer 4, WAV files automatically download and play in ActiveMovie windows (just as video clips do). Other browsers may use a plug-in to play WAVs, or they may be opened in MediaPlayer, a utility program that comes with Windows 95/98.

*To save a WAV file in an ActiveMovie window, right-click the WAV window and choose **Save As** from the pop-up menu that appears.*

Streaming Audio

Streaming audio works like streaming video (described previously in this chapter). The most common format for streaming audio is RealAudio. When you click a RealAudio link on a Web page, a tiny setup file is downloaded to your computer, RealPlayer (the utility used for RealAudio and RealVideo) automatically launches, and the audio plays as it downloads. If you don't have a copy of RealPlayer, you can get one at RealNetworks' site (**http://www.real.com/**).

Interactive Video

Interactive video is similar to streaming video, except for the following:

➤ It is live rather than prerecorded.

➤ Viewers can comment and direct the action in real-time by typing into a chat window.

If special software is necessary, it can usually be obtained by clicking a link on the site's Web pages. Otherwise, Java applets are used to handle the video transmission. As long as your browser supports Java, you may not need additional software.

Finger in the What?

Amsterdam Tonight (**http://www.amsterdamtonight.com**) offers live sex shows and is an excellent example of interactive video. If you use Internet Explorer as your browser and want to hear the action as well as see it, you must launch Speak Freely (an audio chat program) prior to launching Internet Explorer. You can learn about Speak Freely in Chapter 19, "Erotica" (Netscape Navigator users, on the other hand, can hear the audio without launching any additional programs.)

Web-based Chat

In the past year or so, Web-based chat has gone a long way toward catching up with standalone chat programs. Chats that you can participate in using nothing more than your browser are now predominantly Java based. The better examples of Java-based chat (such as Yahoo! Chat) offer many of the same features found in standard chat programs, such as the ability to change fonts and colors, send private messages to other users, and view participants' profiles.

On the other hand, chats that are *not* Java based are best avoided. It's not uncommon to have to click the **Refresh** button repeatedly to see new messages, for example. As a result, you will find it exceedingly difficult to carry on anything that resembles an interactive conversation.

Yahoo! Chat uses Java to implement features found in the best of the standalone chat programs.

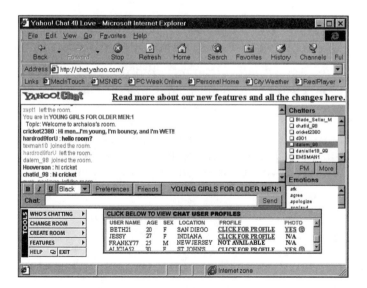

Tips for Better Browsing

By clicking links, clicking buttons, and choosing menu commands, you can accomplish just about everything you would normally want to do with your browser. The more you know about your browser's capabilities and commands (some of them are well hidden), however, the more productive your surfing sessions will be. The following tips and techniques will help you save time and avoid unnecessary Web-related aggravation.

Opening Links and Pictures in a New Window

If you routinely use a single browser window to enlarge thumbnails and to explore new links, you already know that method has the following drawbacks:

➤ After you click the **Back** button, you frequently have to wait while the originating page's thumbnails and banners are reloaded and redrawn.

➤ If you went to a different Web site, the original one may have to reload in the same fashion.

➤ You cannot continue to do work on the original page until it has reloaded.

You may not know it, but you can have *multiple* browser windows open in most browsers. Thus, while you're reading one Web page, your browser can be loading a different page in a window in the background. To accomplish this, do the following:

➤ **On a Windows PC** To open a page or picture link in its own window, right-click the text link or thumbnail, and then choose **Open in New Window** from the pop-up menu that appears.

➤ **On a Macintosh** To open a page or picture link in its own window, click the text link or thumbnail and—while holding down the mouse or trackball button—choose **Open Link in New Window**, **New Window with this Link**, or a similar command from the pop-up menu that appears.

You can also create new browser windows by just choosing **File**, **New**, **Window**, or **File**, **New Window**. Doing so creates a duplicate of the currently active browser window.

Every new browser window that you create operates independently from every other browser window—the same as working on several memos or letters in your word processor, for example. When you are ready to get rid of a browser window that you no longer need, click its **Close** box.

How Many Windows Can I Open?

That depends on the browser you use and the amount of memory that the browser has available to it. Check the Options or Preferences for your browser to see whether you have an option to specify the number of browser windows (sometimes called *sessions*) that can be open at one time. If you don't find such a setting, you can have as many windows open as memory allows.

Multiple Simultaneous Downloads

Like a good sex partner, Internet system software for the PC and Macintosh can manage more than one task at a time. Although you may be able to do only one thing at a time (walking *and* chewing gum can be a chore for some folks), your Internet programs have no such limitations. When you ask your Net software to simultaneously complete several tasks (such as check for new email and open a new page in your Web browser—all while typing to a friend in a chat program), your computer switches as needed between all these tasks. Things may slow down noticeably, but they will all eventually complete.

Therefore, if you're on a thumbnail page, you might click (or right-click) *four* thumbnails—one by one—and choose **Open in New Window** for each one. Similarly, if you find several interesting links to other sites, you can use the same procedure to open them all—without losing sight of the original page.

Downloading Pictures (Rather Than Opening Them)

Some browsers have a command that enables you to download a picture or photo directly to disk—without opening it in a new window. In Internet Explorer 4, for example, you can right-click on a thumbnail or text link for a picture, choose **Save Target As**, select a destination drive and folder for the picture, and then click **Save**. Because this process doesn't open a new browser window or change the contents of the current window, this is the fastest way to deal with pictures that you are sure you want to save.

Using a Picture as Your New Wallpaper

Wouldn't it be cool to use a sexy picture as your *wallpaper* (the background pattern for the desktop on your PC) on your home computer? If you have Windows 95 or higher, use Internet Explorer 4 or Netscape Navigator as your browser, and think that you can work with those kinds of distractions, you can easily accomplish this feat by right-clicking any picture that you see on a Web page and choosing **Set as Wallpaper** from the pop-up menu that appears. The screen is automatically redrawn using the current picture as the wallpaper.

Later, if you find that your boss, spouse, girlfriend, or boyfriend isn't amused, you can switch the wallpaper by following these steps:

Another Way to Set Wallpaper

Open the **Display Control Panel**, click the **Background** tab, and then click the **Browse** button. Locate the picture file on your hard disk that you want to use as wallpaper, and then click **Open** and **OK**.

1. Click the **Start** button on the taskbar.
2. Choose **Settings**, **Control Panels**. The Control Panels folder opens.
3. Double-click the **Display Control Panel** to open it.
4. Click the **Background** tab.
5. Choose a new picture file to display as your wallpaper, and then click **OK**.

Using a Web Page as Wallpaper

If you have Internet Explorer's Active Desktop feature enabled, you can optionally choose an *HTML file* (a Web page) to use as your wallpaper. To restore the original Internet Explorer 4 wallpaper, choose the *wallpapr* file from the Wallpaper scrolling list box.

You can use pictures as the background for your desktop. This Hajime Sorayama drawing makes a wonderfully distracting wallpaper.

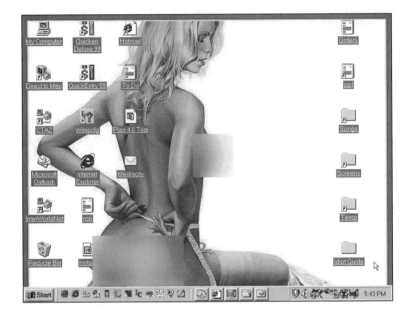

A History Lesson

Did you stumble upon an amazing Web site the other day, but now you've forgotten its name and address? It's easy to do if you surf a lot. By default, every browser automatically records a list of the Web sites and pages you have recently visited.

*Click the **History** button on the Internet Explorer 4 toolbar to reveal the History pane (on the left side of the browser window). Choose the site or page you want to revisit from the alphabetic list of sites you have previously visited.*

History pane

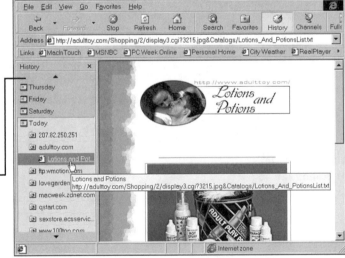

If you use Netscape Navigator, choose **History** from the Window menu to view a list of recently visited Web pages.

The Least You Need to Know

➤ You need an advanced Web browser, such as Internet Explorer or Netscape Navigator, to fully experience the graphics and multimedia of the World Wide Web. Newer computers frequently come with one of these programs pre-installed.

➤ Moving from one Web page to another is done by clicking text or graphic links or by typing an address (URL) in the browser's Address or Location box.

➤ You can store addresses of Web pages that you want to revisit by saving them as *bookmarks* (Netscape) or *favorites* (Internet Explorer).

➤ Designers often put tiny representations of pictures called *thumbnails* on their pages. After you click a thumbnail, a full-size copy of the picture appears for you to view and optionally save to disk.

➤ You can also download programs and other files from Web sites. All you have to do is click the appropriate link and tell your computer where you want to save the file. The final step for many downloaded files is to use a utility program such as WinZip or StuffIt Expander to convert them to programs and documents that are ready to be used on your computer.

➤ Depending on the browser you use and other software installed on your computer, you may be able to download and play video and audio clips, as well as streaming video and audio.

➤ Although Web-based chat used to be extremely clumsy, it has made significant advances. The better Web chat sites rely on advanced Java applets to provide program features that make it easy and fun to chat using a browser.

YOU TYPE REAL SEXY...

Chapter 3

Newsgroups: Dirty Discussions and Plentiful Pictures

> **In This Chapter**
>
> ➤ Read online discussions
>
> ➤ Peruse pictures posted by other people
>
> ➤ Put your own messages and pictures where people can find them

A *newsgroup* is the Internet equivalent of a giant bulletin board. Anyone can see messages and pictures put on a newsgroup, and anyone with the computer equivalent of a thumbtack can put up his or her own messages. Your computer *is* that thumbtack. A $2,500 thumbtack.

On the Internet, you can find thousands of different newsgroups, many of which are about sexual topics. No matter what your sexual special interest is, you can most probably find a newsgroup for you. The server computers on the Net share the messages, so people in different places can get to them. Most newsgroups consist of messages that are passed back and forth over a network called *Usenet*, which is part of the Internet.

Does the Newsgroup Reader Read Them Aloud?

A *newsgroup reader* is a program that can help you locate newsgroups with topics of interest to you, bring the messages that you're interested in to your machine, and help you post your own messages. If you are accessing the Internet from your home computer, you received a newsgroup reader as part of your Internet software package. Newsgroup readers are built in to most versions of Netscape Navigator, Netscape Communicator, Internet Explorer, and the AOL software; within the next few years they will probably even start including it with Hostess cupcakes. It's common stuff.

If you are using a computer at work, the newsgroup reader may not be installed on your PC. Downloadable freeware and shareware newsgroup readers are available for Windows, UNIX, and the Macintosh.

Step 1: Telling the Funky Reader Where It's At!

Before your newsgroup reader can read messages from the newsgroups and send messages to the newsgroups, it needs to know the location of a *news server*, a computer that stores copies of all the newsgroup messages. When you installed your Internet software, you probably gave the computer this information; it's part of the standard installation process for most systems, and is even built in to the software for some of the larger ISPs.

Who's Counting?

Sex is by no means everything. It varies, as a matter of fact, from only as high as 78 percent of everything to as low as 3.10 percent.

—James Thurber & E.B. White, *Is Sex Necessary?*, (1929)

If your newsgroup reader asks for the address of your news server when you start it, or if the program later tells you it cannot reach the news server, you may have to add the news server's address yourself. The place to set it will be part of an Options, Configurations, or Preferences command, depending on which program you're using. Your ISP or your company's network manager should be able to give you the address. This address will have two parts: a name for the computer you'll be reaching (which may be a word name like **news.gertler.net** or a numeric name like **234.201.114.009**) and a *port number* (which will just be a number, usually **119**). Enter this info.

Step 2: Picking Your Newsgroup (Not Picking Your Nosegroup!)

The next step is to select which newsgroups you want to follow. Every newsgroup reader handles this differently, although for the most part they aren't very good at helping you find what you want. (Look for a command that says Subscribe or Join. Don't worry—you won't be charged for subscribing or joining Usenet newsgroups.)

If your newsgroup reader and your Web browser came together (and they probably did), a handy Web page can help you find the ones you want. Surf over to **http://www.newsville.com/search.html** and type a word related to your interest (such as **blonde** or **oral**) into the Search field. Click **Go**. A list of newsgroups with that word in it will appear. Click a newsgroup on that list, and your newsgroup reader will *try* to get to the messages in that newsgroup. (It is possible that your particular news server doesn't handle messages from that group; I'll get to how to deal with that later on.) The news reader should also add that newsgroup to the list of newsgroups you read.

Selecting Sexy Sections

To get you started, here are a list of some of the sexually oriented newsgroups on the Web. The ones with "binaries" in the name are where you'll find pictures; the rest of them will have mainly text messages:

➤ alt.sex.advocacy

➤ alt.sex.anal

➤ alt.sex.biblical

➤ alt.sex.bondage

➤ alt.sex.breast

➤ alt.sex.brothels

➤ alt.sex.buxom

➤ alt.sex.cd-rom

➤ alt.sex.commercial-sites

➤ alt.sex.couples

➤ alt.sex.erotica

➤ alt.sex.escorts

➤ alt.sex.exhibitionism

➤ alt.sex.femdom

➤ alt.sex.fetishes

➤ alt.sex.first-time

➤ alt.sex.gangbang

➤ alt.sex.girls

➤ alt.sex.graphics

➤ alt.sex.historical

➤ alt.sex.homosexual

➤ alt.sex. kinky

➤ alt.sex.lesbian

➤ alt.sex.magazines

➤ alt.sex.marketplace

➤ alt.sex.masturbation

➤ alt.sex.men

➤ alt.sex.movies

➤ alt.sex.oral

➤ alt.sex.orgy

➤ alt.sex.phone

➤ alt.sex.pictures

➤ alt.sex.prostitution

➤ alt.sex.safe

➤ alt.sex.services

➤ alt.sex.sm

➤ alt.sex.society

➤ alt.sex.sounds

➤ alt.sex.spanking

➤ alt.sex.stories

➤ alt.sex.strip-clubs

➤ alt.sex.super-size

➤ alt.sex.swingers

➤ alt.sex.toons

➤ alt.sex.trio

➤ alt.sex.video-swap

➤ alt.sex.voyeurism

➤ alt.sex.wanted

➤ alt.sex.watersports

➤ alt.sex.women

➤ alt.binaries.pictures. erotica

➤ alt.binaries.pictures.erotica. amateur

➤ alt.binaries.pictures.erotica. anime

➤ alt.binaries.pictures.erotica. blondes

➤ alt.binaries.pictures.erotica. bondage

➤ alt.binaries.pictures.erotica. exhibitionism

➤ alt.binaries.pictures.erotica. female

➤ alt.binaries.pictures.erotica. girlfriends

➤ alt.binaries.pictures.erotica. latino

➤ alt.binaries.pictures.erotica. male

➤ alt.binaries.pictures.erotica. pornstar

➤ alt.binaries.pictures.erotica. voyeurism

➤ alt.binaries.pictures.bisexuals

➤ alt.binaries.pictures.celebrities

➤ alt.binaries.pictures.girlfriends

➤ alt.binaries.pictures.personal

➤ alt.binaries.pictures.sex

➤ soc.sexuality. general

➤ soc.sexuality.spanking

Step 3: Getting Messages (Not as Fun as Getting Massages)

Generally, if you are connected to the Internet when you open a newsgroup in your newsgroup reader, the program will automatically start retrieving the messages posted to that group. Otherwise, you may have to connect to the Internet and click the newsreader's **Get** command.

Depending on how you have your newsreader's options set up, the newsreader will retrieve one of two things:

1. If your newsreader is configured for reading messages *online* (while connected to the Internet), the newsreader will display the title of each message on the newsgroup. Then, when you click on the title of a given message, it will retrieve and display that message. This is a good method if you don't expect to read most of the messages.

2. If your newsreader is configured for *offline* message reading, it will download all the messages and store them on your hard disk. After it has finished, you can disconnect from the Internet and read your messages. This is a good method if you expect to read most of the messages but don't want to tie up the phone line.

To change whether your reader downloads just the headers or the entire messages, use your newsreaders **Options** or **Preferences** command.

Messages in this newsgroup

The newsreader part of Netscape Communicator looks like many newsreaders, with a list of message titles on one part of the screen and the currently selected message in another.

Name of this message

When it was sent

Sender

Newsgroups it was posted on

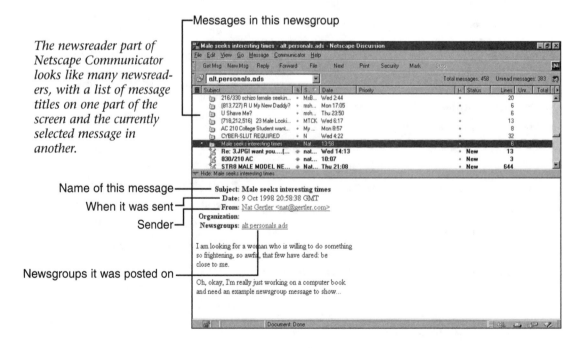

Step 4: Reading the Messages and Looking at the Pictures

After you click the header to pull the message up on your screen, you'll find a number of pieces of information displayed. Generally, you'll see at least the following:

➤ **Subject** This is the title of the message. If it starts with Re:, it is a reply to another message. If it ends with what looks like a fraction (such as [3/5]), it is part of a long message that was broken up into several parts. [3/5] is the third message in a five-message set.

➤ **Sender** This is the name or email address of the person who posted this message to the newsgroup. Don't count on it being accurate; people who are involved in sex-oriented newsgroups often use fake names and addresses to preserve their privacy.

➤ **Newsgroups** It's possible to post the same message to several newsgroups. This will list all the newsgroups that the message is on.

If it is a text message, the text will be displayed. If it's a message with a picture on it, the picture may be displayed, or you may see a link to click to get the picture loaded and displayed.

Photos are encoded using one of two systems that converts them into a bunch of unreadable text, one called *uuencoding* and the other called *MIME*. Most modern newsgroup readers have the built-in capability to turn the text back into a picture. Because photos use up a lot more file space than text does, photos are frequently broken up into several messages. If you select the first message of the series, most modern newsreaders will automatically load all the messages and rebuild the picture.

If your newsreader doesn't have decoding capability, your best bet is to upgrade to a newer newsreader. Although this may seem like a hassle, your other option is to download the program *uudecode* from somewhere (it's free). To use it, save all the messages that make it a photo, run them through the uudecode program to turn them into a graphics file, and then run another program to view the results—that is, unless it's a MIME-encoded picture. In that case, you will have to run it through a MIME-decoding program. That's far too much work to see a naked person ... or at least too much to see a *picture* of a naked person.

Step 5: Posting Your Own Messages

If all you do is read messages without ever posting your own comments or photos, you are what Internet users call a *lurker*, which would be an odd thing to put on your résumé. If everyone were a lurker, there would be no messages to read. What fun would that be?

Participating in newsgroup discussions is easy:

➤ To respond to something in the message currently displayed on your screen, use your newsgroup reader's **Respond** or **Respond to Group** command. (**Respond to Sender** will just email the message to the person who posted the message, assuming that person didn't use a fake address.)

➤ To start a new discussion in the newsgroup you are viewing, use the **New Message** command.

When you do either of these things, a message editing window appears. If you are replying to a message, a title for the message will appear in the Subject field. Otherwise, you will have to enter a title into that field. Type your message into the message area, and then click the **Send** command to post your message. (Some newsgroup readers or online newsgroup sites also offer a Preview option.)

To post a picture, instead of typing your message, click the **Attach** command. A file browser opens, enabling you to select a file from your hard disk. Pick the file with the picture you want.

Secret Identity Time!

Several good reasons exist for not having your real name and email address on your messages. First, there's privacy, especially when it comes to sexual matters. Second, using your primary email address invites unsolicited advertisements or annoying mail (known as *spam*). Marketers scour Usenet for valid email addresses to add to their lists. Some Web sites, such as Deja News, offer private email boxes that provide you with a "posting address" and filter out spam. Use your newsreader's **Option** command to configure a fake address.

Netiquette: Sex Is No Excuse for Rudeness

If you are going to participate in online discussions, you should watch the rules of *netiquette*, or civility on the Internet. The most important ones for newsgroup posters are as follows:

➤ **Keep your posts in the right newsgroup** The **Alt.sex.swingers** site is probably not the right place to post your recipe for strawberry-flavored cheeseburgers. Nor is **rec.cooking.cheeseburgers** the place to invite people to your orgy. (**Alt.sex.swingers.cheeseburgers** might be okay, but sadly it doesn't exist [yet]. It might be a nice place for people who like all sorts of buns.)

➤ **Avoid posting pointless insults** Even if you disagree with someone, keep your messages on the topic at hand. Otherwise, the discussion tends to degenerate into an ongoing exchange of invective (what newsgroup users call a *flame war*).

➤ **Post photos *only* in picture-oriented newsgroups** If the newsgroup doesn't have "binaries" or "pictures" in the title, you shouldn't post photos or graphics files there. Many people read newsgroups using relatively slow connections, and a picture in what is supposed to be a text-only group will waste a lot of their download time.

➤ **Keep your pictures small, both in file size and dimension** This ensures that the images will download quickly and fit on the viewer's screen. (See Chapter 5, "Other Useful Utilities," for tips on how to do this.)

➤ **Quote the message you are replying to** Because of the way Usenet works, passing messages from computer to computer, messages show up on different computers in different orders. People may be reading your reply to someone's message without being able to read the message to which you replied. If you quote the relevant portions of the message you respond to, others can follow what you say much better. If the original message is long, however, it's good netiquette to "snip" the parts that aren't relevant to your reply.

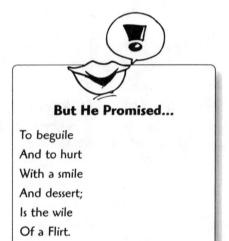

But He Promised...

To beguile

And to hurt

With a smile

And dessert;

Is the wile

Of a Flirt.

—J. Ashbey-Sterry

Getting Newsgroups from Somewhere Else

Because thousands of newsgroups exist, many news servers choose not to provide access to all of them. In the case of the news server at your job, it's probably against company policy to allow access to non-business news groups, particularly groups that include adult material. The men and women who operate commercial ISPs don't want newsgroups that none of their customers read taking up space on their server. In other cases, they may choose not to carry a group because they have moral qualms with its contents or fear that it might get them in trouble with local authorities.

Just because your news server doesn't receive a specific group doesn't mean there isn't a way to work around the problem.

Say "Pretty Please"

The first thing to do is ask your ISP if it can add the newsgroups you want to their server. This is often all you need to do, especially with smaller ISPs.

Get a Different News Server

You could switch ISPs to get a different news server. Even if you want to stay with your ISP, however, you may be able to arrange to use another news server.

Pull up **http://www.newsville.com** on your Web browser, for example. This is a home site for a service that, for a monthly fee, will let you configure your newsgroup reader to get the messages from their server. They carry a large range of newsgroups, including sex and picture newsgroups, that many other servers don't carry.

Webify Your Newsgroup Reading

If you surf on over to **http://www.dejanews.com**, you will be able to read newsgroup messages over the Web, without needing a newsgroup reader or a news server. Click the link marked **my deja news**, and you will be taken to an online form that you can fill out if you want to regularly read the news via the Web. Or if you just want to quickly stop in on a certain newsgroup and see what's going on, click the **Browse Groups** link.

Need to Know More?

If you want to know more about Usenet and newsgroups, point your Web browser to **http://sunsite. unc.edu/usenet-i** for the Usenet Info Center.

Deja News supports only text messages, however. If you want to see the pictures from Usenet on the Web, you can sign up with one of several Web services that give you access to Usenet pictures, such as **http://www.pictureview.com** or **http://www. justpics.com**. These sites involve a fee, so they are basically fee-charging photo archives like the ones discussed in Chapter 8, "Free, 'Free,' and Commercial Web Sites."

Searching the Newsgroups

At Deja News (**http://www.dejanews.com**), you'll find a plethora of tools that enable you to search through the newsgroups for certain information. You can use the Search feature, for example, to find any current messages containing specific words. Type **sex marshmallow**, and Deja News will generate a list of all the current messages that have both words in them, so you can do your research on your favorite personal food fetish... or on determining the gender of those marshmallow Easter candies shaped like baby chicks.

News servers don't keep old messages around forever. After a few weeks, old messages are generally wiped out to make room for new ones. Deja News, however, has cataloged old messages going back several years. Click **Power Search** and you can select a time period of messages to search, as well as to limit your search to certain newsgroups, certain authors, or even certain languages. Keep in mind that anything you post will also be archived.

I'm Coming, Soon

Don't knock masturbation—it's sex with someone I love.

—Woody Allen

The Least You Need to Know

➤ *Newsgroups* are online discussion areas. Many of them have sexual content, and some of them have pictures.

➤ You need a *newsgroup reader* to read newsgroups. Most Web browsers come with a newsgroup reader built in.

➤ To read the messages on a newsgroup, select that newsgroup in your reader and choose the **Get Messages** command.

➤ To post a message on a newsgroup, use either the **Reply** command (to respond to a message) or the **New** command (to start a new discussion).

➤ There are accepted rules of *netiquette* (Internet etiquette), such as not posting pictures to a non-picture newsgroup.

➤ Not all news servers carry all newsgroups, but you may be able to get the ones you want added to your server.

➤ Deja News (**http://www.dejanews.com**) is a good source for reading, posting, and searching for newsgroup text messages through your Web browser.

Chapter 4

Email: Mail You Can Use with Ease

In This Chapter

➤ Read private messages sent to you

➤ Send private messages to someone else

➤ Get your own private email account

So you find someone online, maybe on a newsgroup, maybe in a chat room. You meet an exciting online mate, someone you want to exchange your deepest, dirtiest secrets with. But how do you go about it away from the prying eyes of other computer users?

Email—It's Nothing Like a She-male

Email, which is short for *electronic mail*, is just messages sent from one person to another over the Internet. When you set up your computer for the Internet, you received an email address. That's the thing that looks something like **yourname@ somecompany.com**—the @ sign is a real giveaway that you're looking at an email address.

Email is the single biggest reason that people are getting online. Companies want to be able to have workers quickly exchange messages. Grandma wants to be able to keep in touch with little Chucky at college (while Chucky would rather that Grandma went back to real letters, which tended to come with $10 bills). The evil, maniacal *Complete Idiot's Guide* editors snorted gleefully when their writers got email, because they knew that if the writer claimed the work was done, they could actually force him to deliver.

So What Does That Have to Do with Sex?

Email is the best-kept secret in Internet sex. Millions of people are involved in online affairs, sending smutty little (or sometimes very large) messages to each other. People who would never dream of downloading dirty pictures are creating their own written pornography to share with someone they lust after or someone they have never even met. Flirting via email can range from friendly, romantic notes to full-length sexy scenarios, describing fantasy with copious erotic detail. Some people who are shy in person or awkward on the phone become quite libidinous in email, where they have time to build their words in private.

Hey Rizzo, You Seen My Lighter?

It is the socially inept girl with few alternatives who is most frequently involved in necking sessions. The popular girl gets a reputation for being a pleasant companion, a good sport, and an interesting person.

—*The Art of Dating*, Evelyn Millis Duvall, Ph.D., & Joy Duvall Johnson (1958)

Consider the case of Mary, a mid-40s, bisexual, female teacher from the West Coast. During her libidinous years, she thought she had done everything. Then in a private newsgroup, she finds herself exchanging humorous messages with Daniel, a shy man in his mid-20s with an unlikely job as clerk at an adult bookstore. They send each other a couple of friendly, joke-laden emails. The tone grows from friendly to politely flirty. Then to suggestive. Then to hot and descriptive. She tends toward quick ideas and appreciation, whereas he pours out long, detailed scenarios of just what they should do in the impossible event that they actually meet. Then it moves on to a mixed email/phone relationship; on the phone, she takes control, and teaches the inexperienced man much of the reality of sex with spicy tales from her background. And then the unexpected happens; her travels bring her into his area. An energetic, torrid, kinky weekend solidifies their lusty friendship, which leads to years of occasional shared nights out eating, dancing, being entertained at a strip club, or (even better) just staying in.

Of course, your email lover doesn't have to be the proper stranger. It can be a midday surprise for your current squeeze, or a great (and cheap, compared to phone calls) way to stay in intimate contact with a traveling spouse. It has been used to restart old relationships and transform long-time friendships.

Using Standard Email Software

Whether you are using the computer at work or at home, if it is set up to use the Internet, it has almost certainly been properly set up for email. The common online software, whether it be AOL or a Web browser, generally comes with an email program to help you get your email and create and send email. (It is often just another feature of the same program that handles your newsgroups, as discussed in the preceding chapter.) Current Internet programs often have as many features as Swiss army knives.

To check your email, connect to the network (at work, you are probably always connected) and run your email program. Most email programs will give you a visual or audible signal to tell you there is mail waiting for you, ranging from a simple "ping" to AOL's famous "You've got mail!" The command to actually retrieve and view your mail changes from program to program, but it is usually something obvious like **Get mail** or **Open mailbox**.

Your mail is shown on a list, including the title of each piece and its author. Click a title to view that mail. To reply to an email message, use the **Reply** command. (Beware of the **Reply All** command, which will send your response to everyone that the initial message was sent to. You don't want to accidentally broadcast an intimate response to a non-intimate message.)

To create a new message, click **Create**, **Compose**, or **New Message**, depending on the software you are using. There will be a Subject field for you to enter a message title and a To field for you to enter an email address. Almost every email program has an *Address Book* feature that enables you to keep a list of the people you share email with and their email address, so you can select their address from a list instead of having to memorize it.

Whether you are replying to or creating a new message, use the **Send** or **Queue** command to get your message on the way to its recipient.

And Here's What I'd Look Like with Brad Pitt's Head...

If you have some digital pictures on your hard disk (either ones you have scanned in yourself or ones you have downloaded), you can send them with your email message. To do this, click the **Attach** command. A directory browser will open up, enabling you to select which file you want to attach.

You should try to keep the size of the file you are sending small. (See Chapter 5, "Other Useful Utilities," for tips on how to do this.) You also want to make sure that the file format is one that the recipient's computer can understand. Stick with JPEG (.jpg) or GIF formats because all Web browsers can show those, and many mail programs will display them.

You can attach more than one file to a single email message, and you can also use this technique to send non-picture files, such as word processor files or programs.

Come Up and Queue Me Sometime

Some tips on being arousing in email include the following:

➤ Know what the person you are emailing is into, and write toward that. You can probably be comfortable being suggestive toward rather vanilla sex at first. Build toward explicitness. If you want to experiment with something non-traditional in your email, touch on it in one note and see what reaction that gets, instead of building a fantasy around it. Remember, one person's exciting fetish can be the source of someone else's utter disgust.

➤ In addition to building fantasies, share actual experiences. Many people have interesting stories about sex. You can start off a good conversation exchanging stories about how you lost your virginity or the wildest thing you ever did.

➤ Don't try to cover everything in one message. If you are email-compatible with someone, you will have many opportunities in later messages to bring up every little thing that gets you thrilled.

➤ When describing fantasy scenarios between you and your email partners, focus on describing your own actions and emotional reactions and their actions. Don't describe their physical or emotional reactions. "You lick my earlobe and it thrills me," for example, is fine; but don't say, "I lick your earlobe and it thrills you." Just say, "I lick your earlobe." Any reaction you describe may not match the way they really react, and thus will make it hard for them to feel part of the fantasy. Let them imagine their own reactions.

➤ Similarly, don't physically describe people in your writing unless you know what they look like. You can still use non-specific complimentary terms—just make sure they aren't descriptive. You can refer to a woman's "lovely body" or a man's "handsome chest," but avoid "curvaceous body" and "muscular chest."

➤ Adjectives and descriptive phrases are your friends. They are like the smooth caresses that keep sex from being just a sudden, jerky collision. "I run my hand along your thigh," for example, doesn't hold an erotic candle to "Slowly, I glide my extended fingers across the lovely bared expanse of leg, my fingertips just barely making contact with your delicious flesh."

➤ Check out Chapter 19, "Erotica," for the addresses of some Web sites with more tips on erotic writing.

➤ Have fun! Writing the message and imagining the recipient reading the message should be a thrill.

Web-based Email: The Cyberflirt's Friend

So, you're on the Internet, and you have your email software and your email address. You have all the email access you could possibly want, right?

Probably not. If you use email from work, your email may be being read by the boss (who may be surprised to learn why you bought a case of Silly Putty and a spatula the other day).

It may be a violation of your terms of employment to use the email system for non-business items. And your company probably doesn't want its company name in an email address that is being posted in a message on the Stuffed Animal Fetish bulletin board.

If you use email at home, you may not want to have your lusty reminiscences with your old lover in the same email file that your kids are going to check when they want to know whether Grandma has emailed them. And although you're being a sexual explorer in cyberspace, you may not want an email address with your real name on it, for privacy's sake. (In the wrong hands, your email address can be used against you.)

So what you need, ideally, is another email address—one that doesn't have your name or the company's name, and one that doesn't have to go through your email software, which stores the mail on your hard disk.

What Is Web-based Email?

A number of systems these days offer free, relatively anonymous email addresses. To check your email, you go to their Web site, type your email address and a password, and voilà: Your Web browser displays a full email interface. Click here to read your email, or click there to compose and send a message. These Web sites are usually easier to use than many standalone email programs.

And better yet, they're *free*. These Web servers make their money by showing you ads while they display your mail.

So Where Is This Free Email?

Some sites specialize only in email; others offer email as part of a collection of Web site services, including news reports, search engines, stock quotes, free Web site storage space, and more. Here are some of the more popular email sites:

➤ **http://www.hotmail.com**

➤ **http://mail.yahoo.com**

➤ **http://www.iname.com**

➤ **http://www.zdnetmail.com**

➤ **http://email.angelfire.com**

MSN Hotmail is probably the best known of the free Web-based email services. As with most of the services, the interface is simple and easy to use.

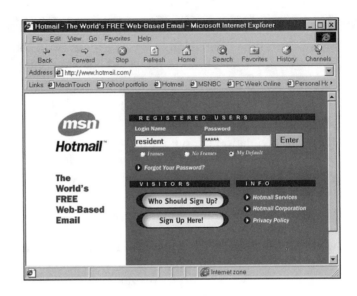

Eek! They Want to Know My Name!

To sign up for the free email from one of these sites, just click the link marked **Sign Up** or **Register** on the Web page. This takes you to a form that you have to fill out.

The form asks you to pick your own email address (the first part, that which comes before the @). They will want you to pick a password.

Privacy Has Limits!

A privacy policy is not going to protect you from having your information revealed if the police get involved. Be naughty, but don't be felonious!

The site will probably ask for more detailed information, however, such as an existing email address. Often they'll ask for your real name, address, and even your salary range. The email address is a genuine need, so they can help you remember your password if you lose it. The rest they are gathering for marketing purposes. What they want to do is send you junk mail (although usually they will put a carefully worded phrase with a check box that enables you to choose not to get junk mail).

What they won't do is to let other users know who is hiding behind your email name. Almost all these places have a posted privacy policy that promises, in detail, not to reveal that information. (If you give them a fake name or address, however, you would not be the first one.)

Other Facts That Make Web-based Email WHEEEEmail!

Besides privacy, a number of additional benefits make Web-based email worthwhile, such as the following:

➤ You can check your email from any Web terminal. When you are traveling, you can stop at an Internet café or a library to keep up your correspondence.

➤ If the person you are exchanging email with uses the same Web-based email service, new messages will usually show up in that person's mailbox instantly. This is better than a standard email service, where messages may take hours to move from one computer to another.

➤ The address belongs to you. If you have an email address through your company or through your ISP, that address will probably stop working when you change jobs or ISPs. However, your Web email address keeps working.

With all these benefits, it often makes sense to have two Web-based email addresses: one private one for play, and one with your name in the email ID to use for more practical matters.

Dealing with Spam

After your email address appears anywhere online, whether it be on a newsgroup posting, on a Web page, or as part of your company's online directory, you will start getting *spam*, which is the Internet name for email ads sent to you without your requesting them. These things are a pain in the neck. They use up your online time and your disk space, and they trigger your "You have mail" chime when there is really nothing of interest waiting for you.

Some of the most common instincts in dealing with spam are actually bad ideas:

➤ **Don't respond via email** If they actually put a valid return address on the spam, their computer will detect your response and put you on a list of people who read and respond to spam—a list that they use to send you even *more* spam! Many spammers use forged return addresses, however, which means you may be helping them fill up some innocent person's mailbox with angry email, or that your reply will just bounce back to you.

➤ **Don't visit their Web site to find some way to complain** They may be making their money by showing you ads; if you visit their site, you're helping them.

➤ **Never accept their offers** Most of what they push are obvious scams, like quack medicines and get-rich-quick schemes. Even if the spam is advertising something of interest, like an adult pictures site, any company that sends out spam doesn't deserve your business.

What can you do? Delete the message. If you are getting annoyed with the spam, check your email program (or email Web site). It may have *filtering* features that enable you to choose not to see certain email, based on who sent it or based on certain words that tend to show up in the subject line of spam messages.

Some spammers include information at the bottom of their message about how to get yourself off their mailing list. Opinions are mixed as to whether following those instructions is likely to decrease the amount of spam you receive.

The Least You Need to Know

➤ *Email,* electronic mail, is individual messages sent from one person to another.

➤ When you sign up with a service provider, it will assign you an email address and give you software to send and receive email.

➤ To compose a new message, use the **Compose** or **New Message** command in your email software. Type the user's email address, the subject of the message, and the text, and then use the **Send** command.

➤ To add a file (such as a picture file) to an email, use the **Attach** command.

➤ Free Web-based email services are a handy tool to protect your privacy.

➤ Never respond to spam (unsolicited email ads).

Chapter 5

Other Useful Utilities

In This Chapter

➤ View pictures from your hard disk

➤ Break downloaded archives into individual files

➤ Conserve hard disk space

Downloading erotic pictures and stories can very quickly leave you with a lot of files on your hard disk. Unless you have some way to manage those files, you will have trouble finding the one you want, and they can end up filling your hard disk.

A number of programs are designed to help you view images in files, find the ones you want, organize them, and reduce the amount of space that they take up.

Picture Viewers

Although most of the pictures that you download can be viewed using your Web browser, that really becomes clumsy when you have a lot of pictures to look at. The process of opening each picture file is a long one. A good picture viewer program can make that easy, however, and do a lot of other things for you as well.

Many picture viewer programs are available, with different capabilities. Many of them are shareware, which means that you can try them out to see whether you like them before you decide to buy. The following sections examine a free viewer built in to Windows, how to use your Web browser to view saved files, and some more-powerful commercial viewers.

Windows File Browser: Free and Easy

If you're using Windows 98 or Windows 95 with a recent version of Internet Explorer installed, you have a simple and quick file viewer already on hand. Although it doesn't have all the advanced image-viewing capabilities of some of the commercial viewers, it is a good thing to start with.

To use it, double-click the **My Computer** icon on your desktop. A window opens up, displaying a list of the disk drives and other storage devices on your computer. Double-click any of the devices, and the window displays a list of files and folders on that disk. Double-click any folder to get into that folder to view its files, or use the **Back** button to get out of a folder that you have gotten into.

Click **View** on the menu bar. On the menu that appears, see whether a check mark appears next to **as Web Page**. If there is, just click **View** again to make the menu go away. If the check mark isn't there, click **as Web Page** to select that viewing option.

Select any picture file by clicking its icon. The picture in the file appears on the left side of the window. Unless it's a very small picture to start with, the image will be reduced; you should still be able to see which picture it is, however.

The Web view enables you to quickly see a small version of pictures saved on your hard disk.

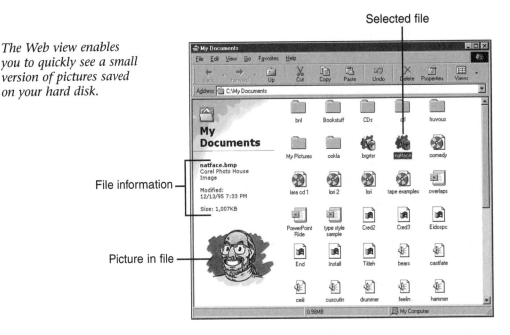

Using this method, you can quickly find the file that you want to view. After you do, double-click the file's icon, and Windows opens up a program to display that file.

Phinding Photos Among the Philes

If you have photo files mixed in with other types of files in the same directory, choose **View, Arrange Icons, by Type**. All the JPEG photo files will be grouped together on the display, and all the GIF files will be together in a separate group.

Looking at Saved Photos with Your Web Browser

Your Web browser can display your saved photo files. It's not a very good tool for searching through files, but if you know the file you want (and it's in one of the formats your Web browser supports), it works nicely.

To open a file using your Web browser, choose **File, Open**. (On most Web browsers, Ctrl+O works as a shortcut for this command.) Depending on the browser you use, your browser may open a directory navigator immediately, or you may have to press **Browse** or **Choose File** to open up a directory navigator. Use that directory navigator to locate the file you want, and then double-click the filename. The photo displays full-size in your browser window.

Remember that if all you want do is look at hard disk files, you don't need to be connected to the Internet. If starting your browser automatically starts your Internet connection, click **Cancel** or **Disconnect** on the dialer window to keep from tying up your phone line and possibly running up your Internet bill.

Turbo Browser: Not Just an Anagram for U.R. Robots Brew

Turbo Browser, manufactured by Pacific Gold Coast, is more than just a picture viewer. It's a full file-management utility for Windows 95 and higher, enabling you to look at the contents of many types of files, including word processing documents, spreadsheets, file archives, Web pages, and many more.

Turbo Browser is available in a free trial version that will run for a month. If you want to continue to use it after that, you must register it, which will cost you around $60. To download Turbo Browser, surf over to **http://www.pgcc.com/turbobrowser/downloads.html** and click one of the download servers listed. Your browser will start downloading the program and may ask you where to store the file, which is only about 1.5 megabytes. That shouldn't take more than about 15 minutes to download.

Where Do I Put Downloaded Programs?

If you are using a Macintosh computer or Windows 95 or higher, the best place to put these downloaded installation programs is on the desktop. That way, it will be easy to find the installation program to run it and later to delete it. Your browser will enable you to select this from the locations to store files; with some browsers, you can use the **Options** or **Preferences** command to set that as the default place for files; with others, you select the storage location each time.

Installing Turbo Browser

To install Turbo Browser, find the file that you downloaded using either Windows Explorer or the My Computer file browser. Double-click the file's icon, and the program starts trying to install itself.

Farrah, Cheryl, Pamela

"...if people think I'm sexy, that's wonderful. If I can help anybody get through puberty, I say 'good!'"

—Cheryl Ladd

The program asks twice where to put some files. The first time, it's just looking for a place to put files it needs for installation. Just click **OK** to put them in the current directory, and then click **OK** again when it tells you that it has finished extracting the files. The second time, it's asking about the actual program files, and suggests your main Program Files directory. Click **Next** to start the installation.

Using Turbo Browser

To start the program, click the **Start** button on the taskbar, and select **Programs**. From there, select the **Turbo Browser** folder and, from there, select **Turbo Browser**.

The Turbo Browser display looks a lot like a Windows Explorer display, with a pane on the left where you can select a disk drive and directories, and a pane to the right that shows all the files in the currently selected directory. What makes it different from Windows Explorer is the third pane; click on any filename, and the contents of that file display in the third pane.

Zoom in   Rotate

Select a directory   Select a file   Zoom out

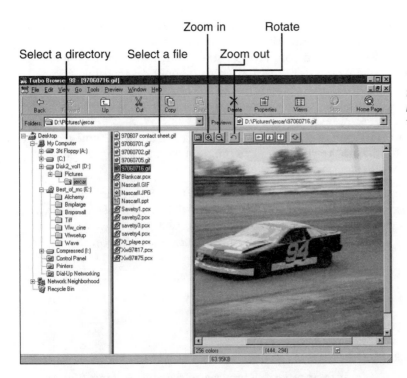

When you downloaded the file marked Racy Picture, *this wasn't what you had in mind...*

If you have a picture file selected, a series of buttons appear above the image. One button enables you to zoom in on the image, another button enables you to zoom out, and a series of buttons enable you to flip and rotate the picture in various ways.

Press **Ctrl+Shift+M** and the first two panes disappear, leaving more room to see the image. (Press **Ctrl+Shift+M** to get those two panes back.) Select **File**, **Print** to print the image.

Turbo Browser has many other fine features; exploring the menus, experimenting with files, and looking through the Help file will teach you more about those.

The Positives of Quick Vue Plus

Quick Vue Plus is a program that takes a very different approach toward picture viewing. Rather than creating its own program to find files like Turbo Browser, Quick Vue Plus enables you to use your existing file browsing tools, adding to them the capability to quickly display a file. The program can also enhance your Web browser, adding the capability to view many additional file types.

Quick Vue Plus is based on an older program called Adobe File Utilities. Versions of Quick Vue Plus are available for UNIX and for Windows 95 and higher. For Windows users, a free trial version will work for 30 days. After that, if you want to use it you will have to get the unlimited-use version, which costs about $50.

75

To download the trial version, go to **http://www.inso.com/forms/trialform.htm** and fill in the form there. Click the **Submit** button, and you will be shown a link to download the product. Click this, and your browser starts downloading the program. Your browser may ask you where to store the file, which is about 4.5 megabytes.

Installing Quick Vue Plus

If you are planning to install this version, make sure you have at least 20 megabytes available on your hard disk before you start. The program won't use up all that space in the end, but it needs it to perform the installation.

Find the file that you downloaded using either Windows Explorer or the My Computer file browser; it will be named something like `Q450e32e.exe`. Double-click the file's icon, and the program will start trying to install itself. You must step through a number of screens by clicking **OK**, **Yes**, or **Next**, depending on the screen. During this process, the installation program detects your Web browsers (and other compatible programs) and enhances them.

After the installation is complete, you can delete the file you had downloaded, freeing up several megabytes of disk space.

Using Quick Vue Plus

While using Windows Explorer or another file browser to see a list of your files, right-click any filename or icon. The menu that appears will include a **Quick View Plus**; select that command, and a window will quickly open up to display the document. This works not only with picture files, but also many types of word processor and spreadsheet files, among others.

To view hard disk files from your Web browser, use your browser's **File**, **Open** command. Select the file you want to view. Quick Vue Plus automatically detects the type of file and displays it. You can also view files from the Web that end in .dxf, .img, .pcx, .pict, .wmf, .tga, .targa, and .pic, and many others.

Zipping, Stuffing, and Squishing Files into Less Space

Files are a lot like donuts: A lot of nothingness takes up a lot of space. If you squish them down, they take up a lot less space. And if you have to deal with a whole dozen of them, they are easier to transport if you find something to put them all in, instead of carrying them one by one.

File compressors (also called *archiving utilities*) are a type of program that enables you to squish all the nothingness out of your files and to combine several files to store in one file. Then, when you need to use the files, not only can the compressor get them from the combined file, it can also unsquish them, restoring them to their pristine state. (That's something you can't do with donuts.)

These utilities have three primary uses for the adult Internet user. One is just to save space on your hard drive; by compressing your own files, you save a lot of room. Another is that these utilities also enable you to put a password on the compressed files. Because no one can uncompress the files without the password, this keeps prying eyes out of your stored files.

The third use is that many Internet sites store their files compressed into groups. This not only saves space on their file server, but it also saves a lot of downloading time because the file is compressed. It's also a lot easier for you to download a single file that holds 40 pictures of buxom babes than it is for you to start 40 separate downloads, one for each picture file.

Don't Believe Everything Your Hear

"He had heard, as all people do hear at some time or other, that sex can be learned from the gutter, so he set out to make a comprehensive survey of the gutters of eighteen large American cities."

—*Is Sex Necessary?*, James Thurber & E.B. White (1929)

If you download one of those compressed files, you need a file compression program to get at the files. Luckily, there is one standard program for Windows users and another one for Macintosh users; get the program for your computer, and you should be able to handle most of what's out there.

WinZip for Windows

Most compressed files you'll download are *Zip files*, which end with the .zip extension. A number of programs can create these files or pull the original files out. (In fact, the Turbo Browser program discussed earlier in this chapter can handle Zip files; so if you are using that, you don't need a separate file compression utility.)

The best known and most powerful program for handling Zip files is WinZip, which can also handle a number of other types of compressed files. Surf over to **http://www. winzip.com** to download it, and double-click the downloaded file's icon to start the installation. The file size is about 1 megabyte.

Free UnZipping!

If all you are interested in doing is unzipping other people's zipped files instead of zipping your own, you can use a free UnZip utility from **http://www.camdevelopment. com**.

After you have installed WinZip, you can open any Zip file just by double-clicking it. WinZip automatically starts up and displays a list of the compressed files. You can double-click any file to quickly view its contents, or use the **Extract** command to copy it from the Zip file into its own file. WinZip has a built-in tutorial and help system to guide you through the details of its many features.

As this WinZip file display shows, compressing files can save over 80% of the space they take up, although compressing JPEG files will save considerably less space.

File size before compression

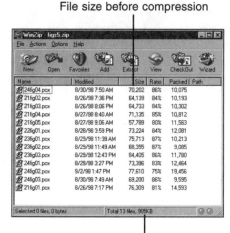

Space it takes up in zipped file

You can use the trial version of WinZip for three weeks before deciding whether you want to keep it. If you like the program, registration costs $29.

StuffIt for Macintosh

StuffIt is the standard Macintosh file compression software. Several versions of this program are available. StuffIt Expander can only take files out of a compressed file. It cannot make compressed files. However, it's free. Surf over to **http://www. aladdinsys.com** to download it.

From the same site, you can also download DropStuff With Expander Enhancer, which when combined with the StuffIt Expander enables you to compress files. This is a shareware program, however; after 15 days, it will cost you $30 to continue using it. For about $70 to $80, you can buy StuffIt Deluxe, which has all those features and more.

All versions can understand BinHex, MacBinary, and StuffIt files, which are the three most important formats for downloading Macintosh programs. The commercial versions can also understand Zip files and several other formats.

Automatic Unsquishing!

Some compression utilities configure your browser to automatically decompress any compressed file you download. If your browser is not configured like this, you can configure your Web browser to automatically start your file compression program whenever you download a compressed file. Use the file compression program's **Help** command to be shown information on how to do this.

The Least You Need to Know

➤ You can double-click the Windows **My Computer** icon to bring up a file browser that enables you to quickly see small images of photos stored on your hard disk.

➤ A Web browser's **File, Open** command (**Ctrl+O**) can be used to view saved pictures.

➤ Picture viewer utilities such as Turbo Browser and Quick Vue Pro make it easy to quickly look at the contents of your picture files.

➤ File compression utilities enable you to squish several files together into one file that takes up less space, or to unsquish files out of those compressed files.

➤ The standard Windows file compression utility is WinZip. The StuffIt family of products is the standard for the Macintosh.

Chapter 6

Finding Sex Sites on the Web

In This Chapter

➤ Following links and clicking banners

➤ Using recommended site lists

➤ Using search engines

If you have surfed the Web at all, you know that sex sites are everywhere. As you soon discover, however, all sex sites are not created equal. Many do not have the type, quality, or quantity of material you seek. That's why it helps to know the techniques you can use to find the best sex sites.

Click, Click, Click: Links and Banners

When searching for new Web sites, you occasionally run across Web addresses in magazines or on television that you can type into the Address box of your Web browser. Similarly, friends may email addresses (also called *URLs*) to you that you can copy and paste into the Address box. More common, however, is just clicking a text or graphic *link* in a Web page to go to a new site.

Banners are graphics links (usually rectangle-shaped) that advertise other sex sites. Clicking a banner transports you to a different sex site.

Banners serve two purposes for a site owner. First, sites often swap banners with one another as sort of a cooperative advertising program. Second, when you click a banner and arrive at the new site, you may be generating a tiny amount of revenue for the referring site. These *clickthroughs* enable many of the smaller sites—particularly the free ones—to stay in business.

Because the pages of sex sites are often overflowing with links and banners, following these links is an easy way for you to explore new sites. Note, however, that these links often lead to pay sites. After touring the site and checking out a few samples, you may be asked whether you want to dig out your credit card to pay for a membership. The choice, of course, is always yours.

Clicking Is Faster Than Copy and Paste

In most current email programs, you don't have to copy and paste URLs. If a Web page address appears in the text of an email message, you can just click it to instruct your browser to go to that Web site.

It's alive!

Banner ads for sex sites often contain animations depicting sex acts, designed to draw your attention. Not surprisingly, this works—at least the first few times you see one.

Because they can be money-makers, it's not unusual to find lots of banners on some site pages.

The Best Names for Sex Sites

Adult movies often have corny or unusual names designed to attract attention. Sex sites are no different. A few of the more creative Web site names we came across include the following. (We won't vouch for the site content, however.)

➤ Heh! That's My Wife! (**http://www.ungawa.com/aesc/wife1.htm**)

➤ Girl Germs Posters (**http://www.positive.org/Home/posters.html**)

➤ Vertical Smiles (**http://verticalsmiles.com/**)

➤ Jessica Grabbit (**http://www.jessicagrabbit.com/home.html**)

➤ ohyes-OhYes.com (**http://www.ohyes-ohyes.com/**)

➤ Saving Ryan's Privates (**http://www.stiff-one-eye.com/saving/**)

Sex Site Lists

Clicking banners invariably leads to an unending stream of pay sites. If you are interested in free sites (or at least some free sample pictures), you can consult one of the many sex site lists available on the Web.

Persian Kitty's Adult Links (**http://www.persiankitty.com/**) is the premier page for exploring sex sites. With listings for around 1,700 links, you are almost certain to spot something that appeals to you. To keep the list manageable, sites are split into several broad categories, such as "Free Sites with Images" and "Amateur, Voyeur, Exhibitionist Pix." Each link description includes the number of pictures and movie clips you can find at the site.

Sites have to ask to be listed in Persian Kitty's Adult Links and must abide by these restrictions:

➤ The site must not require an *adult verification system* for you to gain admission.

➤ The site cannot employ obtrusive *pop-up consoles* or exit consoles. (A *console* is a small window that automatically pops up when you go to or leave a particular Web page. It may contain links to pages or advertisements, for example. Pop-up consoles are often annoying and intrusive.)

➤ The site cannot contain illegal material such as child pornography. Sites that contain celebrity nudes and porn star home pages also are excluded.

Because the list changes daily, you will want to return to Persian Kitty's on a regular basis.

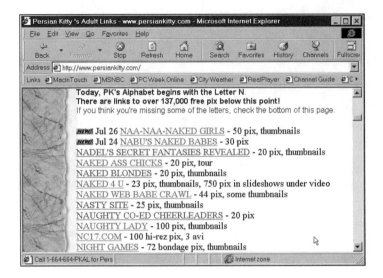

If Persian Kitty doesn't satisfy all your needs, Table 6.1 has some other site lists that you may want to peruse:

Table 6.1   Sex Site Lists

Site Name	Web Address	Description
69 Sex Sites	**http://www.69sexsites.com/**	Links and comments for a limited set of hetero-sexual, gay/lesbian, bd/sm, and transgender sites
AdultSeek	**http://www.adultseek.com/**	View links by category or search using key-words; provides site descriptions
Babe 911	**http://www.atch.com/ babe911/**	Bikini and adult site links organized by cate-gory; some commentary
Helmy's 4adultsonly V4.0	**http://www.4adultsonly.com/**	Links by category; view samples from picture sites
Amateur Hardcore's A-Rated Hot Spots!	**http://www.amateurs.com/ amateurs/hotspots.htm**	Links by category with comments; offers pic-ture searches for paying members
Jane's Net Guide	**http://www.janesguide.com/**	Detailed reviews of Sex selected Web sites

Site Name	Web Address	Description
Naughty Lynx	**http://naughty.com**	Search site that works like Yahoo!; excellent site descriptions
QuikSex! Adult Search Engine	**http://www.quiksex.com/**	Links by category with comments
Sexhound	**http://www.sexhound.com/**	Sniff out new sites with their search engine or by clicking category links
Star-Rated Adult Link Listing	**http://www.ohyes-ohyes.com/**	Star ratings of selected sites
Sticky Links	**http://www.stickylinks.com/**	Hundreds of links by category; raw, straight-ahead commentary
The Ynot Adult Network Smart List	**http://ww2.ynotnetwork.com/ smartlinks/**	Extensive site list organized by category; notes whether sites include thumbnails, videos, require membership, and so on
Zweistein's Erotic Links	**http://huizen.dds.nl/ ~milacku/list.html**	800 links, arranged alphabetically by site name

The List of Lists

Although everyone eventually settles on his own preferred source of new sex sites, you might want to refer to Yahoo! for some additional suggestions. Type the following address in your Web browser to see a massive list of sex link directories:

http://www.yahoo.com/Business_and_Economy/Companies/Sex/ Directories/

Search Engines

Whether you're a novice or an experienced Web surfer, you probably have used popular search sites such as these:

AltaVista (**http://www.altavista.com/**)

Excite (**http://www.excite.com/**)

Lycos (**http://www.lycos.com/**)

Yahoo! (**http://www.yahoo.com/**)

Where Oh Where Has My Little Lamb Gone?

You can also use some of the search engines, such as AltaVista, to search for matches in newsgroups.

These general search sites are commonly referred to as *search engines*. They enable you to search the Internet for Web pages that contain information that matches the *keywords* (search strings) you type.

You may already have used search engines to find sites that mention topics such as stamp collecting, baseball, butterflies, art deco, psychotherapy, or any of a million other subjects. Not surprisingly, these same search engines prove useful in finding sex sites. In fact, many of the sites discussed in this book were found using search engines. If you get tired of blindly following links from one sex site to the next, give a search engine a try. The site descriptions provided by search engines are often more elaborate than those that accompany the links and banners in sex sites.

In Yahoo!, entering the search phrase "sex sites" yields an extensive list of links to sex directories. To go to any of the found sites, click the underlined or highlighted text.

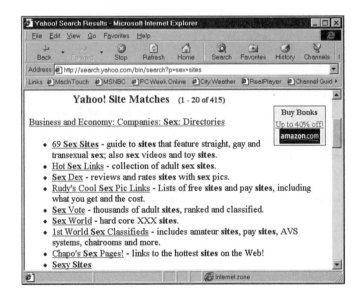

Searching with Internet Explorer

If you use the latest version of Internet Explorer (Microsoft) as your Web browser, you can take advantage of its built-in search feature. Click the **Search** button on the toolbar to open a search pane on the left side of the document window. To conduct a search, choose from any of the search engines listed in the drop-down menu; type a search word, phrase, or list of keywords in the box; and click a button to begin the search. After a few seconds, matches (also called *hits*) appear in the search pane. To view any of the listed Web pages, click its link in the search pane. Because the search pane doesn't change as you explore the links, you never have to click the **Back** button to refresh the link list.

You can also do a search of Yahoo! by typing search terms in the Address box at the top of the Internet Explorer 4 window. Just type a question mark (?) followed by your keywords (such as **? oral sex**), and then press **Return**.

Click the **Search** button to show or hide the search pane

Address box

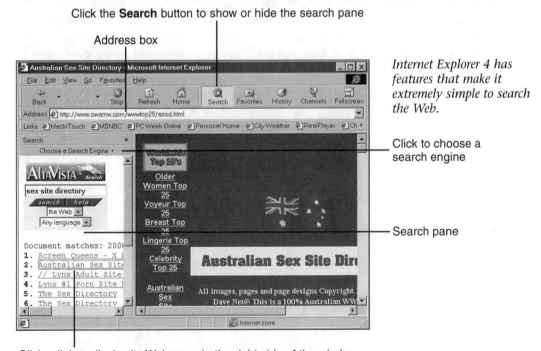

Internet Explorer 4 has features that make it extremely simple to search the Web.

Click to choose a search engine

Search pane

Click a link to display its Web page in the right side of the window

Occasionally, you run across a sex site that has a built-in search engine. To see an example, go to A411 Adult Links (**http://www.a411.com/links.html**). At A411, you can perform a simultaneous search of 16 of the top Web search engines, such as AltaVista and Lycos.

People Just Like You and Me

If you think you're alone in your interest in Net sex, think again. Go to the following Web page to see how many other people are using Magellan to locate sex sites: **http://voyeur.mckinley.com/cgi-bin/voyeur.cgi**.

The Least You Need to Know

➤ Sex sites often contain links and banners you can click to visit new Web sites.

➤ You can find many extensive lists of sex sites on the Web. Each may include hundreds or even thousands of sex-oriented sites. The better ones include site descriptions, as well as information concerning whether the site offers picture *thumbnails*, the number of free pictures, types and number of movie clips, quality and speed ratings, and so on.

➤ Although you might not think to look there, general-purpose search sites, such as Yahoo! and AltaVista, can be very helpful in finding sex sites.

Chapter 7

Safe from Prying Eyes

In This Chapter

➤ Monitoring your children's Internet activities

➤ Protecting your privacy

This chapter provides some suggestions for ways to keep your children from getting at the same Internet content you are viewing and for keeping your online activities private.

Child's Play (Restricting Access)

In many households, children are free to wander the Internet as they please. As this book demonstrates, however, you probably prefer they not see plenty of Internet material. The simplest way to restrict your kids' Internet activities is by doing one or both of the following:

➤ Use a Web rating system to restrict the sites that they can and cannot view.

➤ Install software that enables you to control their other Internet activities, such as the amount of time they spend online, whether they will be allowed to enter certain chat rooms or channels, and the types of personal information they are allowed to reveal while online.

Web Rating Systems

You can choose from several major Web rating systems. The way they typically work is that every Web site gets a series of numeric ratings for the amount and type of objectionable material it contains, such as sexual and violent content. If you want to restrict your child's access to certain types of Web sites (those that show partial or frontal nudity, for example), you just specify a low Nudity rating in your browser's Options (for Internet Explorer users) or in an ancillary program such as Cyber Patrol. If the child then attempts to go to a rated site that includes nudity, he or she is prohibited from entering the site. As an example, let's look at how one of the major Web rating services works.

RSACi (Recreational Software Advisory Council on the Internet) does not rate Web pages. Webmasters rate their *own* pages, submitting numeric ratings for violence, sex, nudity, and language on a five-point scale (see Table 7.1). Each Webmaster is then responsible for embedding the site's ratings in the Web page code so that they can be read and responded to by browsers and parental control programs.

Table 7.1   RSACi Ratings

	Violence Rating Descriptor	**Nudity Rating Descriptor**	**Sex Rating Descriptor**	**Language Rating Descriptor**
Level 4	Rape or wanton, gratuitous violence	Frontal nudity (qualifying as provocative display)	Explicit sexual acts or sex crimes	Crude, vulgar language, or extreme hate speech
Level 3	Aggressive violence or death to humans	Frontal nudity	Non-explicit sexual acts	Strong language or hate speech
Level 2	Destruction of realistic objects	Partial nudity	Clothed sexual touching	Moderate expletives or profanity
Level 1	Injury to human being	Revealing attire	Passionate kissing	Mild expletives
Level 0	None of the above or sports related	None of the above	None of the above or innocent kissing; romance	None of the above

Internet Explorer 4 includes support for the RSACi ratings. To use them, choose **Internet Options** from the View menu, click the **Content** tab in the dialog box that appears, and click the **Enable** button in the Content Advisor section. If it's the first time that you are enabling the Content Advisor, you will be asked to type and confirm a supervisor password. Only someone who knows the supervisor password can modify these options or turn them on or off. Click the **Settings** button and adjust the sliders to determine the levels of violence, sex, nudity, and language you want to allow.

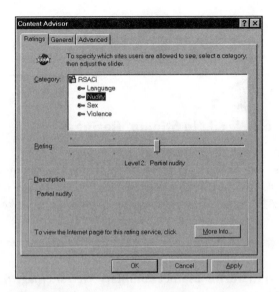

To set a rating, click a category and drag the slider until the desired rating text is shown.

After you finish setting the ratings, click the **General** tab. You can check two User Options:

➤ **Users can see sites that have no rating** If you don't check this option, your children can only go to RSACi-rated sites. Although this will prevent your kids from seeing most of the sexual content on the Web, it will also keep them from seeing virtually *anything* on the Web. This is because non-sexual sites seldom submit ratings to RSACi—or any other rating service, for that matter. On the other hand, checking this option will enable your kids to visit any Web page that has not been rated—including many sex-oriented sites.

Microsoft Wins...for Now

At present, Internet Explorer has built-in support for site ratings; Netscape Navigator 4 does not. However, it appears that Navigator 4.5—when released—*will* support SafeSurf site ratings (discussed later).

➤ **Supervisor can type a password to allow users to view restricted content** This is the supervisor's "ratings override" option. If you want to look at an unrated site or a site with ratings that exceed your settings, all you have to do is type the supervisor's password.

As you can see, relying on the RSACi ratings to control your kids' Web activities is an iffy proposition. To make it work for you, we suggest that you enable ratings and check only the supervisor option. Then when your child wants to see an unrated site, he/she must ask you to enter the password.

Ratings? We Don't Need No Stinkin' Ratings!

Because it is in the interest of sex sites to prohibit children from viewing their pages, you would think that they would be eager to be rated. Sadly, few sex sites bother to turn on content ratings. As a test, I randomly checked 40 of the sex sites in this book. Only three had RSACi ratings. Trusting in rating systems alone to keep your kids from entering forbidden sites is probably a mistake.

SafeSurf (**http://www.safesurf.com**) is another voluntary Web site/page rating system. In addition to rating pages for adult or controversial content (such as drug references), Webmasters are asked to determine the appropriate age range for viewing their site. If you use Internet Explorer, and would like to use this standard with your browser, you can download the ratings system from the Safesurf Web page. Netscape Communicator 4.5 will have it integrated automatically.

Helpful Software

Rather than trusting in rating systems to do the entire job, you should consider installing additional software to help monitor what your kids do online. Cyber Patrol and Net Nanny are two popular programs.

Cyber Patrol

http://www.cyberpatrol.com/

You can use Cyber Patrol ($29.95, PCs and Macs) to block or allow access to Web sites based on their content, such as the presence of nudity, profanity, and explicit sex. Cyber Patrol also does a lot more, however. You can pick the times of day when Internet access is permitted. You can specify text strings that will be jumbled when typed by your child during a chat or on a Web form (such as his/her name, street address, phone number, and your credit card numbers). You can prevent access to Internet Relay Chat channels, and prohibit him/her from running particular programs on your computer.

Cyber Patrol offers a free seven-day demo that you can download from **http://www.cyberpatrol.com/download.htm**.

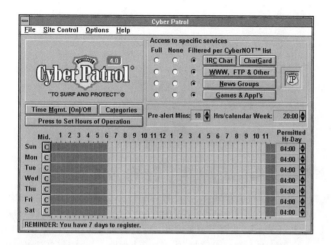

A quick glance at the Cyber Patrol window will show the monitoring options that are enabled, as well as your child's online time schedule.

Net Nanny

http://www.netnanny.com/

Net Nanny ($26.95, Windows 3.1x/95/98) can block, monitor, and filter anything happening on your PC—regardless of whether your child is connected to the Internet. Not only can it monitor what he or she sees on the Web, it can eliminate the capability to send or receive certain types of information and graphic images. Words, phrases, content, and Web sites that you have deemed inappropriate for your child can all be monitored. You specify the action that will be taken for each type of violation, including making a note of it in a log file, masking out the prohibited words with *x*'s, displaying a warning, or shutting down the program.

Web site monitoring is based on "can go" and "cannot go" Web site lists. You can download these lists from the Net Nanny site and modify them as you see fit. If you have more than one child, you can set up different allowable actions for each one. (This can be very helpful when your children's ages are disparate.)

Net Nanny offers a 30-day, full-featured evaluation copy of their software. You can download it from **http://www.netnanny.com/downloads**.

Things Your Children Should Know About Using the Internet

Chances are, because you are interested in the Internet, your kids will be, too. Children are inquisitive, curious, and they love to explore. They will also imitate Mommy and Daddy, for better or for worse. Unfortunately, children can also be very naïve.

Discuss the following situations with your kids:

➤ Going to a Web site that looks like it is for adults

➤ Receiving email from a stranger

➤ Being asked for personal information

➤ Someone using bad words or saying things that make them uncomfortable

➤ Meeting FTF (face to face)

Going to a Web Site That Looks Like It Is for Adults

Your kids are going to surf. No matter how hard you try, you can't watch over their shoulders every second that they are online, and no matter how good your filtering and ratings system is, adult sites still slip by. You need to come to an understanding with your children that when they pull up a Web site that looks like it is for adults (define that however you like), they need to use the back button right away.

Receiving Email from a Stranger

When people post messages to newsgroups using their real email address, they start getting unsolicited email (sometimes within seconds, it seems). Sometimes that email is going to be an invitation to visit a site that you would rather have them not see. Teach your kids not to respond to email, not to click any links in an email, and especially not to open any attachments nor install any software sent to them by strangers.

Being Asked for Personal Information

Predators may use many pieces of information to track your child down. Tell your child to *never* give out his or her real last name, address, phone number, password, or any other personal information.

Someone Using Bad Words or Saying Things That Make Them Uncomfortable

If your young children see something on the Internet that makes them feel uncomfortable, they should come get Mom or Dad so that you can talk to them about it. This could be anything from naked people to the ad for the latest horror movie. And, if you allow your children to chat, they should know that they shouldn't converse with people who use bad words.

Meeting FTF (Face to Face)

Let your kids know to never, never, never agree to meet someone that they have met over the Internet face to face. You should meet in a public place and tell the other child to bring along his/her parents as well. If the "child" is too old to bring along parents, well, maybe you don't want your child to meet that "child."

Protecting Your Privacy

Most people prefer to keep some aspects of their lives private. This includes financial records, medical histories, and even personal data such as phone numbers and street addresses. Sex is no different, especially if you have children who are naturally curious about what Mom and Dad keep in the bottom dresser drawer—or stored on the family computer. Here are a few ways to protect your privacy:

➤ Clearing the Documents (Windows 95) and Recent Documents (Macintosh) folder

➤ Clearing your browser's History

➤ Making files invisible

➤ Encrypting or password-protecting files and folders

➤ Protecting chat transcripts

➤ Emptying your Trashcans and Recycle Bins

➤ Removing the Iomega Zip drive

➤ Installing Windows NT

America Online?

If your family accesses the Internet through America Online, see Chapter 9 for information on preventing children who use the account from viewing adult material.

Clearing the Documents (Windows 95) and Recent Documents (Macintosh) Folder

One of the great features of Windows 95 and current versions of the Macintosh OS is that the operating system can automatically keep track of the most recent documents you have opened—enabling you to quickly reopen them in a subsequent computing session just by choosing their names from a menu. Although this can be a great time-saver, it does have one tiny drawback. It offers anyone else who sits down at your computer the ability to open those same files—without even having to know their location on your hard disk. If you spent the last several hours viewing and downloading pictures from Betsy's Sex Palace, for example, you might not want to make it so easy for your kids to deliberately—or accidentally—view those same pictures.

The Documents folder holds the last 15 documents you have opened. To see them, choose the **Documents** folder from the Start menu.

*By opening the
Documents menu, anyone
can see the documents you
have recently worked on
or viewed.*

To clear the contents of the Documents folder, follow these steps:

1. Click the **Start** button, and choose **Settings**, **Taskbar**, **Start Menu**. The Taskbar Properties dialog box appears.

2. Click the **Start Menu Programs** tab at the top of the dialog box.

3. In the Documents menu section of the dialog box, click the **Clear** button.

4. Click **OK** to close the dialog box.

But I Deleted Those Pictures Right After I Looked at Them!

Sorry, Charlie. Although deleting or moving the original files will keep you or anyone else from opening them by using the Documents menu, it does not remove their names.

The Recent Documents folder on aMacintosh serves the same function as the Documents folder in Windows 95. To clear the Recent Documents folder on a Macintosh computer, do this:

1. Open the **System** folder on your startup hard disk.

2. Open the **Apple Menu Items** folder.

3. Open the **Recent Documents** folder, and select all the files.

4. Drag the files to the Trash and then empty it (by choosing **Empty Trash** from the Special menu).

Don't Remember Those Documents

If you don't want to employ the cumbersome procedure for emptying the Recent Documents folder, you can stop the Macintosh from listing *any* recent documents. Click the **Apple** menu, and choose **Apple Menu Options** from the Control Panels folder. Then you can either remove the check mark from **Remember recently used items** or set the **Documents** setting to **0** (zero).

Clearing Your Browser's History

Another useful software feature that can leave footprints in the sand, so to speak, is your browser's *history*. As you hop from one Web site or page to another, your browser makes a record of each page you have visited. Later, if you want to visit the same site again, you can just choose it from the browser's History list or menu.

If the sites you normally visit are adult sites, you may want to make a practice of clearing the History after every surfing session. The procedure for clearing the History is slightly different in every browser.

➤ **To manually clear the history in Internet Explorer 4** Choose **Internet Options** from the View menu. In the General section of the Internet Options dialog box, click the **Clear History** button.

The Days to keep pages in history setting determines how long pages are remembered before they are automatically deleted.

Get Rid of Your Cache, Too

It's also a good idea to periodically clear your browser's **Temporary Internet files** (found in the Internet Options dialog box in Internet Explorer and under Edit, Options, Advanced, Cache in Netscape Navigator).

➤ **To manually clear the history in Netscape Navigator** Select **General Preferences** from the Options menu, click the **Appearance** tab, and click **Expire now**.

Set the **Visited links expire after *n* days** field to whatever you want. When that number of days has passed, all older links are automatically deleted.

➤ **To manually clear the history in Netscape Communicator** Select **Preferences** from the Edit menu, click the **Navigator** category, and click **Expire now**.

Set the **Visited links expire after *n* days** field to whatever you want. When that number of days has passed, all older links are automatically deleted.

Making Files Invisible

In most operating systems, you can make any file or folder invisible. Regardless of whether you are looking for them on the desktop or in an Open dialog box, invisible files and folders aren't shown, unless your computer is explicitly told to show them.

To make files or folders invisible under Windows 95, follow these steps:

Sometimes Smaller Is Better

You may want to reduce the number of days that the history is recorded—changing it to **1** or **0**, for instance. The shorter the time period chosen, the more frequently your browser will automatically clear it.

1. Double-click the **My Computer** icon on the desktop, and go to the folder that holds the files or folder you want to hide. (Alternatively, you can run Windows Explorer by choosing it from the Start menu on the taskbar.)

2. Choose **Folder Options** from the View menu.

3. Click the **View** tab in the Folder Options dialog box.

4. In the Hidden Files section of the dialog box, make sure that **Do not show hidden or system files** or **Do not show hidden files** is selected. Then click **OK**.

5. Select the files or folders you want to hide. To select multiple items, you can Control-click them.

6. Right-click the selected items, and choose Properties from the menu that appears.

7. In the Attributes section of the dialog box that appears, click the **Hidden** check box, and then click **OK**.

8. Choose **Refresh** from the View menu. Any files or folders that you have hidden will suddenly disappear.

When you want to look at any of these files or folders again, repeat steps 1–3, choose **Show all files**, and click **OK**. To permanently change them back to normal files and folders, continue with steps 5–6, and then click to remove the check mark in the Hidden attribute.

On a Macintosh computer, the procedure is a little different. Although the Macintosh OS does support invisible files and folders, there is no operating system-based command you can use to make items invisible. Instead, you need a separate utility program, such as FileTyper (**http://www.ugcs.caltech.edu/~dazuma/filetyper**). To make a file or folder invisible in FileTyper, you just open it from the current file list, set the **isInvisible** attribute, and click **Change**. If you later want to open the file to view or work with it, run FileTyper again and remove the check mark from the **isInvisible** attribute.

Encrypting/Password-Protecting Files and Folders

Making files and folders invisible is not foolproof. Encryption or password protection software is a more secure way of protecting your privacy.

Because you have so many encryption and password-protection programs out there to choose from, it's difficult to recommend any single one. Here are a few general tips, however:

A Couple of Definitions

Password-protected files can only be opened by entering the correct password. *Encrypted files* are opened in the same manner, but the files are scrambled to prevent them from being read or viewed without your permission.

➤ Assigning different passwords to every file will quickly create a nightmare situation. Imagine trying to remember 50 different passwords! A better approach is to install a utility that enables you to easily encrypt or password-protect the contents of selected *folders*. That way, anything you toss into the folder will automatically be protected.

➤ When dreaming up passwords, be original. If someone is trying to guess your passwords, your age, birth date, kids' names, phone number, street address, and so on *will* be tried—especially if it's your kids who are trying. They're not dummies.

➤ Different utilities offer different levels of protection. Read the program's documentation thoroughly before you decide that it affords adequate security.

➤ If email security is a concern, look for an email program or an add-on that supports encryption.

You can also use password with Zip files by using the built in features of PKZIP (**http://www.pkware.com**) or WinZip (**http://www.winzip.com**).

To begin your quest for a freeware or shareware encryption/password utility that meets your needs, try these Web sites:

➤ Windows 95/98 (**http://www.winfiles.com/apps/98/encrypt.html**)

➤ Macintosh (**http://hyperarchive.lcs.mit.edu/HyperArchive.html**)

Emptying Your Trashcans and Recycle Bins

When you delete something, remember that it's not really gone.

In many e-mail programs, it is a two-step process to delete messages. Initially, deleting a message in Microsoft Outlook or Outlook Express merely moves it to the Deleted Items folder. To *really* delete the messages, you have to open the Deleted Items folder and delete them a second time, or you can quit the program, which—if your Options are set correctly—automatically trashes all deleted messages.

Operating systems such as Windows 95/98, Windows NT, and Macintosh have their own Recycle Bin and Trashcan. Instead of being for email messages, however, they are for your deleted files. Make sure to empty these frequently as well.

Using an Iomega Zip Drive

Even after you have taken several, if not all of these precautions, your files can still be accessed. The only way for you to know for sure that your files are not being accessed without your permission is to remove them completely from your computer. Why not invest in an Iomega Zip drive and use the 100MB floppy disks to save your sexy files? So long as they are with you, they won't be with somebody else.

Installing Windows NT

Let's face it, Windows 95/98 has no security at all. You can set up different passwords to keep personalized desktops for every person that uses your computer, but if someone just presses the Escape key at the logon screen, your computer starts Windows and he or she has access to all the files on your hard drive.

For real security, install Windows NT. It requires a username and password to log in to the computer, and if your hard drive is formatted with NTFS (a special hard drive format used to limit access to unauthorized users) you can deny access to your folders on the hard drive.

The Internet and the Workplace

"Well, I finished lunch 20 minutes early today. There's still time for a little Web surfing...guess I'll see what's new at **www.smutland.com.**"

Stop! Before you fire up your browser or a chat program, be *sure* you know your company's Internet usage policy. There are several excellent reasons for abstaining from sex-related Net activities during business hours, including the following:

➤ In some companies, if what you're doing on the Net *is* not business-related, it can be grounds for suspension or dismissal.

➤ Supervisors may have installed software to monitor employee computer usage, or a copy of your browser's History file might reside on the company network. You should also know that recent court decisions have given employers the right to view employee email.

➤ Displaying sexual material on your screen where other workers might see it could be construed to be sexual harassment.

Know Your Software

Although you may spend hours each day in your favorite chat and instant messaging programs, it's extraordinarily important to know the features each program offers. Unless you have thoroughly explored the Preference and Option settings, you may be placing yourself in jeopardy every time you use these programs.

As an example, ICQ (a popular instant-messaging program) has features that can cause serious grief for its users. First, the default Preferences setting is for ICQ to record a history of messages for each of your online contacts. Unless you routinely delete these histories, anyone who has access to your computer can read your private conversations. Second, although ICQ's chat capabilities have made it a favorite among chatters, the last person to leave an ICQ chat session has the option to save the entire conversation as a transcript.

Other types of Internet software can also pose problems:

➤ Most email programs automatically keep copies of all sent messages. You may want to turn off this option or manually delete selected messages.

➤ Beware of Newsgroup readers. Even if you delete all newsgroup messages and headers at the end of every session, your list of subscribed newsgroups remains. Do you want your kids to know that you checked out **alt.sex.stories**?

The moral here should be obvious. *Read the documentation and Help file for every Internet program you use.* If an option or feature looks dangerous and you have no control over it (such as the ability of chat participants to save transcripts), you can either avoid that part of the program—assuming that's possible—or just chuck the program.

Sharing a Windows PC with Your Kids

So many people are sharing PCs these days that Microsoft decided to make it easy to keep everyone's stuff separate. If you use Windows 95, you can set up your PC so that every user has his/her own preferences and a password. To enable multi-user settings, open the **Users** Control Panel and walk through the dialog boxes.

The Least You Need to Know

➤ While Net sex is a great entertainment for adults, it's not what you want your kids to see. You can combine the content rating features of your browser with a commercial monitoring program to handle this situation.

➤ If you want to maintain your privacy, you should make it a regular practice to clear your Documents (PC) or Recent Documents (Macintosh) folder, and delete your browser's history or cache.

➤ Other things you can do to keep your children from finding sexual documents on your computer include changing file and folder types to hidden (PC) or invisible (Macintosh) and installing password-protection or encryption software.

➤ It's generally a good idea to restrict your Net sex activities to the privacy of your home. This is *not* appropriate in the workplace.

➤ If you want to keep your computing activities separate from those of your children, consider setting up your Windows PC for multiple users.

THAT'LL
BE
$ 8.95,
PAL.

Chapter 8

Free, "Free," and Commercial Web Sites

In This Chapter

➤ How Web sites are paid for

➤ Getting value for your money

➤ Keeping an eye out for scams

Offering erotic material of various sorts is one of the biggest businesses on the Internet; and make no mistake, it is a business. Almost every time you see a Web site dedicated to arousing material, someone is aiming to make money off of the site.

Why Aren't There More Sites for the Fun of It?

From time to time, people decide to take advantage of free Web space they have, and some photos that they happen to have access to (legally or otherwise), and put up a nice, noncommercial Web site just because they enjoy the material so much. These sites almost always disappear quickly. Why? Because generally when somebody is given free Web space, it's with the expectation that it won't receive many visitors. It doesn't put much of a stress on a service provider's equipment to have up some pages that get visited maybe 10 times per day.

When word gets out about a good sex site (and word does seem to spread), however, a lot of people come to visit. Suddenly, a thousand visitors per day stop by, each downloading a megabyte worth of pictures. This uses up a lot of the service provider's resources, and they are apt to give the person running the site two choices: either take the site down, or start paying big bucks like a commercial site.

Most choose the first option, taking the site down. Some pay, and then support their site by putting up advertising for other sites or by charging for access. In other words, they become commercial sites.

A few noncommercial sites do survive, but those are mostly ones that carry only stories, not photos. Story sites don't attract as many people, and a 10-page story uses up less computer resources than a single photo.

"But They Said the Site Is Free!" They Would Lie!

Plenty of sites will tell you that the site is free. Does this mean that you aren't going to pay anything to see it? Possibly. Does this mean that they aren't making money from you seeing it? Definitely not.

Let's consider some of the ways sites make money.

The Banner Ad Model

Many sites make their money by running banner ads for other Web sites. What kind of Web sites? Sex sites, of course. On these sites, it's often slow to see what you want to see, because every time you try to bring up a photo, you're also spending online time bringing up an ad.

These sites sometimes make money each time an ad displays. In most cases, however, money only changes hands if you click on a banner, which will take you to the advertiser's site. If you're on an ad-supported site and appreciate what you're getting, you should click on a banner from time to time. You usually don't have to sign up with the pay site for the ad site to make the money. And be forewarned: Even the paid sites have ads on them, although not generally as many.

The Pretty Catalog Model

Some Web sites offer free pictures and stories as a lure to get you to look at things they have for sale. Usually, these sites are built around a single beautiful model or set of models; you can view photos of them at no charge, and then if you want, you can buy videos, or photo sets, or products such as sex toys or lingerie. Check out **http://www.jtl-productions.com/jtl/April/Aprila.htm** for an example.

Does the fact that it's a catalog mean that it's not worth looking at the pictures? Of course not, as many a man who has flipped through the Frederick's of Hollywood catalog will attest. (And to stave off the next question: of course they do, at **http://www.fredericks.com**.)

These sites seem to be on the wane, however, as more of the stars of erotic videos or strip clubs are starting membership-only sites.

The "It's Free, If You Prove You're an Adult" Model

Many sites advertise themselves as being "100% free" (as if being "43% free" would mean something). But when you try to get in to see the pictures, they ask for verification that you're an adult. How do you verify that? By giving them your ID number from Adult Check or one of several other adult verification services (AVS).

You don't have such verification? Well, just follow the links on the site to get some. So you get taken to the verification company's site, and that site verifies that you're an adult...by taking your credit card information, to which they charge $15 to $20 for a year's membership. With that membership, you can access any site on the membership list. With Adult Check, that's thousands of sites. Much of that fee is given back to the site you first signed up with. That's how sites make money.

At many of those thousands of sites, you'll discover that what you get is a dozen or so pictures. That's it. After all, you have already paid what you're going to pay; they have no reason to give you value.

You Can Leave Your Hat On

Brevity is the soul of lingerie.

—Dorothy Parker

Even if you have an adult verification ID, some sites want more money from you. You may discover that your ID lets you see only a portion of what they have to show you. If you want to see everything, you have to pay an additional membership fee directly to the site. You surf on back to Adult Check to see whether they know about this problem of small sites and partial access. They do, of course, and they have a solution. It's the Adult Check Gold membership, which gets you full access at the many Adult Check Gold-based sites, sites that they tell you they picked as the best sites of their membership and have at least 200 pictures. Of course, this runs you another $15 or so per month, some of which is given to the Gold-approved sites, which is how they make their money.

Is signing up with an age verification system worth it? Probably, as it does give you access to tens of thousands of pictures. Stick to one AVS and explore its sites before you sign up for a bunch of different verification systems. Don't even consider upgrading to the enhanced memberships until you've tried out the basic for a while.

(And if you think that the sites really are just trying to verify your age by this system, realize that many of these sites offer explicit sample photos that you don't need to be a verified adult to see.)

The "Free for a Whole Week" Model

Many membership-only sites offer free one-week trials. Approach these with caution.

To receive a "free" membership, you actually have to sign up for a paid membership and provide your credit card number. The first week is free, and then if you don't cancel, your card will automatically be charged each month for your membership. Sounds easy enough, and it's not that uncommon a business strategy. Plenty of magazines offer a free first issue, expecting that most people won't bother to "cancel" after they receive a bill and the second issue arrives (thus obligating them to pay).

Before you decide to accept a trial membership for one week with plans to cancel it when the week is through, read the fine print. Don't be surprised if you see a clause stating that you have to cancel a subscription at least three days before a billing period, or you will be billed. So if you wait until day six to cancel your subscription, you will be billed for the next month, and that can be a $25 charge.

Even when you do go to cancel, they usually get you again. The information on how to cancel is frequently hidden. Trying looking in the site's Member Services or Frequently Asked Questions (*FAQ*) areas first. If you cannot find the information on canceling there, try getting on the site as a nonmember, and click the links for joining. Generally on the same page as the form you fill out to join, you will find some text about canceling the subscription, and some of this text will be a link. Click this link, and your browser will either display a cancellation form or will open up an email window, which you can fill in with your request for cancellation and your membership information.

The "Free If You Use Our Special Browser" Model

If someone offers you free access to a site but says you need to use a special browser or connection software, beware! A major scam was perpetrated a while back where someone offered special software of that sort. What they didn't reveal was that the software would change the access number your PC would use to dial in to the Internet. Instead of calling your service provider's local number, your computer would dial up a number in Eastern Europe. When you got your next phone bill, you would find charges for a few hundred extra dollars for your Internet use; meanwhile, somewhere in Eastern Europe, someone who got a cut of that phone charge (the European equivalent of a 900 number) was getting rich indeed.

What Do You Get When You Pay by the Month?

The big sex sites, the ones that do most of the advertising, charge on a monthly basis for access. Prices range from $10 to $25 per month, with discounts if you buy a several month subscription. As noted earlier, these places generally offer a free one-week trial (billed as "limited-time offers," although they've been offered continuously for years), which you should be careful in accepting.

The big sites offer a range of content, which may be something for everyone...or something for everyone but you.

Pictures

Large picture archives are the rule for these places. They usually contain thousands of pictures. Generally, these places have pictures for a range of tastes, and their photos are often larger photos than you will get from the free sites. The larger pictures take longer to download, but the better pay sites use faster servers than the free sites, so you actually can get pictures in reasonable time. When the Internet gets bogged down (as it often does), however, these can still be slow.

Video Clips

Film clips (generally of hardcore action) are a staple of these sites. Frequently, these clips are about 30 seconds long, although you can find some that continue for several minutes. These come in two forms: *streaming* clips (which you watch as the computer sends it to you) or *downloadable* clips (which you must download completely before viewing). The clips are almost always displayed in a small window. The clips usually do not include sound because that would slow things down further.

Some sites use their streaming clips to try to extract more money from your wallet. Watching the clips is free, but an ad next to the clip will let you know what video the clip was taken from, and how to order it.

"Live" Shows

The live show is something fairly interesting, and is worth experiencing. In some remote building in who-knows-where, there's a cramped, badly decorated room where someone is displaying himself or (more often) herself in various ways in front of a video camera linked to the Internet. Some of these shows involve multiple people engaging in faux intercourse, and some even show people having real sex (although not as many as claim to).

The basic display takes up one-tenth to one-sixth of your screen. Some add other features as well. On a few, the added feature is sound. More commonly and more interestingly, however, they add online chat.

That's right, you get to converse not only with other people worldwide who are watching the show, but also with the performer. Generally, most of the chat involves viewers commenting on the beauty of the performer and requesting that she show or do certain things. Sometimes the performers type responses, and sometimes they do what is requested.

It's an interesting experience, typing to a sexy woman who is sitting (or lying) there with a keyboard. You can see her face and body, but she knows you only by what you type. Some people find this an interesting novelty. Other people take a liking to the performer and log on regularly for her performances. (That's not hard to do, because typically each room has a limited staff; so a performer might work five four-hour sessions a week.)

109

Forgive Me, Again!

The sinning is the best part of repentance.

—Arabian proverb

Again, these chats are used as a way to get you to spend more money. Generally this is by offering some sort of upgrade. For a hefty per-minute charge, for example, you can get into the chat of what was not a public chat room, or receive audio from the room, or move from a softcore room to a hardcore one, or even enjoy a one-on-one chat with the performer. More about those in a bit.

If you really like these live feeds, you might sign up for several pay sites to sample more live feeds…only to get a big surprise. Few of these sites have their own live feeds. Instead, they license a deal with a site that specializes in live acts. As such, you are likely to see the same feeds again and again on the various sites you've signed up for. You really don't need a subscription to more than one big pay site for this service.

Other Stuff

The big sites like to boast about their huge range of features. Some of those attractions have limited entertainment value such as online games (for example, a slow-playing blackjack game with naked women on the playing cards), member chat rooms, online magazines (mostly just more pictures), and prose stories (usually downloaded from Usenet). Let the buyer beware.

Payment Plans

When you sign up for your seven-day free trial (which, as noted earlier, you should be sure to cancel well before the end of the week, if you're going to cancel at all), you will be offered a choice of several renewal terms. Typically you can sign up for the monthly rate or you can sign up to pay every three months, at only twice the monthly rate; or you can sign up for 12 months for the price of six! Great deals, eh?

Don't fall for it. Stick with the month-by-month payments.

The reason sites offer those deals is because they know you will likely become bored with their material before the month is through. Sexual material online has novelty value for many folks, but that value ultimately wanes in the face of slow downloads, choppy video, or the eventual feeling that all content is basically the same.

If, after a month, you decide that this is a service that you want for a full year, you can switch to the annual payment then. (If the site doesn't want to let you do this, just cancel your account, and then start a new one.) It will cost you only a little more, total. But if you end up paying for that full year and decide that you didn't want it, you'll have some pretty strong regrets. (And, there's always the risk that the site will go out of business before the year is up, sticking you with a big credit card bill and no service.) Most site owners are honest, but these aren't Fortune 500 companies you're dealing with, so be cautious.

Interview with a Live Nude Woman

"Hailey" performs for the Las Vegas Cabaret site. With your monthly fee at any of several sex sites, you can join a group typing requests and compliments to her as she poses, grins broadly, and types replies. For four to five dollars per minute, you can type to her or even speak on the phone to her while she fulfills your requests on a private video feed. To be honest, she wasn't actually nude while I typed to her. Perhaps that shows just how dedicated I am to my work—I typed for 10 minutes without asking for more of this beautiful student with flowing red hair than some typed replies and one nice smile.

Can I ask you some questions for The Complete Idiot's Guide to Sex on the Net?

Yes. I'm reading their books on relationships and politics right now.

What is it like dealing with people who can see you but you can't see them?

I prefer it. I don't think I would be able to dance in a club. Here, I am all alone in a room. It almost makes it unrealistic, I imagine. I also think (hope) that the video quality is such that they would *not* recognize me on the street.

I imagine it's very safe here, so even if the guys do get weird, you're okay.

For the most part, yes. One or two have gotten a bit close, actually.

How long have you been performing?

I've been here about three weeks now.

Any idea what your fans are like in person?

I imagine lonely, married (unhappily, perhaps), the rest is a smorgasbord. I think some are low income, some higher....

At four dollars a minute for the one-on-one, I should hope they tend toward the higher.

Some really seem to get hooked. Surprisingly.

About how much time do you spend with clients doing one-on-one during a shift?

Not very much. All of the girls seem to have a few people that really like *only* them...they tend to call semi-frequently...for longer periods of time. (Grieg is playing...I love this song.)

Well, I see my time is running out. Thanks for your answers, and don't lose your joy!

Don't lose your heart out here! Bye bye!

Credit Cards and Security

The standard method of payment for pay sites of any kind is via credit or charge card (although many sites now do support an "electronic check," where they can transfer money directly from your checking account). The important disadvantage of this method is that you can't challenge an electronic check as you can a credit card debit if you think you have been ripped off (which sounds pretty scary to me, but if you don't have a credit card, it may be needed). And whenever you are giving out your credit card information, particularly to someone you cannot see, you should be cautious.

If the site is well-established and has been around for a while, it is not likely that they're going to use your credit card number to order stereo equipment or a gross of donuts or something like that. You still have to be worried about Internet credit card number thieves, however. People do find ways of getting credit card information that has been sent across the Internet. If they get your number, they may well go on a donut-buying binge that could bring your credit rating to its knees.

To protect against theft and fraud, the brains behind the Internet came up with a security system that encodes sensitive information passing between two computers. This *Secure Transaction* system works great, but both your browser and the Internet site have to support the system. Current versions of the major browsers support the Secure Transaction feature, so you're probably covered from your end. You just have to make sure that the Web site is holding up its end.

Many sites let you choose between a Secured Transaction and a Non-Secured Transaction. If given this choice, of course you want Secured. Some sites don't even offer a choice, automatically going with Secured. Some sites *say* that they're offering you a Secured Transaction, but they *aren't*. The owners of those sites should be taken out back and spanked (although some of them might actually like that).

Luckily, you don't have to take their word for it. Your browser will let you know whether you are properly linked to a secured site. It may show a dialog box stating that you are switching into a secured mode. Even if it doesn't, you can tell by checking a lower corner of the browser window. Current versions of Netscape and Internet Explorer show a closed lock if in Secure mode. (Older versions of Netscape show an unbroken key.) Also, the displayed URL will start with **https** rather than the usual **http**.

Other Credit Card Problems

When you do charge a membership fee or product that you purchase online to your credit card, pay attention to the name that they tell you it will be billed under. These sites know that you may not want people who see your credit card bill to know what naughtiness you've been up to, so they bill it to an innocuous name. In some ways, it may be handy not to have Big Nate's Slut-O-Mania listed on your credit card bill, but it can be confusing later when you try to figure out why you're being billed by Respectable Office Supplies, Inc.

If you do find that you have been billed for something beyond what you ordered, you are in a good position. Because they don't actually have your signature, the credit card company is likely to side with you on any dispute. However, don't expect your credit card company to side with you if you make a habit of disputing charges.

What Do You Get When You Pay by the Minute?

A variety of online sex attractions charge by the minute. Some of them give you things that you can receive less expensively as part of a pay-per-month package, such as being part of a chat group watching or interacting with a performer, or watching live sex. Others take things one step beyond, such as providing a private video session.

Some of the private video sessions advertised on the Web aren't on the Internet. Instead, when you get to the site, you find that you have to download a custom viewer program, which is designed specifically to work with that site. This can actually work to your advantage: By using custom software, the site can use a more efficient method of sending video and avoid the slowdowns caused by Internet congestion. Be aware, however, that your modem may be dialing a long-distance call to reach the service. (Although compared to the five bucks a minute you are slamming down for a naked conversation, that may be a bargain.)

Minute Details

Places that charge by the minute generally have you purchase a fixed amount of time instead of running the meter like a taxicab. The packages vary widely. One site may offer five free minutes in addition to however much time you buy. (This means that if you buy five minutes at $5 each, you're actually getting 10 minutes for that $25 total; but if you buy 45 minutes, you end up with 50 minutes for $225, which is much more expensive per minute.) Another site might require you to pay a $10 "registration fee" before you can buy any time at all.

Some sites offer volume discounts. Ten minutes may be $20, 30 minutes for $40, and three full hours for $100. Before buying that much time, make sure that it's *bankable*, that the site will keep track of how much time you have left. That way, you can use some time now and return later. Otherwise, you'll have to sit there and watch your screen for the three hours straight to get your money's worth (not that there's anything wrong with that, if that's your desire [except for the possible eyestrain]).

The Least You Need to Know

➤ Almost all sites with sexual and erotic pictures are for-profit, making their money through membership fees or from advertising.

➤ Some free sites make money by getting you to pay for adult verification services, which will let you into a large number of sites with limited content.

➤ The sites with the most content (in terms of libraries of pictures, videos, and live sex feeds) charge on a monthly basis.

➤ Read the fine print before you accept a free trial offer; you often have to cancel your account days before the trial is over to avoid being charged for a subscription.

➤ When giving credit card information over the Web, make sure you have a secured connection. You can tell this by checking for the image of a closed lock or an unbroken key in a lower corner of the browser window.

➤ Much of the content in the pay-per-month sex sites is duplicated on many other sites, so there's often no need to join more than one.

➤ If you buy a large amount of time for a pay-for-minute adult service, make sure the time is bankable so that you don't have to use it all at once.

Chapter 9

Sex and America Online

In This Chapter

➤ Connecting to the Internet from America Online

➤ Browsing the World Wide Web from AOL

➤ Sending and receiving email

➤ Reading newsgroups and viewing pictures

➤ Running other Internet programs while in AOL

➤ Exploring sex-related areas within AOL

America Online (AOL) provides one of the easiest means for newcomers to begin exploring the Internet, and its popularity continues to grow by leaps and bounds. In a recent interview, AOL officials said they expect that *half* of all new Internet users over the next several years will choose AOL as their online service provider. Regardless of whether they remain loyal customers, many computer users get their first Internet experience with America Online.

This chapter provides much of the information you need to start using key areas of AOL, including surfing the World Wide Web, sending and receiving email, viewing newsgroups, and chatting. If your primary interest is learning about AOL chat rooms and procedures, be sure to read Chapter 25, too.

That's What Friends Are For

Harry Burns: "No man can be friends with a woman he finds attractive. He always wants to have sex with her."

Sally Albright: "So you are saying that a man can be friends with a woman he finds *unattractive?*"

Harry Burns: "No, you pretty much want to nail them, too."

—*When Harry Met Sally*, 1989

Passwords Are a Secret

Never give your password out to anyone online—even if that person says he/she is an AOL official or if they have a screen name that implies they work for AOL, such as Supervisor175. Under no circumstances will anyone from AOL ever ask you for your password. If you ever get such a request, you should assume that the individual is an imposter.

AOL and the Internet

As recently as only a few years ago, AOL was just a massive content provider. The service was sold to users based on its ease of use, coupled with the fact that its content was available *only* to its members. It was modeled after the much smaller *bulletin board systems* (BBS) that were common in the early days of computing—a place to download files and programs of all sorts and to exchange messages among users.

As the Internet grew in popularity, AOL became a gateway to the Net. For novice users, this meant that they could access Internet content, such as Web pages and newsgroups, through AOL's familiar interface. The following sections explain how to do this.

AOL and the World Wide Web

To view Web pages, click the **Internet** button on the Welcome or Channels menu, choose **Internet Connection** from the GoTo menu, or type the keyword **Internet**. Then click **Go To The Web**. AOL's proprietary Web browser appears. To go to a particular Web page, type or paste the address into the Address box.

Click to go to previously viewed page

Show the Favorite Places list   Set browser preferences

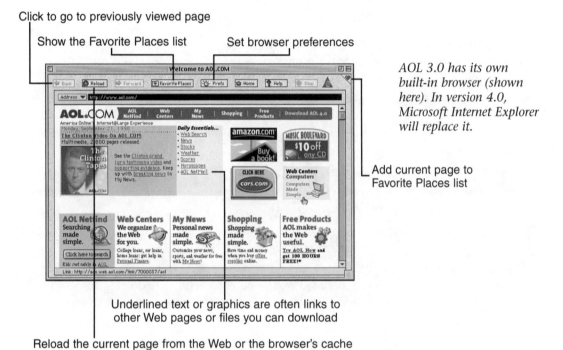

AOL 3.0 has its own built-in browser (shown here). In version 4.0, Microsoft Internet Explorer will replace it.

Add current page to Favorite Places list

Underlined text or graphics are often links to other Web pages or files you can download

Reload the current page from the Web or the browser's cache

To make it easy to revisit your favorite Web pages and sites, you can add them to the Favorite Places list. To add a Web page, visit the page and click the heart icon in the upper-right corner of the browser window. The next time you want to go to the same Web page, click the **Favorite Places** button at the top of the browser window, highlight the desired Web page, and click the **Open** button.

You can download programs and files of all types by clicking text and graphic *links* in the browser window, as explained in Chapter 2.

Favorite Places Mishmash

Keep in mind that the Favorite Places list stores Web page addresses and the names of your favorite AOL areas. To distinguish one from another, you may want to follow AOL's convention of adding **(Web)** after the names of all Web pages.

Click...Don't Type!

If you see a Web page address in a received email message (Web addresses are shown in AOL mail as blue underlined text), you can click the text string to launch the AOL browser and view that Web page. To add a Web address to one of your own messages, select it in the Favorite Places menu and drag it into your message.

AOL and Email

Email (or electronic mail) is a text message sent over the Internet. As an AOL subscriber, you can exchange email with anyone on the Internet—not just other AOL members. For more information about email, see Chapter 4.

To read incoming mail, click the **You Have Mail** icon on the Welcome screen or choose **Read Mail** from the Mail menu. The Online Mailbox window opens, listing all new, old, and sent mail. To read a message, double-click it or select it and click the **Read** button.

Messages can also contain *attachments* (computer files, such as pictures, word processing documents, and so on). To see whether the current message has one or more attachments, click the **Files** tab at the top of the message window. To download the attached files to your hard disk, select their filenames and click **Download Now** (to download them immediately) or **Download Later** (to download them later during this or another online session using the Download Manager).

If you elect to download the file immediately, a standard Save dialog box appears. Choose a hard disk and folder in which to save the file. If the file is a picture, AOL displays it in its own window. Other file types, such as text files, are just saved in the location you specified.

Files for which you have clicked the Download Later button can be downloaded at your convenience. To do so, choose **Download Manager** from the File menu, highlight the files (or folders) that you want to download, and click the **Download** button.

Spam...It's Not Just for Lunch Any More

One serious drawback of being an AOL subscriber is the ungodly amount of unsolicited email messages you receive. This junk mail is commonly referred to as *spam*. Although most such mail *is* sex related, its sheer volume can make it hard to pick out the *real* messages—ones from friends, relatives, and associates.

The best way to avoid spam is to create additional AOL names and keep their use separate from your main name. To keep a name private, *never* do any of the following while logged on with that name:

➤ Join a chat session

➤ Create a member profile

➤ Join email mailing lists

➤ Post messages to newsgroups or message boards

If you want to participate in any of these activities, be sure to do so with a screen name that you don't mind making public. That name *will* receive loads of spam.

Posting messages to newsgroups—particularly sex-related ones—will ensure that you receive an unending stream of spam. (Sex site owners routinely scan newsgroup posts for email addresses.) One way to avoid this situation is to post *all* newsgroup messages through the DejaNews Web site (**http://www.dejanews.com**).

Finally, AOL enables you to list the people from whom you will accept mail. All other mail is automatically rejected. Using this feature ensures that you can always receive important mail without having to wade through spam.

To set this email option, follow these steps:

1. Choose **Mail Controls** from the Mail menu.

2. Click the **Mail Controls** button in the window that appears.

3. Select the username for which you want to set mail controls. Click the **Edit** button.

4. Choose the option to **Allow email only from selected AOL members, Internet domains and addresses**.

5. In the box provided, type the email address of the first person from whom you want to allow mail. Click **Add**. Repeat this step for all other mail recipients.

6. Click **OK** to accept the new Mail Control settings.

To reply to the current message, click the **Reply** button, type your reply, and then click **Send Now** (to send it immediately) or **Send Later** (to send the message during your next Automatic AOL session). To configure AOL to automatically send and retrieve waiting email, choose **Setup Automatic AOL** from the Mail menu.

You can also *forward* received mail—in the event that you want to share a message with someone else (a great joke, for example). To forward a message, open it, click the **Forward** button, choose recipients, enter any new text that you wish to add, and then click **Send Now** or **Send Later**.

To create a new message, choose **Compose Mail** from the Mail menu. A blank message window appears. Enter the recipient's full email address (such as **WildBill@ jnet.com**), a message title (in the Subject box), and the text of the message.

Remembering Email Addresses

Few email addresses are actually designed to be remembered. And many of them are so lengthy that you won't want to type them even if you *can* remember them. The smart way to handle email addresses is to store them in your AOL Address Book. Once stored, you can just drag the addresses into the Address section of any message. (To help you remember each person, you can also store a picture in the address page—*any* picture.) To select an address or manage the contents of your Address Book (adding, deleting, or updating addresses), click the **Address** icon (when composing an outgoing message) or choose **Address Book** from the Mail menu.

Just as you can receive attached files, you can also attach files to any outgoing message (exchanging pictures with your friends, for example). Just click the **Attach Files** button in the message window and choose the file or files you want to send. (Note, however, that some Internet service providers limit the size of message attachments. If a file is too large, the message may be rejected. Normally, however, this is only an issue with files larger than 1 or 2MB.)

A Lifesaving Tip!

Did you ever wish that you could yank back an email message that you sent in anger or that was addressed to the wrong person? No need to click your heels three times, Dorothy; you can *unsend* messages as long as the recipient is an AOL user and that person hasn't already read the message. Choose **Read Mail** from the Mail menu, click the **Sent Mail** tab, highlight the message, and click **Unsend**.

AOL and Newsgroups

Although the quality of sex-related newsgroup postings has slid downhill in the past couple of years, newsgroups still remain relatively popular. AOL subscribers have complete access to a huge set of newsgroups—if you know the tricks.

To reach the newsgroups area, click the **Newsgroups** button on the Internet Connection screen or use the keyword **newsgroups**.

The first step in reading or posting to newsgroups is finding some that interest you. You can *subscribe* to as many newsgroups as you wish. (Subscribing merely means that you want to follow the newsgroups, not that you are actually *joining* anything.)

Unfortunately, AOL filters the list of newsgroups that they follow—eliminating those with an obvious sexual bent. Although such newsgroups are still hosted by AOL, you must know the name of each one that you want to add to your list of subscribed newsgroups. The Expert Add feature enables you to add virtually any newsgroup—as long as you know its exact name. (If you're short on ideas, names of sex newsgroups are scattered throughout this book. Alternatively, you can search for newsgroup names at DejaNews.)

After subscribing to one or more newsgroups, it's a simple matter to read any of the messages (called *posts*) contained in them. From the Newsgroups screen, click **Read My Newsgroups**. Select the first newsgroup you want to examine, and then click **List All** or **List Unread** (to list only those messages you haven't previously read).

Reading newsgroup posts.

Read the highlighted message

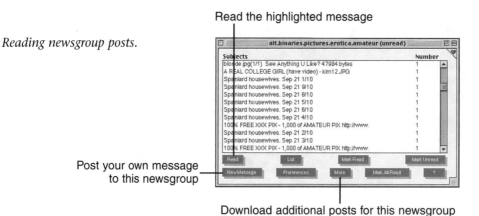

Post your own message to this newsgroup

Download additional posts for this newsgroup

When you see a message that looks interesting, double-click it to read it. If a file is attached (typically, a picture), a new dialog box appears. Click **Download File** to download it to your hard disk. As it downloads to your computer, the image appears in its own window. Close the window after you finish looking at it. (Note that posts with attached messages usually list the filename in the message header, such as Kim157.jpg. Graphic files are generally named with .jpg or .gif extensions.)

It Won't Let Me Download Images!

By default, new AOL accounts are not allowed to download binary files from newsgroups (such as pictures, sound files, and programs). If you want to download such files, you must change the Parental Controls on your account. From the Newsgroups window, click **Parental Controls**, select the account to unblock, click the **Edit** button, remove the check mark from the **Block binary down-loads** check box, and click **Save**.

If you decide that you would like to contribute your two cents' worth to a newsgroup (perhaps answering another subscriber's question or posing one of your own), click the **New Message** button at the bottom of the current newsgroup window. Creating a newsgroup post is just like writing an email message, except that all you need to enter is a subject and the text of your message.

Although it is possible to attach files to your posts, AOL makes it more trouble than it is worth. Instead of just choosing files to attach (as you would in an email program), AOL expects you to manually *encode* each attachment and paste it into the text of your message. If you feel a pressing need to send files to newsgroups, search for a *uuencoding* program on AOL. (Go to keyword **"Software Search"** and search for **uuencode**.) Otherwise, you are better off skipping it and contenting yourself with just looking at pictures posted by others. (Let's hope AOL 4.0 provides this file-posting capability instead of making us do all the work.)

Running Other Internet Programs

Although you may think that you are locked into Internet features that appear in AOL's colorful windows, that's not the case. As long as you have sufficient memory (RAM) in your computer, you can run any of the other Internet programs discussed in this book ... *at the same time as AOL!*

Start by logging on to AOL. The moment you are connected, you can launch any other Internet programs that you like. You might, for example, want to use a browser other than AOL's built-in one. If you have favorite non-AOL chat programs, such as LOL Chat, feel free to run them, too. (As long as you remain connected to AOL, you can run other Net software. Be sure to quit the other programs *before* signing off from AOL, however, because signing off terminates your connection to the Internet.)

No Alternative Newsgroup Readers Allowed

If you want to view newsgroups and use AOL as your Internet service provider, you must do so using their clumsy newsgroup reader. You cannot run an external newsgroup reader (such as Outlook Express or Free Agent) to view newsgroup content.

Sex Within AOL

In addition to Internet access, AOL has content areas and chat rooms available only to its customers. This chapter shows you where to find the best sections of AOL and explains what you can do there.

Censorship and AOL

America Online views itself as a community. And like any other community, this one has an established set of standards (go to keyword **"Terms of Service"**). Although discussions about sexuality from a medical standpoint are okay, *having sex online is not.* Although limited artistic nudity is permissible in photos and drawings, partial or full nudity is banned. And typing certain dirty words in a public chat room will get you banned. Given that AOL derives a massive part of its revenues from people involved in sexually explicit chats (in the private rooms and using Instant Messages), these puritanical rules may seem a bit hypocritical. Nevertheless, if you get caught, don't be surprised if there are consequences—such as losing your account. For more information, go to **http://www.aolsucks. org/censor/**.

Keywords: The Fastest Way to Travel

If hunting for the right AOL screen or menu command gets tiresome, you can use the Keyword command to quickly get to most AOL areas. Choose **Keyword** from the GoTo menu, click the **Keyword** button on the AOL toolbar, or press **Ctrl+K** (Windows) or **Command+K** (Macintosh). Then type the keyword(s) for the area you want to visit, such as **local personals**, and click **Go**. (You can also type a URL to go to a particular Web page.)

If you don't know the name of an AOL area or are just interested in finding out whether it has *anything* on a given topic, click the **Search** button in the Keyword dialog box, and then enter a search term. Sexual terms, such as "penis" and "breast" generally lead you to medical areas, however.

Use the Keywords dialog box to quickly get to any significant area of AOL or to search for areas that interest you.

Chatting: The People Connection

This section of AOL (available from the Channels menu or by typing the keyword **people**) is where you can find most of the live chat rooms. For sex-related chats, try the Romance category. (Click **Find a Chat**, click **Romance**, and then click **View** to see a list of chat rooms that you can join. Each room has a limit of 25 participants. If the chosen room is full, however, AOL can help you join another room with the same chat topic.)

As far as sex is concerned, you may have better luck going directly to the member-created chat rooms. (Click **Member Chats** in the Find a Chat window to view a list of all member-created rooms.) Obviously sexual room names will appear, names such as Cyber Cyber Cyber, Submissive Females, and Wild Women.

A Chest of Drawers

Peggy Brandt: "Most of the men in this town think monogamy is some kind of wood."

—*The Mask*, 1994

Other Areas of Interest

Although the Web, newsgroups, email, and chat all have obvious sexual potential, you may also want to explore a few of these other AOL areas:

➤ **Keyword: Love@AOL** Read cyber-love success stories, chat, and browse through the photo personals to see whether you can find your ideal match—or, at least, an interesting date.

➤ **Keyword: Local personals** If you live in a metropolitan area, your city probably has a personals ad section.

➤ **Keyword: Thrive@passion** Get information on STDs, the G-spot, and Tantric sex; pick up some new dating and relationship tips; play games; and choose a romantic travel destination.

Stand Out in the Crowd

To increase the likelihood that someone will want to talk to you in chat, you can create a *member profile* for yourself. That's where you tell your age, sex, location, interests, and so on, enabling other members to learn a bit about you. Choose **Member Directory** from the Members menu, click the **My Profile** button, and fill in whatever details you feel comfortable providing. You will find that without a profile, some people may not want to talk to you.

Having a profile that contains personal information, however, has its risks. You may prefer to restrict such information to people in chat whom you eventually get close to.

*In **Love@AOL**, this simple search feature makes it easy to specify exactly the type of match you're seeking.*

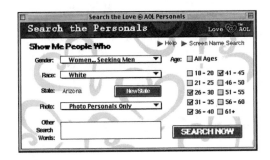

The Least You Need to Know

➤ AOL serves as a gateway to the Internet, enabling you to experience the Web and Usenet newsgroups from AOL's user-friendly interface.

➤ AOL subscribers can exchange email with anyone who has an Internet account—regardless of whether the other person subscribes to AOL.

➤ You can read and post to message groups called *newsgroups*. Some messages contain encoded picture files that you can decode and view with the AOL software.

➤ Sexual content, such as pictures, is hard to find in AOL. Check out several related areas, such as private chats, Love @ AOL, and **Thrive@passion**.

Part 2
A Resource Guide to Sex Sites and Newsgroups

The chapters in this part direct you to some of the best sex sites on the World Wide Web, as well as to many popular newsgroups on sexual subjects. The chapters are organized by content areas, such as amateur photos, sexual humor, and multimedia. Feel free to jump directly to any topic that interests you.

General Picture Sites

This chapter takes a look at some Web sites that feature sexy photos of models, couples, and groups, along with magazines that have an online presence, such as *Loaded* and *Playboy*.

General Picture Web Sites

If you've spent any time surfing for explicit photos, you've noticed that after a while the sites start looking alike. They all divide the photos into similar categories (oral, anal, orgies, and so on); you seldom find cutting-edge lighting or creative poses; and many sites draw from the same sources, such as Usenet newsgroups and scanned magazine photos. We noticed that too, but came up with almost two dozen that stood out from the crowd.

More Picture Sites from Yahoo!

If you would like additional suggestions for general picture sites, visit **http://www.yahoo.com/ Business_and_Economy/ Companies/Sex/Online_Picture_ Galleries**.

Absolutely Different Adult Site

http://www.absolutelyadult.com

Membership site

If you like your sex with nothing left to the imagination, the Absolutely Different Adult Site is for you. In addition to its extensive picture gallery, this pay site offers streaming video, screen savers, desktop themes, downloadable sex games, and adult chat.

Asia Carrera's Buttkicking Homepage

http://www.asiacarrera.com

Commercial site

Asia Carrera, porn star and men's magazine model, has her own site on the Web where you can view several dozen free pics of her, read about how she got into the porn industry, and buy her videos and autographed photos. Asia is bright, articulate, and sexy—truly a winning combination.

Asian Nudes

http://www.asiannudes.com

Membership site

Guests can view a dozen pics and an illustrated erotic story; members receive access to the full site. The women are lovely, and the quality of the photography is very good.

Danni's Hard Drive!

http://www.danni.com

Membership/Commercial site

Large-breasted women dominate Danni's Hard Drive. And the amount of material available to members—including photos of the Webmistress, Danni Ashe—is nothing short of astonishing. You'll see pictorials of models and porn stars, erotic stories, audio interviews, streaming video, live video feeds, and sexy e-zines galore. If you decide to join, you'll find yourself wandering around the site for days wondering whether you'll ever see all that's there.

Play It Again, Sam

"Girls are like pianos. When they're not upright, they're grand."

—Benny Hill, British comedian

Digital Dreamgirls

http://www.ddgirls.com

Membership site

Digital Dreamgirls is the membership site of *Penthouse* photographer J. Stephen Hicks. The site (one of James's favorites) features dozens of gorgeous nude models and amateurs in *large* photo sets—frequently as many as 20–50 shots each. In addition to the photos, there's classy wallpaper for your Windows desktop, out-takes from photo shoots, jokes, erotic stories, an animated strip show, blooper shots, a sex toy mail-order area, and a studio cam section where you can see videos that were made during the photo shoots.

New Math

"Sex appeal is 50% what you've got and 50% what people *think* you've got."

—Sophia Loren

Foxes.com

http://www.foxes.com

Commercial site

Foxes allows you to sample one photo in each of dozens of sets. If you like the sample, you can give them a credit card number and purchase viewing/downloading rights to all the pictures in the set. Set prices range from $4.95 to $9.95, depending on the number of photos.

Karup's Gallery

http://www.karup.com

Membership site

Each week, Karup's provides 30 quality photos of young models and amateurs that guests can download. A one-week trial subscription is $5.95. In addition to gaining access to the photo libraries, members can view video feeds and browse through *VaVoom!*, an e-zine.

Playboy Online

http://www.playboy.com
http:/cyber.playboy.com</bold>

Commercial site/Membership site

Visiting *Playboy*'s site is like reading an online version of the print magazine. The site features articles, reviews, contests, and pictorials—all in the inimitable *Playboy* style. This site should be saved in everyone's Favorites or Bookmarks list.

If content makes a winning sex site, who could possibly have more content at its disposal than *Playboy*? With more than 45 years of monthly issues to drawn on, Playboy Cyber Club is a dream site for the millions of males who grew up with the magazine.

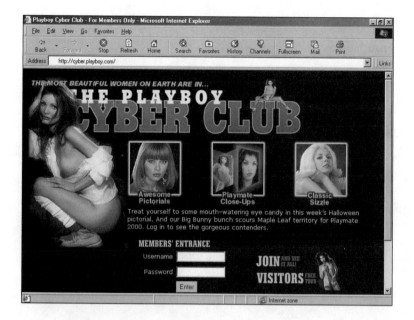

The *Playboy* membership site is resplendent with downloadable pictures of spectacular women—including an immense library of pictorials, some going back 25 years; Playmate personal Web pages; and scans of *Playboy* covers. This site contains so much visual material that new members could spend the better part of a week browsing the site before seeing everything.

If you just want to read (Yes, I know...you only get *Playboy* for the articles), you'll find a complete collection of Playboy Interviews dating back to 1962, as well as advice from the Playboy Advisor. Other site features include a huge online store; live, moderated chats with Playmates and other celebrities; newsgroups; reprints of Little Annie Fanny (my favorite cartoon gal); Playmate audio files; and an art gallery of illustrations from the magazine.

That Was Then

"When you're elected Vice President, you have to give up *Playboy*, which is possibly why you see so few men running for Vice President."

—Spiro T. Agnew

Sizzle

http://www.sizzle.com/

Membership site

As pay sites go, Sizzle has a lot to offer: photo libraries, erotic fairy tales, video streams (including live video from a strip club), 60 hours of interactive video chat per month, and downloadable video clips. Be sure to take the tour. The samples are first-rate.

Tiffany Toyz

http://www.tiffanytoyz.com

Membership site

Tiffany Toyz, a *Hustler*, *Swank*, and *Oui* model, has put together a pay site that promises photos, 13,000 channels of video feeds, 350 movie clips, adult stories, and phone sex. The sample area is small, but does a great job of showing off Tiffany's assets.

Male Bonding on Drugs

Wayne Campbell: She's a babe.

Garth Algar: She's magically babelicious.

Wayne Campbell: She tested very high on the stroke-ability scale.

—*Wayne's World* (1992)

Tokyo Topless

http://www.tokyotopless.co.jp

Free site

Tokyo Topless specializes in photos of large-busted Japanese women. Although the text is mostly in Kanji, the navigation text is in English, so you can move around the site.

Uploaded

http://www.uploaded.com

Commercial site

Uploaded is the e-zine version of a strange, funny U.K. print magazine called *Loaded*. Not your typical men's magazine, the site offers video clips of things exploding (cans of baked beans, a doll house, and a toilet, for instance); an irreverent chat area ("Gender switching, verbal abuse and other nerd habits are encouraged."); and dozens of photos of women who—by all rights—should have serious back problems.

Vertical Smiles

http://verticalsmiles.com

Free site

This site's name immediately got our attention. Vertical Smiles is a free picture site, offering dozens of high-quality photos.

General Usenet Picture Newsgroups

If your quest for general pics on the Web isn't giving you what you want (or if money is a factor), try the following **alt.binaries.pictures.erotica** newsgroups as additional sources:

- ➤ **alt.binaries.pictures.erotica.blondes**
- ➤ **alt.binaries.pictures.erotica.breasts**
- ➤ **alt.binaries.pictures.erotica.brunette**
- ➤ **alt.binaries.pictures.erotica.cheerleaders**
- ➤ **alt.binaries.pictures.erotica.female**
- ➤ **alt.binaries.pictures.erotica.groupsex**
- ➤ **alt.binaries.pictures.erotica.oral**
- ➤ **alt.binaries.pictures.erotica.oriental**
- ➤ **alt.binaries.pictures.erotica.orientals**
- ➤ **alt.binaries.pictures.erotica.pornstar**
- ➤ **alt.binaries.pictures.erotica.redheads**

The Least You Need to Know

➤ Sex sites with photos are readily available on the Web. After awhile, many of these sites start looking alike—featuring similar poses, categories, and even the same pictures. Before subscribing to a photo site, be sure that it offers what you're looking for and regularly updates its content.

➤ You can download sexy photos from many newsgroups. Be aware, however, that much of this material is just illegally scanned photos from magazines.

Chapter 11

Amateur Sites

In This Chapter

➤ Amateur sites on the World Wide Web

➤ Newsgroups where you can find amateur photos

Something about nude amateur photos appeals to us. Maybe it's that the subjects aren't professional models. They're the women who live down the block, our wives, and our girlfriends. Although we don't know them personally, they represent women that we *could* know.

Web Sites

Because personal amateur sites are so simple to start, they are among the most plentiful of all types of sex-related sites. All one needs is a digital camera or a scanner, a cooperative ISP, and an exhibitionist streak.

Until recently, most amateur sites were the efforts of proud husbands and boyfriends who wanted to show off their wives' and girlfriends' bodies. (See what *I* have?) Now, the majority of such sites are money-making ventures in which the softcore pictures are free, while access to the hardcore ones is available only to site members—usually for a fee of between $10 and $20 per month.

Amateur Pages

http://amateurpages.com

Membership site

Amateur Pages currently features more than 20 luscious amateur women. If you spring for a membership, in addition to the numerous preview sets available to all visitors, you can visit each woman's private Web pages, download movie clips, watch 350 channels of streaming video, listen to erotic audio, and flip through the latest issue of *Stroke*, a sexual e-zine. A single membership fee covers all the models' sites.

Bobbi Winters: Naked on the Web

http://www.bigx.com/bobbi_winters

Membership site

For what appears to have been an evolving personal page, this site has class. Maybe it's the attractive layout that caught our eye. (Or it could be the attractive Bobbi.) Each month, Bobbi serves up a new, free pictorial, as well as several photos from a handpicked amateur site.

Web Rings

The Bobbi Winters site is part of an amateur *Web ring* (a group of sites all on the same topic). To view a list of the other amateur sites in this Web ring, click the List Sites link on her home page or go to **http://www.webring.org/cgi-bin/ webring?ring=woracle;list**.

Bobbi's page explains the purpose of the Web ring as follows: "This ring is for Real Amateur Homepages (a site featuring a solitary Amateur female & her friends) or sites that truly promote Real Amateurs (does anything to help amateur homepages to get more traffic)."

College Co-eds

http://www.collegeco-eds.com

Commercial site

This picture site, divided into six areas, contains hundreds of amateur photos—gathered from the Internet and reader contributions—that are free for the downloading. College Co-eds also features free interactive video chat, as well as a pay show. And if you have your own amateur pics to contribute, College Co-eds is buying.

Crazie's Amateur Babes of the Week

http://www.crazies.com/

Membership site

Crazie's is primarily a picture site, offering more than 20,000 professional-quality photos of amateur women and couples, as well as downloadable movie clips. Each week, six new photo series are presented for guests to view. You can download the pictures by clicking individual thumbnails or by downloading a single .zip archive that contains all the pictures for one model. The quality here is consistently high.

If I Had a Hammer

"I could never be a woman. If I were, I would do nothing but sit at home all day playing with my breasts."

—Harris, in *L.A. Story* (1991)

Dream Girls of the Web

http://www.webdreamgirls.com

Commercial site

If you want directions to *a lot* of amateur sites, start your search here. Click the **Index** link for a free, annotated list of hundreds of amateur sites, each featuring a woman who has decided to bare it all on the Web. Alternatively, you can go to the Gallery pages to see a preview of each site before deciding which ones you would like to visit.

Kelley Uncovered

http://www.kelleyuncovered.com

Membership site

According to her bio, Kelley is an A student pursuing her Associate's degree in business. And she appears to have found a way—using the Net—to do a little business before graduating. The site's guest area has more than two dozen photo series. Members get racier pictures, streaming video, audio clips, and access to Kelley's chat room (where she appears weekly).

Princess Olivia's Wicked Web

http://www.princessolivia.com/

Membership site

This subscription site is the work of a delightfully curvy blonde amateur named Olivia. Unlike many picture sites, Princess Olivia's is dedicated exclusively to pictures of Olivia and her husband. Members are treated to a huge collection of R–XXX pictures (close to 1,000) of Olivia posed solo and with her husband, a series of slideshows, and a nice selection of hardcore videos. (The videos include a built-in player, so no additional software is needed to watch them.) And if you're hunting for leads to other noteworthy amateur sites, be sure to look at Olivia's "Friends" links.

Q of Denmark

http://151.196.210.211/~danish/

Free site

"You can never have too much of a good thing." In this personal Web site, Majbritt presents 286 free photos of Kirsten, a pretty Danish girl who thought it would be fun to make her nude debut on the Internet.

Southern Charms

http://www.southern-charms.com/

Membership site

If you're looking for amateur pics, Southern Charms won't disappoint you. Currently, it features more than two dozen women, each offering scores of free pictures as teasers to their membership areas and as enticements to buy their merchandise, such as videos and lingerie.

Texas Sexy

http://209.50.233.50/texassex.htm

Free site

Texas women are special, and Texas Sexy obviously agrees. It provides links to some of the better amateur Web sites that feature women from Texas (models, dancers, wives, and girlfriends). Although the linked sites are mainly membership or commercial sites, each has a nice assortment of free photos. Anyone for nude line dancing?

This Is Your Wife

http://www.btinternet.com/~wmeneilly

Adult Check site

You have to love the title of this British site. Go here to see some *real* amateurs.

Tubetop.com

http://www.tubetop.com/

Commercial site

Tubetop.com is a Web site run by Brandy, a San Francisco party girl. Truly an amazing woman, her body defies description. You will find many free shots of her and her roommate, Danielle. Unlike the typical professional model photos that appear on most sex sites, Brandy and Danielle actually look like they're *enjoying* themselves.

Amateur Site Lists and Newsgroups

For additional amateur sites, try the following links:

- ➤ **http://dir.yahoo.com/Business_and_Economy/Companies/Sex/Online_Picture_Galleries/Amateurs/**
- ➤ **http://www.amateurindex.com**

If you're using a Web search engine, try the keywords *amateur* and *sex*.

You can also find amateur photos in these newsgroups:

- ➤ **alt.binaries.pictures.erotica.amateur**
- ➤ **alt.binaries.pictures.erotica.amateur.female**
- ➤ **alt.binaries.pictures.erotica.amateur.facials**

Amateur Photos in Newsgroups

The photos you will find in amateur newsgroups have followed the same pattern that we have seen in other sex-related newsgroups. At one time, these photos were mainly contributed snapshots of wives and girlfriends. Now, however, they are predominantly recycled photos that have been "borrowed" from Web pages or are posted as advertisements for pay sites.

The Least You Need to Know

- ➤ Amateur sites are plentiful on the Web. A lot of exhibitionists have discovered a way of cashing in on the fact that people like looking at naked women— even if they aren't professional models, and sometimes *especially* if they aren't professional models.

- ➤ Although you can still find free amateur sites, they tend to turn into membership sites when the cost becomes prohibitive or when the profit potential becomes apparent.

- ➤ You can find amateur pics on several newsgroups.

Chapter 12

Of Interest to Women

In This Chapter

➤ Finding Web sites containing erotic stories for women

➤ Finding sexy art and photos of men

➤ Several suggestions of e-zines devoted to women's erotica

Women who surf for sex often find themselves frustrated, because, as in the real world, most sexual material online is designed to attract men. For centuries women have been told to keep their sexuality to themselves. The Net is helping to change that by showcasing erotic material created with women in mind. The guys don't know what they're missing.

So we find ourselves dedicating this chapter to helping women find content that will appeal specifically to them. Don't let yourselves think that the other chapters in this book can't be equally valuable to you, however.

Every Woman's Fantasy

http://www.everywoman.com

Free site

Among women's sites, this one seems to have it all: sex, dating, relationship, and health articles; sex and love quizzes; and humor. The only thing that isn't free at Every Woman's Fantasy is the erotica—you subscribe and they send it to you by email. Be sure to pay them a visit.

K-Web (Kinky Women Expanding Boundaries)

http://www.kweb.org

Free site

K-Web is a site for women who are involved in BD/SM. (We *love* their tag line: "A perverted playground for penisless people.") It has a wide selection of erotic stories, a few pictures of their faithful readers, and some really interesting and informative articles pertaining to the real-life practices and concerns of those in dom/sub relationships.

Lady Lynx

http://www.ladylynx.com

Free site

Lady Lynx has several pages of links to women's erotica, male picture sites, and special interest sites.

I Saw the Light

"I couldn't stop thinking about it. The, like, fact that...that people...had sex. That they just *had* it, like sex was this thing people...*had*, like a rash. Or a...a Rottweiler. Everything started to seem like, pornographic or something. Like, Mrs. Krysanowski has sex. So does Mr. Katimsky. They both have sex. They could...have sex together. Like right now. [groans] I am, like, the *sickest* person."

—Clare Danes, in *My So-Called Life* (1994)

Purve

http://www.purve.com

Membership site

Purve is an *e-zine* (electronic magazine) for women featuring pictures of male models and couples in soft- and hardcore poses, live video feeds, games, desktop wallpaper, greeting cards, erotic stories, and chat. Although you can't see much of the site's content in the free preview tour, guests are invited to join in the free chat sessions.

Scarlet Letters—A Journal of Femmerotica

http://scarletletters.com

Free site

Scarlet Letters is an e-zine with erotic stories, art, poetry, articles, advice, and humor. It is open-minded, intelligent, and sexy. We have yet to look at a page that wasn't worth reading.

Sensual Woman

http://www.sensualwoman.com

Free site

Sensual Woman has several softcore and hardcore pictures of nude men and couples, a page of women's erotica and poetry, and a discussion board.

TheKiss.com

http://www.thekiss.com

This site is the home of the Kissing Tip O' the Day. Here's one you might want to try. Because the tip changes frequently, a new one appears when you actually check out the site.

"The Profile Kiss: Place a series of light kisses along the profile of the face of your love, beginning at the forehead. Conclude with a prolonged kiss on the lips."

Stay Tuned

"Oh, well, there's nothing wrong with G-rated movies, as long as there's lots of sex and violence."

—Elvira, in *Elvira, Mistress of the Dark* (1988)

Out of the Mouths of Babes

"What a day, eh, Milhouse? The sun is out, birds are singing, bees are trying to have sex with them—as is my understanding...."

—Bart Simpson, in *The Simpsons* (1989)

In addition, TheKiss has a virtual e-kissing booth (to send that special someone an electronic token of your affection), kissing products (including a phone that looks like a pair of juicy, red lips), and a page of just-plain-fun kissing stuff. The part I liked best was listening to the Kissing Quotes. Remember the line about kissing from the movie *Bull Durham*? Now you can hear Kevin Costner say, "...and I believe in long, slow, deep, soft, wet kisses that last for three days," over and over again. That alone makes this site a treat.

Beefcake!

If pictures are your thing, you might want to check out a few newsgroups in the **alt.binaries.pictures.erotica.male.*** hierarchy on Usenet.

WWWoman AfterDark!

http://afterdark.wwwomen.com

Free site

This is an excellent search site, providing links to sexual topics of interest to women. With 62 subcategories from which to choose, you are sure to find what you want to know ... or see.

Nancy Friday

http://www.nancyfriday.com

Free site

Nancy Friday is the author of many books about sex. Here, she gives her insights, asks your opinions, and shares information about herself and about sex. It is both a site for her fans and a site with erotic stories and discussions that make you think about sexuality in a way that maybe you haven't before.

California Lesbian's Girl Guide

http://www.girlguide.com/

Free site

This magazine caters primarily to lesbians of Los Angeles. It features many articles about the lesbian community, comic strips, sexy poetry, and other information and amusements. It also has links to other sites of interest to lesbians.

This site's authors are the winners of the Rainbow award, which is "exclusively bestowed upon those gays, lesbians, bisexuals, and transgendereds who have made a contribution to the GLBT Web community through excellence in content, design, creativity, presentation, or overall concept of their Web page."

"Girlfriends" and "On Our Backs"

http://www.gfriends.com

Free site

These two magazines aimed at the lesbian community share the same site. "Girlfriends" is the more mainstream, with articles about health (Ask Dr. Dyke) and visibility of the lesbian and gay community. "On Our Backs" is the "infamous bimonthly" that features more adult content, such as XXX video reviews and erotic photos.

The Least You Need to Know

➤ Although most sex sites seem to be geared toward attracting men, some very smart and very sexy sites have been launched in the past few years that cater to women. You may have to look harder to find them, but you are unlikely to be disappointed. These sites provide excellent incentive to women who might otherwise be reluctant to surf the Web for sex.

Chapter 13

Women with Women

In This Chapter

➤ Web sites that feature women-with-women photos and sexual material

➤ Newsgroups where you can find women-with-women photos

This chapter is about women-with-women sex sites. We chose that description because most of the sites you find on the Web promising "lesbian" or "bisexual" action aren't designed to appeal to lesbians or bisexual women. They're designed to appeal to the typical horny guy. After scouring the Web, we discovered that although women-with-women photos are a common component of many general sex sites, they are seldom a site's focus.

Chastity Has a Whole New Meaning

"Girls who put out are tramps. Girls who don't are ladies. This is, however, a rather archaic usage of the word. Should one of you boys happen upon a girl who doesn't put out, do not jump to the conclusion that you have found a lady. What you have probably found is a lesbian."

—Fran Lebowitz

Women-with-Women Web Sites

This section lists the select set of sites devoted to women-with-women material.

4 Lesbians Only

http://www.4lesbiansonly.com/

Membership site

In addition to their XXX-rated image gallery (samples are available), 4 Lesbians Only offers 1,000 streaming video channels, live video broadcasts, chat rooms, X-rated games, and erotic stories. If you're willing to provide a credit card number, the site offers a one-week free trial (normally about $16 per month).

Dyke Xploitation (Dyxploitation)

http://www.dyxploitation.nu/

Free site

Dyxploitation is a refreshing change of pace after wading through so many sites that merely feature fantasy lesbians (that is, two women waiting for a man to make their sexual encounter complete). Created by and for lesbians, this e-zine includes articles and erotic stories. Visit Dyxploitation and learn something new. (We did. In Issue 2, "jiggle feminism" is discussed.)

Girl Gallery

http://www.girlgallery.com/

Membership site

Girl Gallery specializes in pictures of "amateur lesbians." (James says he'd hate to be considered an amateur heterosexual.) We wonder—because models are invariably paid for photo shoots—if they will now have to consider themselves professional lesbians and give up their right to perform in the Lesbian Olympics. Moving right along....

Girl Gallery is home to 300 pictures of women with women. An Adult Check ID (one of the many age verification systems discussed in Chapter 8) is required to see the entire collection, but you can check out a few images without it.

Lesbian Play

http://www.lesbianplay.com/

Free site

Lesbian Play is a teaser site for The Internet Lesbian Archive (**http://lezar. xxxstorage.com**), a membership photo site. Each week, Lesbian Play serves up two excellent free photo series.

Obsessions

http://www.obsessions.com/

Membership site

Obsessions is hosted by Stephanie, a young woman from Texas. She has plenty of pics, video reviews, streaming video, an e-zine, and links. Guests are invited to take a tour of the galleries. The sample photos are high quality (with an emphasis on blondes). What we saw impressed us. Be sure to also visit Stephanie's friends' site (**http://www.fellony.com**) for more great amateur shots.

One-on-One Lesbians

http://www.1on1lesbians.com/

Membership site

Live video feeds are the big draw of One-on-One Lesbians. Every channel has different women, and site patrons direct the action. (The live, interactive sex is provided by **Sexview.com**, a site owned by Python Video—owners of Live Sex from Amsterdam, as discussed in Chapter 19.) Other features include chat rooms, X-rated games, and erotic stories. Guests are invited to read lesbian-theme erotic stories and view samples from the picture galleries.

Same or Different?

If you read the information for 4 Lesbians Only at the start of this chapter, you will note the striking similarity of these two sites. In fact, both offer the same free one-week trial and use the same billing company.

Women-with-Women Picture Newsgroups

You'll also want to visit the following photo newsgroups:

➤ **alt.binaries.pictures.lesbians**

➤ **alt.binaries.pictures.erotica.lesbian**

➤ **alt.binaries.pictures.erotica.lesbians**

The Least You Need to Know

➤ Relatively few Web sites feature women-with-women photos. After checking out the ones listed in this chapter, picture collectors should visit the newsgroups, as well as the general photo sites covered in Chapter 10, "General Picture Sites."

Chapter 14

Fetishes: Sexual Special Interest Groups

In This Chapter

➤ BBW (Big Beautiful Women) sites

➤ Women with natural breasts

➤ BD/SM (bondage and discipline/sadomasochism) sites

➤ Tattooing and piercing

➤ Cross-dressers

➤ Voyeurism and exhibitionism sites

➤ Miscellaneous sites

In our diverse culture, the word "fetish" has come to mean virtually anything that a person focuses on as being erotic, a kind of a sexual special interest. This chapter leads you to a variety of these sites on the Web and in newsgroups.

BBW (Big Beautiful Women)

Large and bountiful, big and bouncy. Large women have many admirers. Here are some sites for the men who love them.

**Colonel Sanders and the
Farmer's Daughter**

"Kinky sex involves the use of duck feathers. Perverted sex involves the whole duck."

—Lewis Grizzard

Angie's Big Beautiful Women

http://www.boobcity.com/angie/

Free site

Angie's Big Beautiful Women has softcore and hard-core pics of Rubenesque beauties. This site also contains links to other BBW sites.

BBW Lover's BBW Picture Page

http://www.geocities.com/SouthBeach/
Strand/8134/

Free site

This site features 40 amateur photos of big, beautiful women in large, lacy lingerie.

Big Beautiful Women Featured in Video Productions

http://www.proaxis.com/~sherlockfam/bbw.html

Commercial site

You say you like your women on the voluptuous side *and* you're a movie fan? Do we have a page for you! You can view BBW stills from *Monster in the Garage*, *Trailer Park Trilogy of Terror*, *Odd Noggins*, *Look! UFOs!*, and the ever-popular *Mars vs. The Pope*.

Dimensions Online

http://www.dimensionsmagazine.com

Commercial site

Dimensions Online is an e-zine version of *Dimensions Magazine*, a print magazine dedicated to big women and their fans. Be sure to check out the Personals and Exhibits areas.

Natural Breasts

Large, artificial breasts have become a mainstay in North American porn. Many men, however, prefer breasts just as God made them, whether large or small (as Flo and Eddie exclaim in the Frank Zappa movie *200 Motels*: "More than a mouthful is wasted!"). These sites feature women with small or natural breasts.

Little Women Forum

http://lwforum.com/

Membership site

The Little Women Forum proves that a woman doesn't have to be a 38D to be sexy. In addition to photos, there is humor, a BBS, an opinion page, and Nymphette's Naughties (an adult toy store).

Real Boobs

http://www.electricplanet.com/realboobs/

Free site

Real Boobs is a photo site devoted to breasts as found in nature—not surgically enhanced. You choose the pictures you want to view and download by cup size.

BD/SM

Whether you're an expert or just interested in broadening your sexual horizons, here are several good bondage and discipline/sadomasochism sites for you to peruse.

BD/SM Cafe

http://www.bdsmcafe.com

Free site

Hosted by B and Belle, the BD/SM cafe has an extensive list of explicit photo galleries: Male and Fem Dom, Spanking, Best of Bondage, Group BDSM, and Fetish Mania. The site also contains stories, personals, a gift shop, IRC advice, and a fascinating Victorian Vices page.

You Can't Iron on Them

Lovers of small breasts should also check out the **alt.binaries. pictures.erotica.breasts.small** newsgroup.

So Why the Curfew?

"No padlocks, bolts, or bars can secure a maiden better than her own reserve."

—Miguel De Cervantes

Erotic Vox

http://www.eroticvox.com

Free site

Voxanna Michaels began this excellent story site because she wanted to portray "healthy and empowering" BD/SM relationships. All the stories involve safe, communicative, and consensual acts, *and* they are well-written. You will also find BD/SM resources, chat, message boards, a bookstore, and related links.

The Nest

http://misa.ppages.com/

Free site

Sir Sparehawk, Darling, and Morganna Le Fay have put together a BD/SM site that will be useful to dominates and submissives (otherwise known as "tops" and "bottoms" or "doms" and "subs") and enlightening to everyone else. Although most of the pages apply to virtual-time relationships, you will also find picture galleries that illustrate almost every variation of bondage and discipline, a leather braiding forum, and advice for doms and subs. If you would like to know what goes on in BD/SM chat, you can read several transcripts of scenes and collarings that were taken from The Nest's chat room.

Whap! Magazine

http://www.whapmag.com

Commercial site

Women who are dominant over men in otherwise traditional male-female relationships will find this site a treasure. Visit this site to subscribe to or order issues of *Whap!*, the print magazine.

Body Modification

Body modification has been a part of most cultures for thousands of years. In recent times, it has become more common in North America as a means of reclaiming control of the one thing that truly belongs to you: your body.

Many people have altered parts of their bodies for aesthetic or sensual purposes through piercing, tattooing, and other methods. (You don't think most people have their nipples pierced because it looks cute, do you?)

It Hurts So Good

"Pain is used as a test of the ability of the self to control the conflicting imperative of the mind and body. The pleasure aspect is a consequence of having defeated pain, both with the physiological high and the heightened awareness of being resultant from the experience."

—"Body Adornment," by Cordell Terrien, *BME Body Modification* e-zine

Many sites on the Internet discuss body modification. Some are serious, some are fun, some are serious fun. Table 14.1 lists several that represent a cross section of what's available. For more background on the history and sensual aspects of body modification, read the essay by Sander Thomas posted at **http://www.bme.freeq.com/pierce/reclaim.html**.

Table 14.1   Body Modification Sites

Site Name	Address
ASC Tattoo Directory	**http://www.tattoodirectory.com**
Adult Piercing Page	**http://home.maine.rr.com/antigone**
BME Body Modification Ezine	**http://www.bme.freeq.com**
Bodyart Home Page	**http://www.bodyart.com/**
Inkshow.com, Tattoo e-zine	**http://www.inkshow.com**
Passage Body Piercing Studio	**http://www.interlog.com/~passage**
Your Henna Mehndi Tattoo and Body Art Supplies Resource	**http://www.bodyartsupply.com**

Cross-Dressing

Everybody likes to get dressed up now and then. If you're into *cross-dressing* (wearing clothing intended for the opposite sex), take a peek at the sites in Table 14.2.

Table 14.2   Cross-Dressing Sites

Site Name	Address
Emerald Fantasy	**http://emeraldfantasy.com**
The Inner Discovery Network	**http://innerdiscovery.org/gender**
Kerry TV's Lycra page	**http://users.aol.com/kerryjtv**
Lee's Mardi Gras, Drag, and Transvestite Boutique	**http://www.lmgnyc.com**
Photography by Misa Martin	**http://www.users.interport.net/~misa**
Rupaul.Net: The Official Rupaul Website	**http://www.rupaul.net**
Sian-Louise's Lovely Lingerie Homepage	**http://www.geocities.com/ WestHollywood/Heights/5308**
Tri-Ess: The Society for the Second Self	**http://www.tri-ess.com**

Voyeurism and Exhibitionism

Okay, Webster's, do your stuff...

> **voyeurism:** *n. the practice of obtaining sexual gratification by looking at sexual objects or acts, esp. secretly.*

> **exhibitionism:** *n. the attaining of sexual gratification by exhibiting and attracting attention to one's genitalia.*

Sounds like a match made in...well, Gomorrah, doesn't it? Thanks to the miracle of the Internet, voyeurs can now hook up with exhibitionists from the comfort of their homes (see Table 14.3). Ain't technology grand?

Table 14.3   Exhibitionism and Voyeurism Sites

Site Name	Address
Black Widow Cam	**http://www.blackwidow.nu**
Flash Mountain	**http://www.flashmountain.com**
Flasher Contest	**http://home.onestop.net/flasher**
Intimate Friends Network	**http://www.ifriends.net**
Sex Cam Guide	**http://www.sexcamguide.com**
Sexisgood.com	**http://www.sexisgood.com**
The Voyeurweb Homepage	**http://voy.voyeurweb.com**
Web Voyeur!	**http://www.webvoyeur.net**
Webcam Index	**http://webcamindex.com**

And Still More!

In case you think we skipped right past your favorite fetish, browse Table 14.4.

Table 14.4   Other Fetish Sites (By Category)

General Fetish Sites

Site Name	Address
Eric Kroll Photographs	http://www.fetish-usa.com/
Eroscan	http://www.eroscan.com/links/fps/
Fetish Net UK	http://www.fetish-net.org.uk
Fets.com	http://www.fets.com
Interfetish	http://www.interfetish.com
People of Kink	http://www.peopleofkink.com
Worldwide Adult Top 100s	http://www.dangerdave.com.au/wwtop25

Yahoo! Fetish Links (http://dir.yahoo.com/Society_and_Culture/Sexuality/Fetishes)

Site Name	Address
Footjobs	http://www.footjobs.com
In the Feet of the Night	http://www.inthefeetofthenight.com
The Legster	http://www.thelegstersociety.com/
Lower Extremities	http://www.viewsite.com
Stocking Zone	http://www.stockingzone.com
Toe-tally Extreme E-zine	http://www.toetallyextreme.com

Older Women

Site Name	Address
Aunt Fannie's Social Security Club	http://www.auntfannie.com
Aunt Judy's Amateur 30+ Older Women	http://www.auntjudys.com
In Praise of Older Women	http://www.inpraise.com

Sports

Site Name	Address
Diana the Valkyrie	http://www.thevalkyrie.com
Different Loving	http://gloria-brame.com/combat.htm

continues

Table 14.4 Other Fetish Sites (By Category) CONTINUED

Sports

Site Name	Address
Kinky Sports	http://www.kinkysports.com/
Women of The WWF	http://wwfimpact.simplenet.com/ gallery/femalepic.html

Other Fetishes

Site Name	Address
The Belly Button Page	http://members.aol.com/WarrenW999/
Equus Eroticus Magazine	http://www.equuseroticus.com/
Eye Scene	http://www.teleport.com/~lensman/ eyescene.htm
Hall of Statuary	http://php.iupui.edu/~Emhughey
The Long Hair Site	http://www.tlhs.org
Messy Fun	http://www.messyfun.com
Messy Sex	http://www.messysex.com
Navel Base	http://navelbase.com
Silver Smiles	http://silversmiles.simplenet.com
Skin Two	http://www.skintwo.co.uk
Smoke Signals	http://www.smokesigs.com
The Spanking Page	http://thespankingpage.com

Fetish Newsgroups

Not surprisingly, there are plenty of fetish-related forums. Here's a selection to get you started:

- ➤ alt.binaries.pictures.erotica.bondage
- ➤ alt.binaries.pictures.erotica.exhibitionism
- ➤ alt.binaries.pictures.erotica.fetish
- ➤ alt.binaries.pictures.erotica.fetish.feet
- ➤ alt.binaries.pictures.erotica.fetish.latex
- ➤ alt.binaries.pictures.erotica.panties
- ➤ alt.binaries.pictures.erotica.voyeuris
- ➤ alt.binaries.pictures.sex.fetish
- ➤ alt.sex.fetish.fashion

➤ **alt.sex.fetish.feet**

➤ **alt.sex.fetish.hair**

➤ **alt.sex.fetish.panties**

➤ **alt.sex.fetish.smoking**

➤ **alt.sex.fetish.wrestling**

➤ **alt.sex.stories.bondage**

The Least You Need to Know

➤ Many sites on the Web and in newsgroups are devoted to fetishes. No matter what your sexual interests, the Net has enough material to keep you busy for a very long time.

Chapter 15

Cartoons and Anime

In This Chapter

➤ Anime, manga, and hentai artwork on the Web

➤ Adult cartoons and comics

Heavy Metal, Fritz the Cat, and *Who Framed Roger Rabbit?* These three movies—and many others like them—have something in common. They all include scantily clad, sexy 'toons.

Whatever the reason, many of us are enamored by the idea of our favorite cartoon characters cavorting around naked. As luck would have it, you can find an abundance of nude and naughty cartoons and comics on the Internet.

Anime, Manga, and Hentai

If you have seen an animated cartoon show called *Speed Racer,* then you have seen *anime.* This distinctive Japanese art form features colorful cartoon characters with huge, wide eyes. Many people find this art style intriguing, so it's no surprise that the Web is teeming with anime sites. Anime pictures come from many sources, including movies, computer games, comic book scans, and, of course, artists who draw their own.

Blame It on Rio

"I'm not bad. I'm just drawn that way."

—Jessica Rabbit, *Who Framed Roger Rabbit?* (1989)

Although there's little to get excited about where ordinary anime drawings are concerned, there are also anime styles that are overtly sexual. *Manga* and *hentai* are soft- and hardcore anime that feature many of the same cartoon characters, but naked or involved in sex acts.

Warning

You should note that hentai (also called *H-anime*) is a Japanese term that means *sexual perversion*. Although you will see many examples of attractive nudes, you will also find bondage, rape, and tentacles (don't ask). If you're ready to check out anime, manga, and hentai, here some sites you can use as starting points.

Games, Too!

If you want to do more than just look at manga and hentai artwork and movie clips, you can also play computer games. To do so, however, you must pay for a site membership. The availability of manga games may be the biggest draw at many anime sites, because much of the artwork is freely available everywhere.

The Big Kiss Page
http://kiss.03.net.tw/dov/kiss

Free site

If you like anime or played with your sister's Barbie dolls when you were growing up, you *have* to check out this site! *KISS* (Kisekae Set System, not the rock band) is a computer paper-doll program. After downloading a Windows or Macintosh KISS viewing program and a KISS doll, you can dress and undress the doll(s) and put on fashion shows.

Although many of the dolls and clothing sets are similar to kids' paper dolls, others are designed strictly for adults. Adult dolls often come with sexy swimsuits, lingerie, and fetish gear.

Digital Pink

http://www.digitalpink.com

Free site

This well-designed site is a great starting place for picking up some of the best free manga and hentai pictures on the Web. The site's Gallery area contains more than 100 images, divided into three sections: Nice, Naughty, and Notorious. Be sure to look through all three.

Hentai Cantina

http://hentai.wizardtech.net

Free site

Hentai Cantina is another solid source of free manga and hentai pictures. The site contains several hundred drawings, organized in five categories: FF7 (*Final Fantasy 7*), Hentai, *Sailor Moon*, *Rama*, and Assorted Pics.

Hentai Land

http://hentai.land.websx.com

Adult Check site

Although it requires an Adult Check pass to get into this site, they do offer two dozen excellent sample pictures. Hentai Land has thousands of images, as well as movie clips and games.

The Hentai Ring

http://www.altern.org/hring

Free site

The Hentai Web Ring contains more than 100 hentai member sites. Go to this massive links site to reach any of the member sites.

Host Hentai

http://www.hosthentai.com

Pay site

If the guest tour is any indication, Host Hentai makes much of its money by scanning manga and hentai comic books. Each scan shows an entire comic book page.

Features available exclusively to members include a chat area, articles, humor, and an extensive list of hentai links. Plenty of content is also available to guests, including scans from a comic called *Bondage Fairies*. If you're looking for softcore manga or anime, however, search elsewhere. Even the free material at Host Hentai is very graphic.

Ozy's Anime Site

http://www.tasarim.force9.co.uk/ozy

Free site

This small, personal Web site features 30 hand-picked, softcore anime pictures. Ozy has good taste.

Erotic Cartoons and Comics

Have you ever wondered what Veronica and Betty look like without their sweaters? Do you get a funny, tingling feeling when you think about Jessica Rabbit? Well, stop blushing. We won't tell anyone. Here are a handful of sites where you can download adult cartoons and comic books.

Angry Clown Comics

http://www.angryclown.com

Membership site

Angry Clown Comics is definitely worth a quick peek. Although this pay site contains few full-size samples, the comics they offer are colorful and interesting (*Nick Fitts: Private Dick*, *Alien Sex Fiend*, *Freaky Chick*, and *Pizza Girl*).

Cherry Comics

http://www.cherrycomics.com/

Free site

This is the official home page of Cherry Poptart, an adorable 18-year old, or—as the comic's author describes her—"...a really nice girl that swallows."

You can find Cherry Comics at Atomic Books (**http://www.atomicbooks.com** or call 800-778-6246). The specific Cherry page is at **http://www.atomicbooks.com/ adultcomic/cherry.html**. Atomic Books is an offbeat Baltimore bookstore that has a great selection of adult comics and erotic art and other sexy books and magazines.

Nightwing's Cave

http://members.xoom.com/Nightwing316/

Free site

If sexy comic covers are your passion, you will love Nightwing's site! In his spare time (and he must have a lot of it), he scans comic book covers and posts them on this site. If you're curious about which comics actually feature scantily clad females, this is the place to find out.

Playboy-Dark Horse Comics

http://www.playboy.com/darkhorse/

Commercial site

This site is a collaboration between *Playboy* magazine and Dark Horse Comics. Unlike most comic sites—which merely show tiny previews of comic pages—you can read complete stories here, as well as learn about and chat with the artists. The Archives section currently has *Betty Page*, *Ghost*, *Dirty Pair*, *Hellboy*, *Barb Wire*, and *Rascals in Paradise* comics. Among comic sites, consider this one a "must see."

Sir Darcy's Dungeon—Comix Series

http://www.sirdarcy.com/iComix.htm

Free site

It stands to reason that if we searched hard enough, we would find a site devoted to BD/SM comics—and here it is. In addition to scans of comic pages (such as the X-rated Bill Ward comics from the 1960s), you will also find BD/SM and fetish pictorials (*Latex Rubber Nurses*, for example). Even if BD/SM isn't a passion of yours, the site is well worth a look.

Adult Anime, Cartoon, and Comic Newsgroups

If you're hunting for free adult cartoons, newsgroups are an excellent source. Try these for starters:

➤ **alt.binaries.pictures.erotica.anime**

➤ **alt.binaries.pictures.erotica.cartoons**

➤ **alt.binaries.pictures.erotica.cartoons.moderated**

➤ **alt.binaries.pictures.erotica.disney**

The Least You Need to Know

➤ The Japanese art form known as *anime* includes everything from cute drawings of schoolgirls and fairies to hardcore scenes that would be illegal in most countries if depicted in photographs. Few boundaries are not crossed in anime, cartoons, and comics.

➤ Erotic and overtly sexual drawings of famous cartoon characters—particularly Disney heroines—are plentiful in adult comic newsgroups.

➤ Full-length adult comics such as Cherry Poptart and Angry Clown Comics were only found in single-pane–style in *Playboy* and *Penthouse* at one time. Now, they are easy to find and plentiful on the Internet.

Chapter 16

Just for Laughs

In This Chapter

➤ Reviews of some of the best sexual humor pages on the Web

➤ Joining email mailing lists for free jokes

Sex and humor are a natural combination. As long as we're so preoccupied with sex, we may as well have a few chuckles at the same time.

Funny Web Pages

The Web is teeming with sex, so it's only natural that sexual humor abounds, too. (We laugh at everything we love.) The Web is the ideal place to show off, and some of the funniest people in the world are eager to demonstrate just how witty they are. As a bonus, most of the humor sites are free, so you can laugh and smirk to your heart's content.

Don't Save These Sites

Although a handful of Web sites are *devoted* to sexual humor, most of the sexual humor on the Web consists of just single-page giggles and general silliness. Although these one-pagers aren't worth bookmarking, they are great for passing along to friends!

The Dr. Seuss Purity Test

http://www.whocares.com/html/seuss_purity.html

Free site

You can find a gazillion sexual purity tests out there (see **http://dir.yahoo.com/ Society_and_Culture/Sexuality/Purity_Tests** for some examples). You're sure to get a kick out of this one. ("Have you done it on a boat? Have you done it with a goat?" Can *you* pass this test?)

The eXonizer

http://www.global-image.com/eXonizer

Free site

For those of you who think that you already have too much sex in your life, you can use the eXonizer to "automatically strain out lewd, suggestive, or sexually ambiguous words and phrases as you surf."

Just type or paste in the URL of any page, and the eXonizer displays a new version of it with all the bad words replaced with Censored. Click any of the censored words for a cogent explanation of why the word was stricken.

    The word download has been censored because it contains load.

Hoot Island

http://www.hootisland.com

Free site

"Hoot Island is dedicated to the belief that sex can be funny *and* erotic, and that the best sex is often both."

This is one of our favorite Web sites. And there's a lot to see here, including WebGirls ("silly nekkid wimmen"), funny WAV files, CyberSpooge (Hoot Island's version of a porn site—be sure to look at the sample pics), and classic erotica (including a letter from Ben Franklin on how to choose a mistress).

How to Get Rid of a Blind Date

**http://jokes.webdevelop.com/jokes/
archive/blind.shtml**

Free site

If you're not sure whether any of the following suggestions for shedding an unwanted Romeo or would-be Juliet will work, you can choose from among 52 others.

> *Idea #10. Stand up every five minutes, circle your table with your arms outstretched, and make airplane sounds.*

> *Idea #44. Bring 20 or so candles with you and, during the meal, get up and arrange them around the table in a circle. Chant.*

Can We Talk?

"I smiled when I had sex?...You know, that's not the part I remember."

—Joan Rivers, comedienne

How to Satisfy a Woman Every Time

http://klinks.com/totalman/fun/fun11.htm

You will never have to wonder again…. This page contains an extremely long list of ways to satisfy a woman. Some are absurd, some are sweet, many are downright funny, and there's a great surprise ending.

Nude Man Carrot

**http://www.maui.net/~liam/
nudecarrot/nudemancarrot.html**

Free site

More Excuses

If these aren't enough for you, use the random blind date excuse generator at **http://www.halcyon.
com/gwally/cgi-pvt/getout.pl.**

What would you do if you saw a lonely,
naked, little veggie hitchhiking by the side of the road? Offer him a ride, of course. This is a thoroughly silly site chronicling the amazing adventures of an anatomically incorrect carrot.

Vegetable in the raw.

Pornomatic

http://www.maddogproductions.com/pornomatic.htm

Free site

Have you ever wanted to write and star in a porn movie? Here's your chance! You start by making up a title and typing in your name. Next, you choose location, outfit, action, playmates, and so on. Click the button at the bottom of the page that puts it all together, and voilá, there's your script! (It's up to you to audition your co-stars.)

Realsheep

http://www.techstation.com/realsheep

Free site

This is an extremely funny parody of the Realdoll sex doll site (**http://www. realdoll.com**).

Stupid Penis Tricks

http://www.grownmencry.com/hhh/STP.html

Commercial site

What do you do with it, when you aren't doing *it* with it? Think costumes. Think entrees. Think garnish. Think a bag of M&M's, proper trajectory, and the physics of a catapult.

This creative page is part of Heartless's Holey Haven site (**http://www. grownmencry.com/hhh/talk.html**). If you like the tricks, consider popping for a T-shirt or calendar.

Xtra Living—Loveman

http://www.xtra.co.nz/content/special/loveman/

Free site

This is a fun, friendly, little site. LoveMan offers advice to the lovelorn, a "Chick Acquisition Guide" (CAG), a Geek Glossary, the Love-O-Matic love note generator, a Virtual Gift Generator, and the Reject-o-matic (so you can heartlessly dump the person you won by using the aforementioned features).

More Sexual Humor Web Pages

Table 16.1 lists more than a dozen other pages where you can get some yucks.

Table 16.1   More Funny Web Pages

Brenda's Dating Advice for Geeks	**http://home.earthlink.net/~brendar**
The Dirty Joke	**http://www.thedirtyjoke.com**
The Dork	**http://members.aol.com/dorkedom/ entry.htm**
Dr. Ducky DooLittle	**http://www.drducky.com**
Field Guide to North American Males	**http://www.fieldguide.com/**
Flash Mountain	**http://www.flashmountain.com**
Medieval Pick Up Lines	**http://jvj.com/bandgpic.html**
Naked Women (requires Java)	**http://www.twmacinta.com/ detector/English.html**
Oral Pleasure Can Be Yours	**http://www-eden.rutgers.edu/ ~jmcateer/WoH/pyramid.html**
Pick Up Lines	**http://www.geocities.com/ SouthBeach/Lights/7519/ pickup.html**
Playboy Party Jokes	**http://www.playboy.com/ magazine/current/english/ party-jokes.html**
Random Dirty Joke	**http://www.randomjoke.com/ topic/dirty.jhtml**
Random Pick-Up Line Generator	**http://www.halcyon.com/gwally/ cgi-pvt/pickuplines.pl**
Society for the Recapture of Virginity	**http://www.thebluedot.com/srv**
Strange U.S. Sex Laws	**http://www.lectlaw.com/files/ fun23**
Urban Legends Reference Page: Sex	**http://snopes.simplenet.com/sex**
Viagra Jokes	**http://www.net2business.com/ humor/viagra.html**
The Virgin	**http://www.ammoweb.com/jokes/ stories001.htm**

continues

Table 16.1   More Funny Web Pages CONTINUED

World Sexual Records	**http://www.ece.utexas.edu/ ~jmeans/Worldsex.html**
Zack Brown's Underground Origami Page	**http://lynx.neu.edu/z/zbrown/ ug.html**

Joke Mailing Lists

If you have already made some Net friends, your email box is probably crammed each morning with dirty jokes from them. By subscribing to a *mailing list*, you can receive new jokes every day and not have to wait for your friends to annoy you with theirs.

Far too many joke mailing lists abound for us to pick the best. You can learn about many of them at this site:

http://dir.yahoo.com/Entertainment/Humor__Jokes__and_Fun/ Mailing_Lists/

The Least You Need to Know

➤   The main sources of sexual humor on the Internet are in Web pages and email mailing lists.

➤   Unlike most sex sites, the humor sites are typically free.

Chapter 17

Special Interest Sites

In This Chapter

➤ Creating electronic greeting cards for those special occasions

➤ Confidential nude photo processing

➤ Decorating your computer desktop with sexy wallpaper and screen savers

Read on to find the best spots on the Web to create erotic or romantic electronic greeting cards, get 35mm nude shots processed without exposing yourself to local ridicule, and pick up some hot screen savers and wallpaper to adorn your computer screen.

Erotic and Romantic Electronic Postcards

In the past few years, greeting cards have become *very* expensive. Maybe you have grown tired of spending $3 for a piece of paper that will be glanced at and then tossed away. Fight the high cost of sentiment! Hundreds of Web sites enable you to create free electronic greeting cards. As long as your lover has an email account, he or she can know what you have in mind, in as much detail as you care to provide. Note that all the card sites listed in this section contain *free* cards that anyone can customize.

You may ask yourself why Web sites would provide you the opportunity to send these cards free of charge. Well, don't worry. They get something out of it.

➤ They get people coming to their Web site, which will mean that more people will see their sponsors' ads. This means more money for them.

➤ They reason that if you liked sending a free card from their site once, you'll do it again as long as they keep adding new pictures. That's reasonable.

➤ For every card that you send, your recipient has to come to their site to claim it. That means that maybe your recipient will send a card to another friend or back to you. That means more and more people visiting their site and seeing their sponsors' advertising banners.

➤ Every time you type in your email address and the email address of a friend of yours, the operators of the Web site add the address to their database of "customers." They can then send mass email to everyone to invite you back to their Web site to see new photos (and draw more traffic for their sponsors) or to sell you their products. Maybe you'll like them so much that you'll subscribe to their Web site. Or, they might sell your name and email address as part of a large mailing list to other businesses that have similar products to sell.

In spite of this onslaught of marketing strategy, we still send these cards. Why? Well, the value for the "free" cards is (in my estimation) well worth the cost.

Creating an Electronic Postcard

As an example of how simple it is to create an electronic postcard, here's how it's done at Erotic Postcards (**http://www.eroticpostcards.com**). (Needless to say, these hardcore cards should be sent only to someone you know *very* well.)

The lovely Jerri escorts you through the process of creating and sending a card. First, you choose one of 15 X-rated categories for the card, such as **Couples**, **Hooters**, or **Oral Sex**. Second, you pick a picture to illustrate your card. Third, select a font and type color, such as Verdana and blue. Then you type your message, and enter the name and email address of both the recipient and yourself. Finally, you can add a cartoon icon to the card, if you want to. An email message is then automatically sent from the site notifying the recipient that a card is waiting to be claimed.

From some sites, you can also attach a sound file to the card that plays when received. Most provide a "preview mode," enabling you to see—before sending the card—exactly what the recipient will see. Many will also notify you via email when the recipient has come to the Web site and picked up the card.

Postcard Sites

Here are some other electronic postcard sites that you should investigate. Depending on the site, the card pictures and messages range from erotic to kinky to sleazy. Whatever your (or your lover's) mood and taste, you are sure to find something appropriate in one of these sites.

BDSM: A Powerotics Production—POWERotics Postcard Center

http://www.bdsm.com/powerotics/sendcard.html

Membership site

POWERotics offers several dozen images by photographers Tom Mayes, Hans Meijer, and Todd Friedman of BD/SM themes to send to your favorite dominant or submissive. It also includes galleries from the First SmokeShop Collection, The Fetish Club, Vintage Bondage, and Classic BD/SM Anime.

Erotic City Postcard Center

http://www.eroticcity.net/postcards/postcard.html

Membership site

If you're looking for subtlety, you won't find it here. Erotic City has six X-rated pictures that you can use as the basis for free postcards.

Hallmark Connections

http://www.hallmarkconnections.com/

Commercial site

Hallmark? You think we're kidding? This is one of the best sites to find mainstream electronic greeting cards. They may not lead directly to sex, but a card from the "Love:Suggestive" section can bring a laugh and set the stage.

Hallmark has a solid selection of slightly naughty, slightly suggestive greeting cards. The fancier animated cards are $2.50 each, but they also have free cards that you can send.

Kinky Cards

http://www.kinkycards.com

Membership site

No matter what your favorite fetish, you are sure to find an appropriate (or should that be *inappropriate*?) card here. Kinky Cards has more than 1,400 images for you to survey. Latex? Got it. BD/SM? Got it. Erotic photography? Got it. Spanking? Got it. Teddy bears in bondage? Got that, too. (We really *love* the teddy bears.)

Photo Cards—Beautiful, Beautiful Women and Handsome, Handsome Hunks

http://www.netdreams.com/Net.Dreams/9th/postcards/bbw.html

**http://www.netdreams.com/net.dreams/9th/postcards/
hhh.html**

Free site

Photo Cards has pictures of gorgeous women in elegant lingerie and handsome men.
All are pretty and tastefully done. (How did *that* happen?)

Porn Card

http://www.porncard.com/

Free site

Porn Card has the usual softcore and borderline hardcore pictures. Several of the cards
are cropped so that the...uh...interesting parts are off-camera. Categories include
Naughty Birthday, Seasonal Sex Cards, True Studs, and Innocent Fun. This site offers
one vital, original thing: Many of the cards are laugh-out-loud funny.

For example, a woman is lying with her chest across a man's stomach. Her face is offscreen. The caption says: "Happy Birthday! Who's going to blow out your candle this
year?"

Another one shows a couple having sex. The caption says "Happy F*ing Birthday."

SexyCards Online

http://www.sexycards.com/

Free site

This site struck me as original because it looks like a group of friends got together and
shot a roll of film of themselves. They have strange props (sailor hats) and only one
woman is actually showing her breasts. One guy is actually mooning the camera (at
least I think it's a guy—it's hard to tell from that angle).

And a Few More...

You can't have too many electronic greeting card sites in your browser's Bookmarks or
Favorites list. Here are some additional ones for you to visit.

Table 17.1 More Greeting Card Sites

Site Name	Address
E-Kissing Booth	**http://www.thekiss.com/ekiss/**
Virtual Kisses & Hugs	**http://members.tripod.com/**
Kiss Kiss Kiss Postcards	**~catchme/cardss.html**

Site Name	Address
Virtual Hugs and Kisses	**http://www.hugkiss.com/**
Erotic Postcards from the World Museum of Erotic Art	**http://www.opkamer.nl/amea/ sendp.htm**

Nude Photo Processing

Here's the scenario: You and your significant other are nude and in a playful mood. There's a camera in the room. You pick it up and mount it on a tripod. The dog looks at you funny. You set the timer, hop onto the bed, and do cute naked things to each other just as the flash goes off. Giggles ensue. Before you know it, the entire roll is gone.

Now what? The Internet has a solution. Send your film to one of the sites listed in Table 17.2.

Table 17.2   Nude Photo Processing Sites

Site Name	Address
Delilah's Adult and Confidential Photography Processing	**http://www.delilahs.simplenet.com/**
Discreet Photo	**http://www.nakedphoto.com/**
M.O. Photolabs	**http://www.mophotolabs.com**

Is your wife or girlfriend too shy to pose nude? No problem! Technology comes to the rescue. For $20, the digital artist who operates the Web site at **http://www.ragart. com** will "nudify" a scanned photo of your clothed female lover—for better or worse. This is more work than just sticking your lover's head on another woman's body; check out the before-and-after photos at the site.

Wattage Does Matter!

"The difference between pornography and erotica is lighting."

—Gloria Leonard

Sexy Screen Savers and Wallpaper

For those of you who never seem to get enough sexual stimulation, consider moving it onto your computer desktop. The following sites offer erotic screen savers and wallpaper.

Adult Wallpaper

http://www.sagelink.net/teaser/wallpaper/paper.htm

Free site

This site offers two free images of "kaleidoscope" nudes that make excellent tiled wallpaper. Save either or both images to your hard disk, and then follow the instructions in Chapter 2 for "Using a Picture as Your New Wallpaper."

Wallpaper for Macs

Like Windows-reliant computers, Macintosh computers running OS 8 or higher can also display a picture as the background for the desktop. Follow these steps:

1. Click the **Apple** menu, and choose **Control Panels, Desktop Pictures**.

2. Click the **Picture** button, and then the **Select Picture** button. A standard file dialog box appears.

3. Select the picture you want to use.

4. Choose a positioning option from the first pop-up menu.

5. When the picture in the preview window appears as you would like it to, click **Set Desktop** to transfer the image to your desktop.

If you later want to return to a normal desktop (without a picture), click **Remove Picture**.

Desktop Arts and 3D Screen Savers

http://www.artx.com

Free site

If you're looking for sexy—but not outrageous—screen savers or wallpaper, this is the perfect place to start. Desktop Arts features erotic Windows and Macintosh screen savers, wallpaper, and games—and it's all free! There's so much material here that you can easily while away several hours just browsing.

That Picture Paints Only 900 Words

If a picture does a poor job of filling the desktop area, or is exceptionally small, there is a way out. Macintosh and all flavors of Windows enable you to "Tile" the picture, which repeats it all over the screen, instead of just placing it once in the middle. Windows 98 (or Windows 95 with the Plus! package) also enables you to stretch the image to fit your entire desktop.

Intimate Images

http://www.hootisland.com/iip

Commercial/Membership site

Intimate Images Photography has a few very nice pictures of nude women that you can download for free and install as Windows wallpaper or Macintosh desktop pictures. Click **Free Stuff** in the menu bar and follow the instructions.

Nudes.com

http://www.nudes.com/

Commercial/Membership site

At this site, you can order a pair of 20-picture screen saver packages for $9.95. You can choose from 40 categories of high-quality images featuring work by J. Stephen Hicks.

XXX Screensavers

http://www.xxxscreensavers.com

Free site

By the time this book is printed, you will be able to download three types of screen savers to your Windows platform. One is akin to a slideshow, and the others are rotating photocubes and photospheres. At the time of printing, only the photocubes were available. And although only Windows screen savers are available right now, they are also working on versions for Macintosh.

If you get confused about how to download and install these, you can just follow the very good instructions at this URL:

http://www.xxxscreensavers.com/instructions.html

You can also subscribe to receive a new screen saver by email each week.

Sexy Swimwear Screensaver

http://ourworld.compuserve.com/homepages/esmsoftware/swimsuit.htm

Free site

This site gives away a swimsuit slideshow screen saver. As they say, "This screen saver is completely *free* of charge! No expiry, no reminder messages." And aren't those the best kind?

The Least You Need to Know

➤ An electronic greeting card or postcard is the perfect way to say "I miss you," "I want you," or "Have you ever seen anything so perverted in your life? (Let's try it!)" You can be thoughtful without having to leave your PC—and go tromping all over town to find just the right card. Also, you can send sexy cards without having to go to the local "dirty book shop" and take the chance of seeing your second grade teacher there (which, I'm sure would cause permanent mental scarring).

➤ If you've wondered how you are ever going to get those nude pictures from that weekend rendezvous developed, many confidential photo processing labs advertise their services on the Internet.

➤ Wallpaper and screen savers don't have to be limited to soothing mountain scenes and flying Windows icons. Sex is everywhere. Why not on your desktop, too?

Chapter 18

Multimedia: Lights, Camera, Action!

In This Chapter

➤ Finding and playing video clips, audio clips, streaming video, and streaming audio

➤ An interview with the management of Live Sex from Amsterdam, an interactive sex Web site

Gone are the days of plentiful, free online video clips. Because clips tend to be huge (between 200KB and several megabytes apiece), owners of free Web sites soon discovered the cost of letting us download *free* ones. The ISPs complained that too many people were hitting those personal Web pages and reacted by presenting enormous bills to the site owners. So over time, the clips were removed or have been reduced to mere seconds in length. Although you can still download movie clips from some of the subscription sex sites, you are more likely to find streaming video.

The same situation exists with audio files. It takes just as long to transmit a huge sound file as it does a video clip; so finding free, lengthy audio stories such as "How My Boyfriend Deflowered Me in the Back of His Dodge Dart" is less likely. Small sex-related WAVs are still plentiful on the Internet, but you have to hunt for them.

Although free pickings are decidedly slim, we did find several interesting Web sites where you can still download video and audio clips, as well as several examples of streaming video, streaming audio, and live sex. Lights, camera, action!

Movie Clips and Streaming Video

Movie clips are generally playable through your Web browser. Certain types, however, may require a program such as MoviePlayer (to play QuickTime movies on the Macintosh) or MediaPlayer, a utility that comes with Windows 95 and 98. Or you may need an additional plug-in for your browser, such as QuickTime 3.

Tippy, Could You Come Over Here?

"Ecstasy is not really part of the scene we can do on celluloid."

—Orson Welles

Streaming video is often presented using Java, so all you need is a current version of Netscape Navigator or Internet Explorer to view it. Some streaming video, however, is broadcast using VivoActive or RealVideo. If you don't have the necessary applications or plug-ins, see Chapter 1, "Sexual Content on the Net: What's Out There, Where Can I Find It, and What Software Do I Need?" for instructions on what you need and where to get it.

The Hardcore Channels

http://www.hardchannels.com/

Membership site

We take it back. Although there aren't many *free* video clips on the Web, if the following blurb is any indication, there are still plenty *for sale*. "THC presents tens of thousands of fast-downloading, uncensored, hardcore, explicit adult video clips and raunchy video 'freeze frames' that you can watch right on your computer screen, in the privacy of your own home." Your membership entitles you to unlimited downloads.

Hotpants Asia

http://coed-campus.porncity.net/110/

Free site

Hotpants Asia contains a half dozen R- and X-rated AVI and MOV (QuickTime) video clips that you can download for free. Most of the other links in the site—including the ones for free pictures—take you to other Web sites. As a show of gratitude for the free clips, you may want to explore these sites, too.

Kim's Page

http://www.kimspage.com/movie/

Pay site

As a way of advertising her personal Web site and attracting new members, Kim—an attractive 19-year-old exhibitionist—offers six AVI video clips that you can download. The clips are solo performances and are R- to X-rated. Be sure to take a look at the other samples on her home page (**http://www.kimspage.com**).

Scour.net

http://www.scour.net

Free site

If you want some free video or audio clips from all over the Web, give **Scour.net** a try. You enter search terms that describe what you're looking for and **Scour.net** returns a series of matching links. Just click the links to download and play the clips.

Scour.net offers free software that can speed up multimedia downloads. It also provides links to many multimedia players, as well as plug-ins and ActiveX components to beef up your browser's multimedia capabilities.

Sizzle

http://www.sizzle.com

Membership site

If you're into video, a membership in Sizzle will help feed your need. Sizzle has thousands of video streams from which to choose, 3,000 downloadable movie clips, and live strip shows. You will also find a huge picture gallery and an erotic story library to help shift your imagination into overdrive.

185

Smut Archives

http://www.smutarchives.com/freevideos.htm

Free site

This small free site offers a series of XXX video clips (between 800KB and 1MB each), as well as some still-model and couple pictures. You can click the **Live Free Chat** link on the opening page to go to **Sexside.com**, an interactive video chat site (described later in this chapter).

Additional Control over the Videos

In Internet Explorer and Netscape Navigator, the Smut Archives clips play in the browser window rather than as separate, floating windows. You can still resize, save, and set playback properties for the movies by right-clicking them.

Throbnet Websites, Inc.

http://www.throbnet.com

Commercial site

If you're a fan of adultvideos, Throbnet may hold the answer to the current dearth of video clips on the Web. Although it provides no samples for you to view, you can see a still shot from any video before you buy. Clips can be purchased from Throbnet for 50 cents per megabyte.

Pearls of Prose

If you have an interest in erotic stories, you should also check out **http://www.throbnet.com/anonymous_messages**, a section of Throbnet where you can read stories and letters contributed by users hoping to gain free access to the site.

Interactive Video

Web sites that offer *interactive video*, on the other hand, enable you to direct the action. By typing into a chat window, you and all the other members who are online can instruct the models on how you would like them to pose or what you would like them to do. In sites that offer both video and audio (such as Live Sex from Amsterdam), it's almost like being in the same room (but not quite). To prove that what they're seeing is live, many visitors will ask the models to say their name or write specific messages on a piece of paper, such as "I love you, James."

Just Keeping Abreast

"If the effort that went into research on the female bosom had gone into our space program, we would now be running hot dog stands on the moon."

—Unknown

Live Sex from Amsterdam

http://www.amsterdamtonight.com, **http://www.sexview.com**, **http://www.sexplanet.com**, **http://www.xxxhotel.com**

Commercial sites

If you are up for some of the wildest sex on the Internet, check out these interactive video sites run by Python Communications. They provide live, X-rated, no-holds barred sex right in your browser window.

Few taboos exist here. In a typical hour, you are likely to see oral sex, anal sex, masturbation, vibrators, and dildos. As you watch, you can type comments and directions in a chat window, which is shared by all others viewing the show. Sexstar, the show operator, relays the comments to the performers and directs the cameraman to change angles and zoom in for close-ups.

Sex View, Sex Planet, and XXX Hotel simultaneously broadcast the same show, featuring a straight or lesbian couple from the Red Light District of Amsterdam. To subscribe, you buy a block of time. A 60-minute block costs $60 ($1 per minute), for example. The minimum block you can buy is 7 minutes for $19.95 ($2.85 per minute). The more time you purchase, the cheaper the per-minute cost.

If you want additional shows, try Amsterdam Tonight. They broadcast the same live couple show as the other three sites, but also have two "Teaze" shows with solo female performers.

Live Gay Sex from Amsterdam

http://www.queercore.com, http://www.menmenmen.com

Commercial site

Live Gay Sex from Amsterdam features males and costs slightly more than Python's straight sites ($1.50 per minute when purchased in a 60-minute block, for instance).

Netscape Preferred

The Live Sex from Amsterdam and Live Gay Sex from Amsterdam sites are best viewed with Netscape, which automatically handles the audio portion of the broadcast and features a resizable video window. If you use Internet Explorer 4, the video window cannot be resized and audio must be handled by Speak Freely, a separate program that you can download.

Space Amazones

http://www.space-amazones.com

Membership site

Space Amazones is another Python Communications site. Tit Talk, an interactive video chat segment, has two R-rated interactive shows that you can switch between, each featuring a solo female performer who strips, teases, and masturbates as you watch. (These are the same broadcasts as Amsterdam Tonight's "Teaze" shows.)

The shows are only a small part of what's available at Space Amazones. Site membership also gets you more than two dozen RealAudio sex stories, a huge assortment of streaming video channels and clips, browser-based games, screensavers and background images, erotic comic-strip adventures, and a library of hardcore pictures.

Sexside.com

http://www.sexside.com/

Membership site

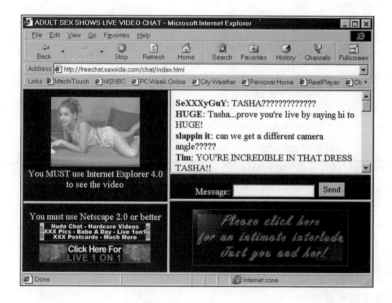

Believe it or not, you can find *free* interactive video sex chat on the Web! As a teaser to its pay chats, **Sexside.com** provides a free chat room in which you can send messages to a live model as she moves seductively on a bed and types occasional replies to the chat participants. (Don't expect any nudity here or much interaction, because this is a free chat on a pay site. But the ladies are uniformly cute, sexy, and provocatively dressed.)

More Live Sex Sites

If you're searching for other interactive sex shows or live performances, enter the following address in your browser:

http://www.yahoo.com/Business_and_Economy/Companies/Sex/Adult_Services/Videoconferencing/

An Interview with Python Communication, Inc. (Live Sex from Amsterdam)

Q: Tell us a bit about the performers. How many live performers do the various sites employ?

A: We can never have too many artists. We always have positions open for good looking, sexy, enthusiastic performers.

Q: How are they recruited and chosen?

A: What we look for in our performers is outgoing and personable personalities and, of course, hot and sexy appearances! Many artists apply for the job because they have seen us on television or in newspaper ads, heard about us via word of mouth, or have been to the Casa Rosso or Banana Bar live theaters in Amsterdam.

If anyone is interested in applying, he or she can send a note and picture to:

Casa Rosso
P.O. Box 16846
1001RH Amsterdam
email: **hr@pythonvideo.com**

Q: What kind of background or personality do you look for?

A: Our artists are just like you and me. And as all people have different backgrounds and personalities, so our artists do, too.

However, they do have some things in common. They all like to be looked at, and they like to be on stage. Moreover, they just work hard to earn a good living.

Q: What does the job description look like?

A: A description of the job: Uninhibited people who can tease and please. Direct interaction with the customers. Must be willing to do almost anything to ensure customer satisfaction.

Q: Are performers given any training before you set them loose in front of a camera?

A: There is no specific training. We hire people who are natural exhibitionists; they love to perform. We just explain to them that the top priority is keeping smiles on our customers faces and have them watch our current "best" performers so they can see what is required. Management monitors the performers to see that they do a good job.

Q: Are there any rules that you've set for the performers?

A: The strict rules we keep are no violence, no bestiality, and no child pornography.

Q: Are some performers solo only, or are all expected to perform in all shows?

A: We have some solo girls who do enjoy doing lesbian shows, but—for the most part—the soloists do solo shows and couples do couple shows.

Q: What's the most unusual request that a performer has received?

A: We get lots of foot fetish requests and— for the gay show—"Can you suck yourself off?"

Q: How do the performers stay fresh? How do they maintain their interest from day to day?

A: Our performers all *love* to fuck, and getting paid for it is just a bonus. We practically have to pay some of them to stop!

continues

continued

Q: Many of the customer requests have to do with proving that this is indeed live sex (holding up cards with their names on them, for example). Can you put this to rest once and for all?

A: Our shows are so unique and incredible, people just can't believe they are watching it live. But we guarantee that our shows are always live and always hot. We have the #1 hottest live, interactive hardcore shows on the Net. We are the *only* live show with no-download sound, and we have the sexiest, wildest performers! This is our promise to you.

A glimpse of the Live Sex from Amsterdam studio, while a show is in progress

Audio Clips and Streaming Audio

Audio sex takes a variety of forms and formats. It ranges from short and often humorous WAVs to the recounting of steamy episodes or actual lovemaking sessions. The most popular formats for downloadable audio clips are WAV and AU—playable by most browsers. Streaming audio is generally in RealAudio format. You need RealPlayer to hear it (**http://www.real.com/**).

Amazing Sex

http://www.amazingonline.com/visitor/eroticsounds/

Membership site

The Visitors section of Amazing Sex is amazingly devoid of samples—*except* for the Erotic Stories area. Here you can find several X-rated RealAudio stories for your listening pleasure.

Summer's Favorite WAV Files

http://www.sagelink.net/teaser/wavfiles/wav.htm

Free site

No WAV collection is complete without a copy of Duckjob, a hilarious audio clip. If you haven't heard it, you can download it (438KB) from a link on this personal Web page. ("Don't move. I'll go get you a towel.") Be sure to check out the other WAVs while you're there. You can also find Duckjob at **http://www.jokefest.com**.

Internet Sex Radio

http://www.radiosex.com/

Free site

The mission of Internet Sex Radio is to provide uncensored information about human sexuality. Kim Martyn, a sex health educator from Toronto, moderates the broadcasts.

To prepare to listen to any of the prerecorded shows, all you have to do is choose your modem's speed from a drop-down list, specify the audio software you will be using (RealAudio or Voxware), and pick the taped broadcast you want to hear. Recent show topics include masturbation, sexual positions, fetishes, bestiality, cyber-affairs, and online dating. The discussions are both informative and entertaining. And they aren't just brief clips. Current programs run from 9 to 22 minutes each. This is nothing like what you heard in your high school hygiene class!

Other Sound Sources

If you have an interest in acquiring some sex-related WAVs, one of the best ways is by using chat programs and requesting them from other users. You will find that many IRC (Internet Relay Chat) and LOL Chat participants are more than happy to exchange WAV files with newcomers.

If you would rather build a collection without relying on the kindness of strangers, take a look at the **alt.binaries.sounds.erotica** newsgroup. You may find RealAudio sex clips there, for example. Or try Scour Net at **http://www.scour.net**.

The Least You Need to Know

➤ Free video and audio are becoming rarities on the Internet. If you are looking for it in quantity (or expecting *quality*), you will have to hunt long and hard. Otherwise, prepare to pay for it.

➤ The latest wrinkle on Net sex is live, interactive video. For fees that can range from $1 to $5 a minute, you can watch and direct the actions of live performers.

➤ You will find RealPlayer an indispensable utility to play streaming audio and video.

➤ One of the best sources of sexy WAVs are the people you meet in chat programs. Ask politely, and many of them will be happy to send you their favorite sound files.

Chapter 19

Erotica

In This Chapter

➤ Erotic art and photography Web sites

➤ Erotic stories and literature on the Web and in erotica newsgroups and mailing lists

---

The sites and newsgroups in this chapter all deal with erotica expressed in art, photographs, stories, poetry, and literature (**erotica**: n. literature or art dealing with sexual love).

As with most of the topics in this book, what is considered erotic is all over the sexual landscape. Photographic images often follow the traditional expression of eroticism—that is, they are predominantly dimly lit, black-and-white figure studies and disembodied body parts. A few sites stray from the mainstream, featuring fanciful artwork, digitally altered images, and the darker side of sex. Erotic stories run the gamut from tales of love and romance to hardcore, "zipless" sex—with nothing left to the imagination. Because each Web site defines erotica in its own terms (and they are all different), you're sure to find something that appeals to you.

Erotic Art

You may be wondering what a section on erotic art is doing in a book about sex on the Internet. In fact, quite a few of the erotic art Web sites we contacted asked us the same question. The answer is simple. Sex isn't just about crotch shots; sometimes it can be cerebral or thought provoking—a feast for the imagination. Art can be the best porn because it inspires your imagination as well as your loins. It may not show you everything that a photo does, but it points you in the right direction.

The Art Pages of Jimu

http://jab.datachan.com/jimu

Free site

Move over, Felix the Cat.

The Art Pages of Jimu is a site filled with Jimu's anime, erotic cartoons, and parody art. It's worth a visit, if only to see "Tinkerbell in Bondage."

Coleman Photography

http://www.globalconnect.net/lcoleman

Free site

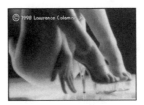

Lawrence Coleman's site is entitled "fineArtfeetfotosforfanaticfemalefootfanciers." Several galleries on this site feature exceptional black-and-white images of women's feet and legs, as well as dance photographs and faces. Great care has been taken to present the subject matter as a true portrait. Mr. Coleman's photographs can be purchased on floppy disk or as 8×10 prints. This site is well worth a look, even if your favorite female body parts are above the ankles.

Distinctive Images Photography

http://www.distinctiveimages.com/

Commercial/Membership site

Doug Lester's photography site contains a section titled "Woman: Studies in Black and White." The pictures are lovely, pure, and simple. The White Silk Collection is a gallery containing images of women draped in semitransparent white silk, effectively creating a soft, subtle eroticism. Additional pictures are available in Mr. Lester's members-only pay site.

Eroticism in Antiquity

http://www.cpu.lu/gka/er_ant.htm

Free site

It's no secret that the ancient Greeks and Romans had tons of buck-naked statuary just standing around taking up space. This site will tell you all about it. In addition to several articles about sex slaves, mistresses, prostitution, and vestal virgins, this site contains many pictures to peruse. Each has a detailed explanation of the myth behind the artwork. (That Priapus ... what a guy!)

Ethos/Eros (Creative Nude Photography Network – Fine Art Nudes)

http://www.ethoseros.com/

Commercial site

This supersite has it all: galleries, links, reviews, videos, books, and anything else you might want to know about the art of nude photography. You can visit more than 100 artists' galleries from this site.

John Carey Photographic Imagery

http://www.sirius.com/~jcphoto/

Commercial site

This site is divided into three galleries: fetish, gothic, and corsets. The color photos are very dramatic; you can't begin to imagine the blood-red lipstick and black hair dye budget for some of the shots, but they *are* interesting. We are far more drawn to the black-and-white work and the sepia-toned vintage images. Carey sells prints, postcards, T-shirts, and calendars.

Ken Marcus Studio

http://www.kenmarcus.com/

Commercial/Membership site

Ken Marcus has photographed women for *Playboy* and *Penthouse*. In this membership site, he shows his unpublished nudes, including bondage and fetish pictures. This site offers a dozen or so free preview images. Mr. Marcus does good work.

Lee Stranahan Erotic Imagery

http://www.stranahan.com/erotica/

Commercial site

These works are based primarily on the model's sexual interests.

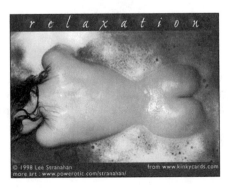

198

This site is another favorite of ours. Most of Mr. Stranahan's models are photographed as they enact their personal sexual fantasies, allowing the viewer a glimpse into the heart of sensuality. It should be noted that many of the women are female submissives, so don't expect soft and fluffy pictures. His galleries feature dozens of strong, provocative images, many available for sale.

Libido: The Journal of Sex and Sensibility

http://www.sensualsource.com/libido/

Commercial site

Libido offers erotic fiction, book reviews, news releases, and some of the finest erotic photography on the Internet. As stated in the Fantasy Photo Gallery, "You'll find photos from a range of sexual orientations and viewpoints that are about the emotional as well as physical side of sex; photos that are playful, funny, lusty, even worshipful." Great site, great pics.

The Maronah Studio

http://www.siserone.co.uk/maronah/

Membership site

"We aim to go beyond the explicit to activate imaginations."

Maronah Studio is a British site with a collaborative approach to erotic art. The preview gallery contains a few tasteful—and decidedly sexy—images. To see the rest, a paid membership is required.

"The erotica we create, while not shying away from all aspects of sexuality, seeks to arouse by evoking rather than merely depicting," the site's creators explain. "Many of Maronah Studio's works are very subtle, requiring the viewer to actively engage with them rather than casually glance. We aim to suggest, remind, and inspire."

Melanie Klegerman's Art and Design: Erotic Art

http://members.aol.com/melaniek73/html/erotic_art.html

Commercial site

This site is filled with bright, cheerful drawings of sexy little fairies, elves, and other fantastic creatures. It is impossible to look at Ms. Klegerman's work without smiling.

Plymouth Rock Art

"Art is so wonderfully irrational, exuberantly pointless, but necessary all the same. Pointless and yet necessary, that's hard for a puritan to understand."

—Gunther Grass

Nerve Magazine

http://www.nervemag.com/

Commercial site

Nerve magazine claims that it plays "less to the groin than the gray matter." They're talking about your brain. If you're looking for intelligent sensuality, this is the site. Check out "Skin: Uncensored Photography" for a wide range of erotic pictures by many artists.

Peter DaSilva Photography

http://www.dasilvaphoto.com/

Commercial site

Corsets, bondage, fetish, erotic nudes, and tattoos are featured in this collection of photographs depicting unconventional sexuality. All of Mr. DaSilva's works can be purchased as photographic prints.

Pornotopia

http://www.pornotopia.com/

Membership site

Don't let its name mislead you. Pornotopia is *not* a typical X-rated Web sex site. You're unlikely to see anything like it elsewhere on the Net.

Pornotopia is a pay site with an extensive gallery of sci-fi/fantasy erotic art images, as well as a lengthy, lavishly illustrated graphic novel. The hardcore pictures are explicit and bizarre. The larger free softcore gallery has colorful poster-style nudes, as well as a few pen-and-ink line drawings. If you like your women bright blue, hairless, and shiny, this is the place to visit.

Roger Moore Fine Art Photography

http://www.interoz.com/gallery/moore.htm

Commercial site

From the quiet sensuality of the sepia-toned Renaissance pictures to the more dramatic contrast of nudes against backgrounds of stone, Mr. Moore's images capture the essential beauty of the human body. The photos can be purchased from this site, and we suggest that you do so.

Roger should be encouraged. Not bad for a guy who was kidnapped and sold to a circus when he was five. He still supports the tattooed man and the painted lady... even buys fancy peanuts for the elephants. (Don't ask. Just read his biography. It's hysterical.)

Third & Fourth Galleries

http://www.3rd-4th.com/erotic.htm

Commercial site

Want to see what great-grandpa had hidden in the bottom of his sock drawer? This gallery has several pictures of authentic French postcards from the early 1900s. These sepia-toned images are subtly erotic and charming. All can be purchased from the site.

Innocents Abroad

"I could take this home, Marilyn. This is something teenage boys might find of interest."

—Vice President Dan Quayle, March 1990 (when purchasing a South American Indian Doll that displays an erection when lifted)

World Art Erotica

http://www.wae.org/

Membership site

Culture? You want culture? Well, pretend you do; it'll impress the neighbors. This is a pay site of erotic art from around the world, but it has a fine free gallery of painting and sculptures from India, Africa, France, Czechoslovakia (Czechoslovakia?), and many other countries. Some of the positions will leave you wondering: "How do they *do* that?"

Other Noteworthy Erotic Art Sites

Table 19.1 lists additional erotic art sites that you should check out.

Table 19.1   More Erotic Art Sites

Site Name	Web Address
AMEA/World Museum of Erotic Art	**http://www.opkamer.nl/amea**
The Erotic Art of Ancient Rome	**http://www.personal.psu.edu/ users/w/x/wxk116/eros/**
Erotic Traveler	**http://www.erotictraveler.com**
Fine Art Nude Photography Network	**http://www.fineartnude.com/ webring/**
Frank Wallis	**http://www.condotiere.com/ audace/ass.htm**
Kassandra	**http://www.kassandra.de/**
Kinsey Institute Exhibits	**http://www.indiana.edu/~kinsey/ events.html**
Nudes and Erotic Fine Art Photos by Ralf Oellerich	**http://www.oellerich.com/**
Sex Art	**http://www.sexart.com**
Sheela-na-gig	**http://www.wam.umd.edu/ ~taramc/sheela.html**

Erotic Art Newsgroups

Although the more than 150 **alt.binaries.pictures.erotica** newsgroups are very popular, few of them contain material that bears any resemblance to that found in the erotic art sites in this chapter. The "erotica" part of the name appears to be a misnomer. What you'll find in most is a mixture of run-of-the-mill porn and ads for X-rated sites. If you're looking for photos and art work that's a bit more artistic, however, it's worth taking a peek at **alt.binaries.photos.nude-art.moderated**.

Erotic Stories, Poetry, and Literature

Now we move on to erotic reading material. To introduce you to the type of erotic wordplay you will see, many of the site descriptions in this section include a brief excerpt from a story.

The Adult Fantasy World of Guillermo Bosch

http://www.guillermobosch.com/

Free site

Mr. Bosch's site is divided into five sections: The Sauce Box (an erotic story e-zine), art, *E-mail: An Erotic Novella*, *Rain* (a novel), and poetry. The writings are plentiful and eclectic in subject matter. Each story is introduced by a sample paragraph, so you can decide whether you want to read on.

> "Dorothy finally smiled and slid out of her blue calico frock. The smooth whiteness of her skin was a marvel to Scarecrow, a beauty beyond beauties. He gasped and reached out for her.

> "They sat by the side of the deserted yellow brick road, Scarecrow working his magic fingers over Dorothy's back and neck and bottom, over her tummy... and ... and ... oh, those beautiful mounds on her chest! 'What could those be,' Scarecrow asked himself? So round and bouncy and smooth with pretty pink tips that Dorothy moaned and sighed when he pinched."

> —*Love on the Yellow Brick Road*, Lucrezia

Adult Story Corner & Jaded Journal Entries

http://www.adultstorycorner.com/

Commercial site

Owned by Lady Jessika and edited by G. Smith, the Adult Story Corner offers over 30 erotic short stories, as well as links to other pages. You will find a few stories of dominance/submission here, but most are your basic vanilla tales with a little fantasy and romance thrown in for good measure. This site is among the best.

> "By now the sun has climbed into the sky and we decide to swim. The water is cool and refreshing as we frolic naked among the waves until we return to the blanket and then slowly dress back in our leathers while still kissing and touching. We walk over to the Harley and I love to watch as you swing your leg over it. You now sit astride with it firmly balanced and held between your strong thighs. You start it and as it jumps to life so much a part of you I climb on. Sliding close to your back opening my thighs to slide them around you I feel so much a part of you. I can feel the engine under me as you slide your hands up and down my thighs and then lean back laughing and say, 'Ready to ride the Harley honey?'"

> —*The Harley*, Lady Jessika

Annie's Diary

http://www.anniesdiary.com

Free site

Annie's Diary contains a series of diary-style erotic adventures, written by Annie, a young, attractive, bisexual woman. Unlike most personal erotic story Web sites, Annie's tales are illustrated with photographs of the women that she has pursued—and frequently caught. Read all about it.

> "As I undressed to put on another outfit, Trista watched me. I could see her looking from the mirror in the dressing room. I smiled back at her and turned around. She was blushing uncontrollably. I asked if she wanted a closer look. Timidly, softly, almost too quietly for me to hear she said yes. I motioned for her to come to me and nervously, slowly she did. I held her in my arms and kissed her softly on the neck.

> "I brushed my lips to Trista's ear and gently whispered, 'Do you want me?' She said yes and we started kissing. We kissed with forbidden passion and a nervous hotness that she had never known before. She told me my kisses were nicer than a man; soft, gentle, but unwilling to let go."

Erotica by Victoria Claire

http://www.accelnet.com/victoria/stories.html

Free site

Victoria Claire writes romantic erotica for women, and she does it beautifully. This site has only a few stories, but they are exceptionally well-written. (*Hint:* You know it's women's erotica if they have dinner first.)

"'Laura.' Someone whispered her name.

"She opened her eyes and saw David standing above her, smiling. He was looking at her face, her eyes, her long tan legs. She practically moaned as she said his name, 'David,' and she wondered how long he had been watching her, perhaps hidden in the shadows near the gate through which he had entered. He refilled her glass and raised it to his lips, licking the remains of chocolate from the rim before he drank. He kissed her gently, all wine and chocolate, as her body responded to the touch of his lips."

—*Wine and Chocolate*, Victoria Claire

Erotica from the Booksmith

http://www.booksmith.com/erotica.html

Commercial mail-order site

Want to buy a book that's all "good parts?" The Booksmith has a *huge* collection of erotic fiction that's certain to appeal to every sexual taste.

Erotica Readers Association

http://www.erotica-readers.com/

Free site

This is an excellent site. It not only offers some of the best erotica on the Net, it also provides book and movie reviews and information for and by writers of erotica. The discussion questions make interesting reading, attempting to answer the age-old question of "What do men and women really want?"

"Theories slipped out of his mind as she moved to lay above him, her hips locking with his. He looked up to see stars fighting each other to be her halo, moonlight begging to be her blanket. He reveled in the disorder and the chaos as his body merged completely with hers. And in the final moments of it all, when he felt his body take the leap into the unknown, he saw it all—quarks to galaxies, atoms to universes. He knew at that moment that everything he'd learned, everything he'd been teaching, was only a thin layer of dry dust hiding the rich, fertile earth beneath. She showed him the rules and the laws and then shattered them with a gentle shudder of her hips and the small cries of ecstasy. The stars seemed to fall like rain onto their bodies and he worshiped it. And her."

—*The Electron*, Adhara Rawcalyn

The Mining Company—Straight Women's Fiction

http://womenserotica.miningco.com/

The Mining Company has a fine collection of erotic stories, but it's not just a story site. It also has links, sexual information, chat, bulletin boards, and articles. It's not just for women either—anyone can easily find something to spark their interest.

> "'I've been watching you for weeks now, you sensed my presence, didn't you? It's time, you know. Are you ready for me?' He smiled, and I saw his fangs for the first time, and I knew he was there to take me as his own.
>
> "What else could I do but nod weakly? I was completely captivated. He moved in closer, allowing his large hands to gently roam over my body. My nipples hardened as he found my breasts and lightly grazed them. My hips thrust forward as he rounded them, then grabbed hold of me tightly. I did not struggle. 'Yes!' I cried. 'I am ready for you!'"
>
> —*Midnight on Bourbon Street*, Amber M.

Romance Fiction.com

http://romancefiction.com/

Free site

Romance Fiction offers free Web-published romance novels. New chapters are added to the book-in-progress every Monday and Thursday. If you are a fan of the genre, you will enjoy this site.

> "'You're mine, Alicia,' he breathed.
>
> Then he placed his lips over hers and kissed her like a man who needed her more than he needed life itself.
>
> Alicia felt her body go up in flames with the words and his kiss. She offered no resistance, opening her mouth to his, fueling his ardor even more. Both of them lost themselves in the taste of each other. It wasn't until Caton moved his lips away from hers to press a kiss to her temple that they both heard the applause from everyone gathered around them."
>
> —*Willoughby Place*, Anne Register-Wang

Don't Tell Madonna

"Agatha Christie has given more pleasure in bed than any other woman."

—Nancy Banks Smith

Sabrina's Erotica

http://www.sabrina.org/sabu.htm

Free site

Sabrina's erotica is just a wee bit off-center. She has a talent for creating unusual scenarios and adds a touch of humor to her stories. They say that sex is the most fun you can have without laughing. Here, you can at least giggle while you *read* about it.

> "'How may I please you?' his deep voice slowly whispered in my ear. 'Do you like tender (pause), or rough (pause), or playful (pause), or kinky (pause), or submissive (long pause), or dominating (pause), or restrained (kiss)?' I nodded. He smiled, 'Then let me take you to my bedroom.' (Chip and Dale: 'After you!' 'Oh NO! After YOU!' 'No no, I insist! After YOU!' 'Then we'll both go at the same time!' 'Absolutely!') He led me into the bedroom and removed my clothes, kissing my body as he uncovered me. (Why don't I EVER wear sexy underwear?) He pulled my hands up to his collar, and I unbuttoned his shirt. I found myself leaning into him, and kissing his neck. I pressed my breasts against his chest, and dragged his shirt off his arms. He pulled me into his body, and I felt the hardness in his jeans.
>
> I suddenly pulled back, surprised at my behavior, and looked into his eyes—his beautiful, warm, accepting eyes. He kissed me once more, probing gently with his tongue. I wanted nothing more than to have this man make love to me. (Bugs and Friends: 'Overture, turn the lights. This is it, we'll hit the heights. And oh, what heights we'll hit. On with the show, this is it!')"
>
> —*First Look*, Sabrina

The Ultimate Internet Romance Book Web Site

http://www.icgnet.com/romancebooks/

Free site

This site is devoted to romance novels and the millions of people who read them voraciously. It features cover pictures, hunky male models, gorgeous buxom women with shredded clothing, authors' biographies, reviews of more than 200 novels, and information for collectors. (*Rachel's aside*: Okay, I know a lot of people read them. And I tried; I really did. But then I came to the phrase: "Ashton vowed that he would ferret out the weasel who stole the jewels...." That was it. I just couldn't go on.)

Other Noteworthy Erotic Story Sites

Table 19.2 lists several other erotic story sites that may interest you.

Table 19.2   More Erotic Story Sites

Site Name	Web Address
Mary Anne's Home Page	**http://www.iam.com/maryanne/**
Notorious Noir—Black Erotic Poetry	**http://www.mindspring.com/ ~derob/noir/**
Orpheus Romance	**http://www.orpheusromance.com/**
Sexy Thinking	**http://www.sexythinking.com/**

Erotic Classics

Where classic erotic books are concerned, you may be able to save yourself a trip to the local bookstore. Some vintage titles are now in the public domain and freely available for downloading from the Internet. No one's erotic education should be considered complete without a solid grounding in the classics.

Fanny Hill, or Memoirs of a Woman of Pleasure, by John Cleland (1749)

http://eng.hss.cmu.edu/fiction/fanny-hill

Free site

Fanny Hill is *the* classic erotic book. If you can't find it in your neighborhood bookstore or library, you can read it here.

> "My breasts, if it is not too bold a figure to call so two hard, firm, rising hillocks, that just began to shew them-selves, or signify anything to the touch, employ'd and amus'd her hands a-while, till, slipping down lower, over a smooth track, she could just feel the soft silky down that had but a few months before put forth and garnish'd the mount-pleasant of those parts, and promised to spread a grateful shelter over the seat of the most exquisite sensation, and which had been, till that instant, the seat of the most insensible innocence. Her fingers play'd and strove to twine in the young tendrils of that moss, which nature has contrived at once for use and ornament."

Vatsayayana: The Kama Sutra

http://www.bibliomania.com/NonFiction/Vatsayayana/KamaSutra/

Kama Sutra means "Aphorisms on Love." It was written between the fifth and sixth century A.D. in Sanskrit, and has since been translated into many, many languages. It is considered the master work of Hindu erotic literature.

"When a man under some pretext or other goes in front or alongside of a woman and touches her body with his own, it is called the 'touching embrace'.

When a woman in a lonely place bends down, as if to pick up something, and pierces, as it were, a man sitting or standing, with her breasts, and the man in return takes hold of them, it is called a 'piercing embrace'.

The above two kinds of embrace take place only between persons who do not, as yet, speak freely with each other.

When two lovers are walking slowly together, either in the dark, or in a place of public resort, or in a lonely place, and rub their bodies against each other, it is called a 'rubbing embrace'.

When on the above occasion one of them presses the other's body forcibly against a wall or pillar, it is called a 'pressing embrace'.

These two last embraces are peculiar to those who know the intentions of each other."

Lady Chatterley's Lover, by D.H. Lawrence (1928)
http://www.bibliomania.com/Fiction/dhl/chat/

"She lay quite still, in a sort of sleep, in a sort of dream. Then she quivered as she felt his hand groping softly, yet with queer thwarted clumsiness, among her clothing. Yet the hand knew, too, how to unclothe her where it wanted. He drew down the thin silk sheath, slowly, carefully, right down and over her feet. Then with a quiver of exquisite pleasure he touched the warm soft body, and touched her navel for a moment in a kiss. And he had to come in to her at once, to enter the peace on earth of her soft, quiescent body. It was the moment of pure peace for him, the entry into the body of the woman.

"She lay still, in a kind of sleep, always in a kind of sleep. The activity, the orgasm was his, all his; she could strive for herself no more. Even the tightness of his arms round her, even the intense movement of his body, and the springing of his seed in her, was a kind of sleep, from which she did not begin to rouse till he had finished and lay softly panting against her breast.

"Then she wondered, just dimly wondered, why? Why was this necessary? Why had it lifted a great cloud from her and given her peace? Was it real? Was it real?"

Women in Love, by D.H. Lawrence (1920)
http://www.bibliomania.com/Fiction/dhl/Women/

"She closed her hands over the full, rounded body of his loins, as he stooped over her, she seemed to touch the quick of the mystery of darkness that was bodily him. She seemed to faint beneath, and he seemed to faint, stooping over her. It was a perfect passing away for both of them, and at the same time the most intolerable accession into being, the marvelous fullness of immediate gratification, overwhelming, out-flooding from the source of the deepest life-force, the darkest, deepest, strangest life-source of the human body, at the back and base of the loins."

Erotic Story Newsgroups

Unlike some sexual topics, erotic stories are alive and well in the newsgroups. Like the ones found on Web sites, the quality varies wildly and you may have to wade through a considerable amount of *spam* (advertisements for sex Web sites, in this case) before finding something that appeals to you. A few of the better story newsgroups include:

➤ **alt.sex.stories**

➤ **alt.sex.stories.moderated**

➤ **alt.sex.stories.tg** (the *tg* stands for transgender)

Sort of Judge Judy

A moderated newsgroup is one that is kept free from spam by a person or team of persons who have to approve of every post to the newsgroup. This is good because it keeps the newsgroup from being overrun by people promoting their Web sites (among other things). It can be a trial, however, because moderators vary by temperament and judgement.

Erotic Mailing Lists

Instead of wading through the Usenet, you might want to subscribe to a mailing list for erotica. Although this is in no way as anonymous as perusing the newsgroups, it may be a bit more convenient.

➤ **Aaron's Adult Story Collection http://www.totallyfreesex.com/ stories/**

➤ **Ken Blue Eyes http://www.geocities.com/SoHo/Coffeehouse/1813/**

> ## The Least You Need to Know
>
> ➤ The two main sources of erotic imagery on the Internet are professional pho-
>   tographers' pay sites and free, personal Web sites that feature scans of artists'
>   works.
>
> ➤ Although our searches didn't lead us to many complete erotic novels, we did
>   find plenty of short stories. They range from tales of romance to graphic sto-
>   ries of lurid—and frequently illegal—sex acts.

Chapter 20

Spice Up Your Love Life

> ## In This Chapter
>
> ➤ The Web contains many shopping malls where you can obtain sex toys and lotions from the privacy of your home
>
> ➤ Add a new element to your sex life by experimenting with accessories (sex toys, lotions, erotic foods, and aphrodisiacs)

Is your sex life in danger of becoming humdrum? You can liven it up by incorporating the products discussed in this chapter: sex toys, lotions and powders, and erotic foods and aphrodisiacs.

Web Sites for the Adventurous (or Frisky)

The Web is littered with sexual shopping malls. We think you will find the following standouts interesting. (You can also find many of the featured items for sale from some of the pay/subscription sex sites.)

Under Lock and Key

You should make sure to never send your credit card number or any personal information over the Web unless you are at a secure Web page when you send the information. You can tell that you are at a secure page if you see a locked padlock at the bottom of your browser.

We also advise against buying from any site that doesn't list a regular mail address and phone number.

If you feel adventurous, ask the operators of the site what they might recommend. Because good adult toy shops aren't readily available in every town, this could open whole new worlds for you. Don't be shy; ask the experts.

Good Vibrations

http://www.goodvibes.com

Good Vibrations is probably the best sex catalog in the world, on par with Blowfish (discussed later). It has an antique vibrator museum that is very interesting and informative. Good Vibes also sells some great books such as the *Good Vibrations Guide to Sex* and select porn videos, which are carefully screened for quality. But they don't just carry porn videos; they also have a wonderful instructional videos section, where they carry titles such as "Bend Over, Boyfriend," which describes how to teach hubby or boyfriend about anal play.

The Adult Toy Shop

http://adulttoy.com

The Adult Toy Shop is not a run-of-the-mill adult toy site. It is well-organized and imaginative, features quality merchandise, and is geared toward couples. They also have instructional videos designed to keep a couple's sex life new and exciting.

Aromatherapy for Lovers

http://homearts.com/depts/relat/aromatb2.htm

The Homearts Network has a few pages devoted to the sensual side of our sense of smell. Scent can be a powerful aphrodisiac, and this site tells which essential oils elicit which responses. They also offer instruction on sensual massage. Can't you just feel the tension melting away?

Astroglide Home Page

http://www.astroglide.com/

Very few sex products do exactly what they are supposed to do and do it well. Astroglide is one of them. It's a water-based, water-soluble lubricant. Sure, others come in flavors and colors, but *this* one is available at most discount stores and pharmacies—and it doesn't get sticky! Visit their home page for excellent information and suggestions on how to use Astroglide. Free samples are also available from the site.

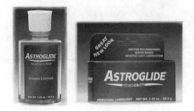

Blowfish

http://www.blowfish.com/

Blowfish is one of the best sex merchandise sites on the Internet. You can see that everything is top quality. In fact, some of the artificial phalluses could easily pass as *objets d'art*. Blowfish has a varied catalog, including vibrators, bondage and related toys, books, magazines, comics, condoms, dental dams, gloves, and much more. Their trademarked motto is "Great Products for Good Sex," and you can tell that they mean it.

Blowfish truly cares about their customers, and it shows in the product descriptions. In the description for their "Honey Mate" product, they even mention that it might set off the metal detector at the airport.

Body Jewelry by Judy

http://www.sexy-jewelry.com/

Have you ever considered getting some body jewelry, but weren't too keen on the idea of having to sit very, very still while someone poked metal objects through your flesh? We don't blame you if you're hesitant—or terrified. Body Jewelry by Judy sells clip-on jewelry that provides the same effect without the pain, holes, or risk of infection. Prices range from $15 to $40.

Let's be real plain here. This jewelry is for your genitals. Judy says, "You can decorate your body in ways you've never imagined with many choices of Clit Clips and Titti Twinklers; Bum Baubles for both sexes; and Frenulum Ticklers to decorate the men."

Kama Sutra

http://www.kamasutra.com/

In business for more than 25 years, Kama Sutra offers an excellent line of scented and flavored oils, lotions, and bath products. They are designed to enhance the pleasure of intimate touch by involving all the senses. The packaging is beautiful, the scents are wonderful, and the flavored oils and lotions add interesting possibilities to massages. (You're on your own for the sense of hearing. Quiet music or a soft moan or two would do nicely, we think.)

Nice-N-Naughty Toy Store

http://www.nice-n-naughty.com/

This is a huge site that sells every sex toy imaginable, as well as a few that you might not want to think about. Some of the vibrators are actually scary looking. Did the Scorpion Wearable Vibe have to *look* like a scorpion? Nevertheless, this is an excellent place to shop. It provides information about how, where, when, and why to use the toys for maximum effectiveness and safety. Nice-N-Naughty welcomes email questions about the merchandise they carry.

Adam & Eve

http://www.aeonline.com/

Adam & Eve is probably the largest and best supplier of adult videos. But that's not all they have: There's leather, latex, and at least 10 different "Throbbing Vibes." Their New Products section contains CD-ROMs, books, magazines, condoms, lotions, lingerie, toys, games, jewelry, and much more.

Their site is complete and well designed, with accessibility for older browsers as well as the latest technology. They even have a search feature; so if you know what you want, you can get right to it.

The Secret Garden

http://www.weballiance.net/wa/secretgarden/

The Secret Garden is a small site with a nice selection of soft bondage gear, vibrators, and lotions. What makes a visit to this site *really* worthwhile is their animated ad for the Fun Tongue. This sex toy looks like the Rolling Stones logo with a sock attached to it...a kind of perverse hand puppet of pleasure.

Advanced Sex

These sites may not be right for everyone, but they sure did catch our eye.

Sybian and Venus II

http://www.sybian.com/

The Sybian and Venus II are the ultimate in sexual aids for women and men. The Sybian was originally designed as a way to enable non-responsive women to experience orgasm. (It also turned out to be one heck of a lot of fun.) Next, the research team at Abco came up with a little something for the guys and named it the Venus II. This device even claims to enable impotent men to have an orgasm. (That's right—orgasm *without* an erection. This, I've got to see.) These are pricey items ($1,395 for the Sybian and $1,095 for the Venus II). You can also find letters and testimonials at the site.

Real Doll—The World's Finest Love Doll

http://www.realdoll.com/

Some things have to be seen to be believed. Start your visit by reading the Frequently Asked Questions document.

Bees Do It

"You are fully functional, aren't you?"

"Of course, but..."

"How fully?"

"In every way, of course. I am programmed in multiple techniques...a broad variety of pleasuring."

"Ohh...you jewel. That's exactly what I hoped."

—Yar and Data, in "The Naked Now," *Star Trek: The Next Generation*

No Respect, Just Dessert

"I'm at the age where food has taken the place of sex in my life. In fact, I've just had a mirror put over my kitchen table."

—Rodney Dangerfield

Erotic Food

The Web sites in Table 20.1 feature items that you can put in your mouth to enhance any sexual encounter. Visit them if you'd like to cook up an amorous surprise of your own.

Table 20.1   Erotic Food Web Sites

Site Name	Address
Aphrodisiac Cuisine	http://www.europeangastronomy.com/archive/EN/chap2/particul.html
Erotic Food	http://very-koi.net/food01.htm
Intercourses: An Aphrodisiac Cookbook	http://www.intercourses.com/
The Santesson Recipe Collection	http://www.santesson.com/recept/aphrlist.htm
Spencer & Fleetwood Rude Food	http://www.rudefood.com
Chocolate Fantasies	http://www.chocolatefantasies.com
The Erotic Chocolate Shoppe	http://eroticchocolates.com
Johan's Guide to Aphrodisiacs	http://www.santesson.com/aphrodis/

Sticky Foods for $200, Alex

"Oh, really? Well, what about that time I found you naked with that bowl of jello?"

—*Real Genius* (1985)

The Least You Need to Know

➤ If you're shopping for sex toys, foods, or other lovemaking accessories, you should check out the shopping malls on the World Wide Web. The companies are very discreet—shipping packages in plain boxes—and the quality of the items is probably much better than what you will find at the corner adult bookstore.

Chapter 21

Let's Play
Dress Up

In This Chapter

➤ Web sites where you can buy seductive clothing, lingerie, corsets, shoes, and accessories

➤ Newsgroups from which you can download lingerie pictures

Clothing and accessories can play an important part in sexual fantasies. Perhaps you can't make love to a real buccaneer or bar wench, but your lover may want to dress like one to please you. The only thing that may be sexier than bare skin is the bare skin you desperately wish you could see.

This chapter lists dozens of Web sites that feature erotic clothing, lingerie, shoes, boots, corsets, and fantasy wear. Most of these sites are mail-order businesses from which you can buy these fashions, although a few sites (and *all* of the newsgroups) contain lingerie and corsetry pictures.

Web Sites

The Web is unquestionably your best source of enticing lingerie—whether you're just looking, collecting pictures, or trying to buy something special. You can purchase lingerie from hundreds of online catalogs. You can also purchase corsets, shoes, and provocative clothing. The following sections describe some interesting sites that you can find on the Web.

Killing Polyester for Leisure Suits

"The origins of clothing are not practical. They are mystical and erotic. The primitive man in the wolf-pelt was not keeping dry; he was saying: 'Look what I killed. Aren't I the best?'"

—Katharine Hamnett

Slingback

You'll also find clothing sites—most notably, collections of shoe and slipper pictures—in the "Foot and Shoe Fetish" section of Chapter 14.

1st Fantasies: Themes, Fantasies, and Romance

http://www.firstfantasies.com/

Commercial site

Did you ever consider acting out your fantasies? Perhaps the thought of dressing as a sheik and harem girl appeals to you. Romantic role-playing is the theme of 1st Fantasies. This mail-order site offers costumes, accessories, props, and fantasy scripts—everything you need for a memorable evening with your lover. Best of all, the outfits and scripts are reasonably priced (patent leather outfits for less than $100 and teddies for $25, for example).

Popular themes include the French maid and the millionaire, sheik and the harem girl, bride and groom, cop and policewoman, female construction worker, racing flag girl, firefighter, and cheerleader. Most of the costumes are designed for women; men's outfits are often limited to decorative thongs. The pictures on the site are often dark and small, but you can still get an idea of what each item looks like.

Everybody's Talkin'

Joe Buck: "Uh...well, sir, I...ain't a f'real cowboy. But I am one helluva stud!"

—*Midnight Cowboy*, 1969

4 Your Eyes Only Lingerie, Etc.

http://www.brcdigital.com/lsfmap.htm

Commercial site

4 Your Eyes Only Lingerie, Etc. is a supersite with more than a dozen catalogs for you to peruse. From the main page, you can click links to catalogs that feature lingerie, lingerie "bouquets," men's and women's briefs and thongs, unisex robes, high heels, body stockings, and sensual day and evening wear (some of which would almost certainly get you arrested in many cities). Most items are inexpensive to moderately priced, so you can indulge yourself without worrying about how much money you've blown on something your girlfriend or spouse will refuse to wear. An online shopping cart records all items that you select and keeps a running total.

4Ever Lingerie

http://www.21stcenturyplaza.com/playstor

Commercial site

Ladies, how adventurous are you when it comes to sleepwear and playing-around wear? 4Ever Lingerie can inexpensively outfit you in tantalizing lingerie that will make the man in your life sit up and take notice (or even *beg*, depending on what you buy). Most items can be had for between $25 and $35 each, plus shipping. The catalog includes a photograph of each item. Many of the most popular selections are available in plus sizes.

You can place your order over the phone or from a secure online order form. When you are ready to add an item to your current order, you click pop-up menus to specify a quantity and color, and then click an **Order Now** button. 4Ever Lingerie's shopping system automatically keeps a running total of all items selected.

@ Corset Home

http://www.danbbs.dk/~dinsen/corsethome/

Free site

This Danish Web site is dedicated to corset fanciers. It includes an extensive dictionary of corset terms, a list of corset manufacturers from around the world, a small collection of recent and historical corset pictures, and an 1880s diary of a young lady undergoing corset training.

Jan. 24, 1884

"After a harsh scolding from the Headmistress, I was ushered into her anteroom where my hands were lashed to a trapeze and I was drawn up such that I could not feel any weight on my feet…after being harshly laced into my correction corsets then left suspended for a while and for three additional adjustments until my waist was reduced to 14 inches. These corsets are most terrible painfully biting into my chest and armpits even when attempting to take a full breath. I was greatly relieved when released into my sleeping stays."

Axford's Corsets Home Page and Online Catalog

http://www.axfords.com

Commercial site

This beautiful, well-designed, English mail-order site has a little something for anyone interested in learning about or buying corsets. The information portion of the site discusses the history of corsets, how they affect sex, and how to put on and wear a corset. Although the online catalog contains about a dozen items (corsets, knickers, bloomers, camisoles, half-slips, maid's uniforms, stockings and suspenders, and wigs) in thumbnail and detailed views, the merchandise appears to be of exceptionally high quality. To make it simple for foreigners to order from Axford's, a currency conversion calculator can calculate the cost of purchases.

If you have ever wondered what it might feel like to try on a corset, here's a brief description from the Web site:

> "Being laced into a corset can be an exquisitely sensual experience; the laces slide across your back as they are pulled gradually in from the top and bottom towards the middle, and the sensation is of being embraced tighter and tighter. You don't have to pull in to a Scarlet O'Hara 18 inches—you may be content with the corset just hugging you or you can lace down to an iron grip."

Baccara Erotics

http://www.baccara.com/cgi-bin/cgi/html_web_store.cgi

Commercial site

Ordering Merchandise over the Internet

Giving your credit card number out over the Internet has its perils. You may feel safer just calling the company's 800 number to place your order (if one is posted on the company's Web page). Check the following sites for some additional helpful information:

The National Fraud Information Center (**http://www.fraud.org**) provides information and news about common online rip-offs.

Scambusters (**http://www.scambusters.com**) offers tips about keeping your credit card numbers safe.

Baccara Erotics is a Dutch sex superstore with online catalogs for lingerie, sex toys, and videos. The catalogs include sections for lingerie, undergarments, latex, and leather goods (including many BD/SM items). Clothing ranges from sexy to raunchy. (Of course, one person's "raunchy" is another's turn-on.) You can view items in thumbnail and expanded views; descriptions, however, are limited to item names and prices.

All prices are listed in Dutch guilders (FL), but the index page does have a calculator to convert currency. Although this is a Dutch site, you can also place orders through an office in Texas—confirming our long-held suspicions of a Netherlands/Texas conspiracy to gain worldwide control of the leather panty market.

Daphne: Ladies' Designer Clothes in Larger Sizes

http://www.daphne1.com

Commercial site

Lingerie isn't only for the slim and petite.
Daphne: Larger Sizes and Daphne: Lingerie For
Larger Sizes are two New York City boutiques
that sell made-to-order clothing for women
in sizes 14–32 (1x–5x). Many of the garments
in the two online catalogs are expensive
($100–$300), but they are positively gorgeous.
Items can be viewed as thumbnails or at full
size.

Jack Holden: "Wo-ow, Angela. You
look different. What happened?"

Angelyne: "I'm dressed."

—*3 Men and a Baby*, 1987

Dark Garden Unique Corsetry

http://www.darkgarden.net/

Commercial site

If you're looking for a custom-made corset, you would do well to consider one from
Dark Garden. After you are through reviewing the general information about the
store, go to **http://www.darkgarden.net/cvs.htm** to see its products. (It can be
difficult to find the link to this page because it is buried in the text rather than provided as a button you can click.)

Corset prices range from $300–$375. Corset dresses (available only with fittings done
in their San Francisco store) range from $800–$1,400, depending on style and fabric.
Items can be ordered online by carefully filling in a detailed measurements form. The
Dark Garden site also provides helpful care instructions for fabric, leather, and patent
leather corsets.

Divaweb Fashions

http://www.divaweb.com/

Commercial site

For the finest in fetishwear, check out Divaweb Fashions. They carry an extensive line of corsets, leather and latex clothing, shoes, and jewelry for both women and men. (Although few of these products appear to be manufactured by Divaweb, you can purchase them all *from* Divaweb. Their online catalog references several sites covered elsewhere in this chapter, such as Dark Garden and Axford's.) You can view items as thumbnails or at full size. Ordering can be done through a secure order form.

Tie Me Up, Scotty!

If you're into *BD/SM* (bondage and discipline/sadomasochism), be sure to take a peek at Divaweb's companion shopping site, Diva After Dark (**http://www. divaweb.com/diva_dark.html**) for the latest in bondage gear.

The Elizabethan Corset Page

http://www.dnaco.net/~aleed/corsets/

Free site

If you're handy with a sewing machine or needle-and-thread, this site may interest you. The Elizabethan Corset Page explains how to make your own corset. In addition to providing patterns, the site includes sewing instructions, wearing information, and links to corsetry supply houses from which you can purchase the necessary materials. You can also read an informative history of the Elizabethan corset, as well as view a selection of corset pictures from the period.

Frederick's of Hollywood

http://www.fredericks.com/

Commercial site

How could anyone discuss lingerie without mentioning Frederick's of Hollywood? We certainly could not. Strolling through the online museum is a blast! By clicking actor and actress names, you can see the Frederick's of Hollywood items that they have purchased or worn in TV shows and movies. (Yes, *actors*! There's a lovely picture of Tony Curtis' strapless bra.) Visit the Models page to learn more about your favorite Frederick's models. You can also request a catalog or find the location of a store near you.

Shopping areas are scattered throughout the Web site. You can click any of the following buttons on the home page to view and purchase merchandise: Shop Online, Store Value Items, and Catalog Covers. You can order by phone or from this secure Web site.

Jack and Jill

http://www.jackjill.com/

Commercial site

Hey Blondie! Drop Your Laundry

"From the cradle to the coffin, underwear comes first."

—Bertolt Brecht

Slinky sleepwear and lacy lingerie are in plentiful supply at Jack and Jill. This huge catalog site is divided into two sections:

➤ **Lingerie Dreams** Bustiers, teddies, baby dolls, camisoles, chemise and sleepshirts, robes, gowns, sexy fashions, clothing, bras, panties, stockings, and garters

➤ **Leather Dreams** Bras, bustiers, cinchers and corsets, hot fashions, teddies, harnesses, restraints, panties and garters, and accessories

Items are priced in the moderate-to-high range and can be viewed as thumbnails or full-size pictures. The clothing is classy, erotic, and sexy—*without* being crude.

If you're in the mood for a special session with your lover, you might want to consider buying a Jack and Jill gift basket of sensual oils, creams, and accessories (vibrators and massage mitts). You can place your order by phone, fax, mail, or use an online form.

Miko Erotic Boutique

http://www.miko45.com/

Commercial site

Curious about how the other half—or whatever percentage they are—live? Miko's catalog offers a little of everything for the well-dressed fetish or BD/SM disciple. In addition to an assortment of lycra and latex fashions, fetish shoes, and gloves, Miko offers some more sinister items such as straight jackets, hoods, blindfolds, wrist/ankle cuffs, whips, and gags. Ordering from the site may be a bit difficult, however, because many of the pictures are dark or only shown as thumbnails. Still, for those curious about BD/SM, Miko's online catalog is a great place to learn the ropes (so to speak).

Odress.com

http://www.odress.com/

Commercial site

Odress.com is a manufacturer of made-to-order dresses inspired by *The Story of O*, a classic erotic BD/SM novel. Prices are in the $200–$400 range. Although each dress is custom made, they all have the following elements in common: "...they leave the breasts exposed and the rear & loins accessible as was the case in the dresses that the women of Roissy wore. Beyond that, there is considerable variation in the designs that may be specified. Most dresses are of two parts: a fitted bodice that closes in the back and is so cut as to leave the breasts exposed, and a skirt that is split waist to hem both in front and in back." A picture page provides examples of some current Odress designs.

Panty-of-the-Month

http://www.panties.com/

Commercial site

When you can't be with her, remind her that you're thinking of her. At Panty-of-the-Month, you can purchase a 3- to 12-month subscription ($90–$300) or a one-time gift set of bra, panty, foods, and other items for the woman in your life. Even though we're talking underwear here, the gift sets have class. In addition to lingerie, they may include items such as chocolate roses, premiere coffees and teas, perfumes, and creams. Orders can be placed via fax, phone, or by filling out a form on their Web site.

The Shoe Palace

http://www.shoepalace.com/

Commercial site

If you're in the market for footwear that will look fabulous while making your toes scream for mercy, visit The Shoe Palace. They have a wide assortment of women's shoes, sandals, boots, and slippers. If you can use some extra height and have a good sense of balance, many of the styles come as platforms or six-inch spiked heels.

To order an item, all you have to do is choose the desired color and size from drop-down menus and click the **Add to Shopping Cart** button. (Note that many styles come only in full sizes.) Because this is a secure Web site, you can safely use it to place your order over the Internet.

SlickChicks Lingerie Boutique

http://www.go-shop.com/lingerie/

Commercial site

SlickChicks is a reseller of the Coquette line of ladies' erotic lingerie and intimate wear. You can flip through their catalog page-by-page or see all items at once as clickable thumbnails that take you directly to the desired page. Items are inexpensive to moderately priced. SlickChicks accepts most major credit cards and is equipped to take orders over the Web.

Stage Clothes, USA

http://www.stageclothes.com/

Commercial site

Whether you're looking for lingerie, shoes, boots, dresses, or bondage wear, you're certain to find something of interest at Stage Clothes, USA. Their online catalog features more than 1,000 items for women and men (in regular and plus sizes). In particular, be sure to take a look at their extensive selection of leather sexwear.

Starkers!

http://www.starkers.com/

Commercial site

> **Bare Essentials**
>
> James Bond: "That's a nice little nothing you're almost wearing."
>
> —*Diamonds are Forever*, 1971

Starkers! specializes in made-to-order corsets and clothing from days gone by. Corset prices range from $275–$400, depending on style and fabric chosen. Most of the clothing is black and elegant—suitable for a night on the town or a fetish ball. Although items can be ordered directly from the Web site, payment must be made by certified check or money order (in Canadian funds).

Veronica's High Heel Palace

http://www.veronicas.com/

Commercial site

Veronica's High Heel Palace sells hand-crafted, 10cm (4.5-inch) high heels in two dozen styles. Prices tend to be high, and the materials are predominantly leather. You can order directly from this secure site. (Note that all prices are given in Swiss francs. See the currency conversion instructions on the site to determine the cost in your own currency.)

Versatile Fashions

http://www.versatile-fashions.com

Commercial site

These online catalogs include moderate-to-high–priced dresses, skirts, corsets, gloves, lingerie, uniforms, and bondage accessories. Many of the garments are made of high-gloss PVC. (Frankly, I'm not sure where one would wear the items found at Versatile Fashions, but they do appeal to me. Rachel says this is not surprising, as I am easily distracted by shiny objects.)

Vintage Elegance

http://www.vintage-elegance.com/

Commercial site

Vintage Elegance is an Alameda, California shop specializing in corsets and lingerie. A basic corset costs from $185–$270. Because corsets must be custom fitted for each person, you are encouraged to come to the shop for a fitting or have them send a mock-up corset to your house.

At present, the catalog is small and obviously a "work in progress," but it shows promise. A beautiful lace Victorian petticoat (one of the few lingerie items currently listed) sells for $189.

Wicked Temptations

http://www.wickedtemptations.com/

Commercial site

Wicked Temptations carries an assortment of sexy women's clothing, ranging from lingerie to dresses and shorts to swimwear. Although most of the fashions aren't appropriate for daily wear, they would be right at home in clubs—well, *some* clubs.

Most items are moderately priced. Dresses typically run about $60, for example; teddies run between $20 and $35. There's even a selection of fashions for men, including several styles of underwear and fetish clothing. You can place orders online, or by fax, phone, email, or mail.

More Sexy Night-Nights

For a list of additional lingerie sites, visit **http://www.yahoo.com/ Business_and_Economy/ Companies/Apparel/Lingerie/**.

Lingerie Picture Newsgroups

As mentioned elsewhere in this book, most picture newsgroups are now filled with *spam* (ads for Web sites) rather than the sexy pictures you might hope to find. Nevertheless, the following lingerie newsgroups may be worth exploring:

➤ **alt.binaries.lingerie**

➤ **alt.binaries.pictures.lingerie**

➤ **alt.binaries.pictures.erotica.panties**

➤ **alt.sex.fetish.panties**

The Least You Need to Know

➤ You can order clothing directly from many Web sites by making choices from drop-down menus, clicking buttons, and filling out online forms. If the site does not support *secure* ordering, you may prefer to order by phone or fax. Always use a credit card instead of sending a check or money order through the mail, because you can dispute the charge if you have problems.

➤ Most Web sites that focus on lingerie are commercial mail-order businesses. If you're just interested in viewing photos of women wearing lingerie rather than buying some, check out the newsgroups and general picture sites (see Chapter 9, for example).

➤ Treat any online store as you would a local business. Be sure to carefully read their terms, such as the return policy, shipping methods available, and additional charges. Save the surprises for the bedroom.

Chapter 22

Up Close and Personal

In This Chapter

➤ Online matchmaking services

➤ Erotic getaways

➤ Polyamory and swinging

➤ Exotic dancers and clubs

➤ Prostitution in Nevada and beyond

Sometimes Internet sex is the goal; sometimes it isn't. If your interests are more in skin-to-skin contact than in cybersex, this chapter will lead you to a variety of useful resources on the Net, including information about erotic getaway spots, swinging and polyamory, personal ads, exotic dancers, and legal prostitution.

Personal Ads

Is there one among us who has never glanced at the personal ads in a metro newspaper, wondering what kind of person would place an ad or respond to one? Well, judging by our exhaustive searches of the Web, we discovered that the answer is...*a lot of people*! The Web contains hundreds of personals sites that make it easy to meet new people—as new friends, for love, and for sex (or for a combination of all three). Here are some of the best. (See Table 22.1 at the end of this section for some other sites worth checking out.)

Adult Friend Finder

http://adult.friendfinder.com/

Membership/Commercial site

When looking for an adult "friend," you can decide up front how far you are willing to take this relationship.

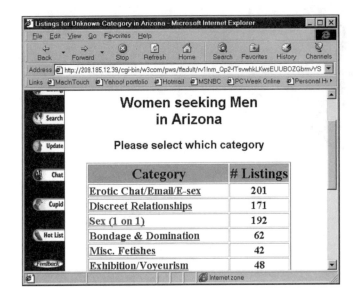

Not just your run-of-the-mill classifieds, the personals at Adult Friend Finder are categorized to show which types of sexual activities each person is seeking.

Basic services are free and include adding your profile to the system, examining up to three user profiles per day and responding to one, receiving reports on individuals who match your desired attributes, and entering the main chat room. For a silver or gold membership, you can do more advanced searches, look at and respond to unlimited profiles, and enter additional chat rooms (using a Java-based chat client rather than the clumsy HTML form reserved for non-members).

ALTernate Lifestyles Internet MatchMaker

http://www.swinger.com/

Membership site

If you're into swinging, are bisexual, or are just "bi-curious," this site may be able to help you find a match. They currently offer a trial membership with access to all features except online chat. Because they take matching people with similar interests so seriously, to gain admission you must answer a detailed questionnaire. Potential matches are ranked by percentage of matching answers.

Classifieds2000

http://www.classifieds2000.com/

Free site

The personals section in Classifieds2000 has a number of things going for it. First, it's extremely simple to use; just click a few radio buttons, pull down some menus, and you're ready to conduct a full-scale search of all matching ads in your state or region. Second, ads clearly list the city where each person lives, so you have a shot at finding a local match. Few of the ads have photos, however.

Know What You're Buying

Many other personals and classifieds sites use the Classifieds2000 database, including Lycos and Excite. If you decide to purchase memberships at more than one personals site, be sure that they don't use the Classifieds2000 database. Otherwise, you're paying twice to see the same information.

Contact Advertising

http://cadv.com/

Commercial/Membership site

If you're into an alternative lifestyle (swinger, gay, transvestite/transsexual, bisexual, or fetish fanatic), Contact Advertising can help you find like-minded people. Through their print magazine, their BBS, and this Web site, you can view personal/swinging ads from all over the United States.

Cupid's Network

http://www.cupidnet.com/

Free site

As a service to love-seekers everywhere, Cupid's Network provides links to dozens of personals sites.

The Extreme ICQ list

http://home1.gte.net/cwbarton/irq.html

Free site

If you're an ICQ user (see Chapter 25) and interested in making some new friends—or perhaps becoming more than just friends—take a peek at this short list of "extreme" ICQ users.

Jailbabes.com

http://www.jailbabes.com/

Free site

From the opening saxophone wail of *Jailhouse Rock*, you just know you're in an entirely different kind of matchmaking site. The purpose of Jailbabes.com is to pair up lonely female inmates with men or women on the outside. Yes, "Release Date" is one of the items listed in every profile.

Jewish Quality Singles

http://www.jqs.com

Membership site

Although you are free to look at as many ads as you like at Jewish Quality Singles, if you want to reply to an ad or post one of your own, you must become a member. Most of the ads contain photos, so you aren't flying blind. One downside: The Search function only allows you to search by age and country, making it difficult to quickly find nearby potential matches.

Finding Someone Local

Although most personal ads list the town or city in which each person lives, you may not have the option to specify a city when conducting a search. Because many of the Search or Browse facilities include a *keyword* option, however, try entering a town or city name there.

Love@AOL Photo Personals

America Online (AOL)

Free for AOL members

Click the tabs at the top of each personal ad to see more information about the person.

If you're an America Online member and like the idea of browsing through tons of singles ads (many with pictures), give Love@AOL Photo Personals a try. You can browse by state or within major metropolitan cities and restrict the profiles listed to particular age groups. And best of all, the price of using all options in Photo Personals is included with your AOL membership. (This may be the single best reason to be an AOL subscriber!)

If you're interested in more traditional personal ads, type the keyword **Classifieds** and click the **Personals** button. You can find additional ads at keywords **Romance** and **DC Personals**.

The Love Garden

http://www.lovegarden.com

Membership site

This is one of our favorite personals sites. Because it requires that all members submit at least one photo, you're never left guessing about a potential match's appearance. At this writing, the site is new and membership is free.

Personals - InfoSpace.com

http://in-115.infospace.com/_1_59061875__info/ newclass/pers_gbl.html

Membership site

Although InfoSpace is actually using the personals database from a service called One & Only (**http://www.one-and-only.com/**), it does a superior job of enabling you to search the database and presenting the results. Placing and viewing ads is free; responding to them requires a site membership to One & Only.

241

Bob and Elizabeth Sound Nice

"Roger Stone, with his wife, placed ads in swinger magazines. That's how square Republicans are. Even when they have a sex scandal, it's with their wives."

—Bill Maher, *Politically Incorrect*

SinCity Personals

http://www.sin-city.net/PersonalAds/

Membership site

If you're into swinging, you'll want to take a peek at the personal ads in the SinCity site. Viewing and placing ads is free; however, only members can respond to ads.

Singles Online

http://www.singlesonline.com/

Membership site

There don't seem to be a lot of members at the moment, but Singles Online is exceptionally easy to use. You can either restrict your browsing to members with photos from a particular state or all members from a state. In addition to guest privileges, members can reply to ads and use additional browsing features.

Swoon: Dating, Mating, Relating

http://www.swoon.com/

Commercial site

How about that? Although Swoon has a commercial side to it (they sell books), the personal ads are free! You can post one, read others' ads, and respond to as many as you like. Browsing is based on area code, so you can be assured of seeing people in your immediate and surrounding area. And there's free chat.

Yahoo! Classifieds

http://personals.classifieds.yahoo.com

Free site

Like many of the other major search engines, Yahoo! has its own classified ads section. As we've come to expect from Yahoo!, the personals section is very simple to use. Searches can be restricted to a specific city or state, as well as to the type of relationship you're seeking (long-term, short-term, pen pal, alternative, or activities partner). You can also perform advanced searches, specifying an age range, ethnicity, religion, and so on. Even if you don't immediately find your soulmate at Yahoo!, it's such a pleasure to use their search engine that you'll find yourself returning to it frequently.

Table 22.1   Other Personal Ad Sites on the Web

Site Name	Address
Adult Personals	**http://www.adultpersonals.com**
Big Date	**http://www.big-date.com**
Dateable.com	**http://dateable.com**
Fantasy Match	**http://fantasymatch.com**
Kinky Contacts	**http://www.kinkycontacts.com**
Kinky Personals	**http://kinky-personals.com/**
Match.com	**http://www.match.com/**

Erotic Getaways

Whether you hope to revive your current relationship or are interested in seeing where a new one will lead, taking off for an exotic vacation or a weekend getaway may be just what the doctor ordered. Here are some super spots that we found on the Web.

Best Beaches in the USA

http://www.petrix.com/beaches

Free site

Something about a day at the beach brings out the romantic side in the most jaded soul. This site lists the best ocean beaches in the United States, based on 50 criteria, such as sand quality, water purity and temperature, wave size, view, and average air temperature. Several pictures of each of the top beaches enable you to check out the surroundings before choosing the perfect place to get away from it all. You will also find five beaches listed as being *especially* romantic.

Gay and Lesbian Active Vacations

http://www.alysonadventures.com/

Commercial site

Alyson Adventures, Inc. is a gay-owned company offering activity-centered vacations.

> "Bike in France, hike in the Alps, climb the Grand Teton, or scuba dive in the Caribbean. Or try a multi-activity vacation, where you'll do something different every day: kayaking, rappelling, mountain biking, diving, hiking, whitewater rafting, and hot-air ballooning, for example."

Sounds like fun.

Hedonism II

http://www.super-clubs.com/SuperClubs/Hedonism.html

Commercial site

Where Do I Put My Name Tag?

"Hey, lemmee ask you a question. In these nudist colonies, do they eat naked in the dining room?"

"I would imagine it's all naked."

"What about the chambermaids? Are they naked, too?"

"They're naked. The gardener's naked. Bellhops. It's one big Nude-O-Rama."

—Jerry and George, *The Seinfeld Show*

Located in Negril, Jamaica, Hedonism II is an adult resort for singles and couples. This place has everything: 22 tropical acres to explore, unlimited food and drinks, two beautiful beaches (one for swimsuit wearers and one nude), water skiing, scuba diving, an aviary, reggae music, dancing, parties, circus training workshops, freshwater pools, quiet moonlit walks, and much, much more. The rooms look very nice. Some come with two twin beds for "friends" who are just traveling together; others include king-size beds and strategically placed mirrors.

Vacations at Hedonism II are "all-inclusive"—that is, meals and activities are included in the price and no tipping is expected. There's more good news, too. The rooms have neither phones nor televisions, so you won't be bothered by the real world.

If you're thinking of traveling alone, you should be aware that you'll be assigned a roommate of the same sex, unless you pay a bit extra for a guaranteed single occupancy. Note, too, that this *is* an adults-only resort, so no one under the age of 18 is allowed.

The Mile High Club

http://www.milehighclub.com/

Commercial site

Oh, admit it. You *know* you've thought about it. The membership requirements are easy enough. All you need is a willing accomplice, an airplane that's at least 5,280 feet above the ground, a vacant restroom, and some discretion.

At this site, you can read about members' experiences, learn what works best, and order Mile High Club hats and T-shirts after your mission is accomplished. (It will also help you learn how to charter a personal flight, if you're not comfortable with becoming a member on a commercial airliner flight.) Happy flying!

Sandals Resorts

http://www.sandals.com/

Commercial site

Sandals Resorts has 10 locations scattered around the Bahamas, Antigua, St. Lucia, and Jamaica. The all-inclusive resorts are for couples only, so you can be assured of romantic settings, replete with private little nooks for you and your significant other. The beaches, accommodations, and activities all appear to be first-rate.

Welcome to the Labyrinth

http://www.inforamp.net/~diva/home.html

Commercial site

Let's say you find yourself in Toronto and are wondering just where to go for some proper bondage and discipline. (Well, it *could* happen.) Just pick up the phone or send an email to the lovely, leather-clad, professional dominants at The Labyrinth, a fully equipped dungeon with an emphasis on safe, sane, consensual BD/SM. Sexual contact is *not* a part of their services.

Polyamory and Swinging

Polyamory is loving more than one person; *swinging* is having sex with someone outside your main relationship with your lover's permission (and in most cases participation). The following Web sites tell you more about both of these lifestyles, which often overlap.

Alt.polyamory

http://www.polyamory.org/

Free site

Sometimes polyamory is defined as an established couple that has sex with others with the approval of their partners. Sometimes it means an emotional attachment to more than one person *without* sexual involvement. Sometimes it signifies a *menage a trois*, a *menage a quatre*, or even a *menage a cinq*. (We could go on—and imagine the polyamorists could, too—but that's as high as we can count in French.)

These are interesting people, and there's a lot of them out there. This home site for the **alt.polyamory** newsgroup contains a FAQ page, a polyamory purity test, a polyamory index, poly personals, events, essays, poly home pages, newsgroup listings, and a polyamory art page.

Loving More

http://www.lovemore.com/

Commercial site

Loving More is a quarterly publication for polyamorists. Here, polyamory is defined as "…all forms of multi-partner relating which are ethical and consensual. You'll find responsible non-monogamous people involved in extended family, open marriage, polyfidelity, intentional singles, communities, intimate networks, tribes and other new paradigm relationship forms." In addition to articles, the site has a list of links, email discussion groups, a message board, and a chat room. You can also purchase books and tapes.

Playcouples

http://playcouples.com/

Commercial/Membership site

Playcouples is a combination chat room, links page, information site, and travel agency for couples who are swingers. In this case, *swinging* means casual sex. (We wish that the swingers and polyamorists would get together and make up a check list so that it would be easier to sort this all out.) Most of the site is devoted to erotic travel for couples. These folks *do* get around.

Exotic Dancers

The Web is the ideal showcase for exotic dancers and strip clubs. See Table 22.2 for the location, prices, and features offered at clubs near you.

Table 22.2 Exotic Dancer and Strip Club Directories

Site Name	Address
Adult Club & Entertainment Directory	**http://www.acedirectory.com**
Exotic Dancer Directory	**http://www.exotic-dancer.com**
Euroamerica	**http://www.euroamericanet.com**
Exotic Nites	**http://www.exoticnites.com**
Ultimate Strip Club List	**http://www.tuscl.com**

Prostitution

Prostitution is illegal in most of the world, although some people believe it shouldn't be. A few counties in Nevada have legalized the practice and, as a result, many Web pages chronicle and critique bordellos in those counties.

Bordello Diaries

http://www.wondersmith.com/bordel

Free site

Blake Wilfong is a devoted bordello customer with a fascinating Web site that details the history of legal prostitution in Nevada, as well as the current facts about the world's oldest profession. You can learn where the best Nevada bordellos are located, how to get to them, what is available when you get there, what it will cost, and who you will find working there. This is an excellent site and a great read.

COYOTE

http://www.freedomusa.org/coyotela/

Commercial site

COYOTE (Call Off Your Old Tired Ethics) is an organization founded to support hookers and fight for the legalization of prostitution, which they believe would create better working conditions. This Los Angeles-based site includes information about the organization, arguments for legalization, some of the group's "favorite hooker jokes," poetry, book reviews, and a history (or "herstory") of prostitution. Another organization for prostitutes and sex workers is the International Sex Worker Foundation for Art, Culture, and Education at **http://www.freedomusa.org/iswface**.

The Golden Years

"When the grandmothers of today hear the word *Chippendales*, they don't necessarily think of chairs."

—Joan Kerr

Sock Shopping Versus Sex

"Sex without love is an empty experience, but, as empty experiences go, it's one of the best."

—Woody Allen

Prostitutes with Home Pages

If you're curious about what a Nevada prostitute's home page might look like, try Sweet Promises (**http://members.tripod.com/ ~sweetpromise/**).

"COYOTE was founded in 1973 to work for the repeal of the prostitution laws and an end to the stigma associated with sexual work. In addition to engaging in public education regarding a wide range of issues related to prostitution, COYOTE has provided crisis counseling, support groups, and referrals to legal and other service providers to thousands of prostitutes, mostly women."

Georgia Power's Bordello Connection

http://www.gppays.com

Free site

A few men who appear to be spending the majority of their days in Nevada brothels "checking out the goods" maintain this remarkable site. The site lists the schedules of many women and provides detailed field reports of their encounters with them. The reports make fascinating reading.

Nevada Legal Prostitution FAQ

http://www.sexuality.org/l/workers/nevada.html

Free site

Many of us have never been with a prostitute or visited a brothel. This well-written *FAQ* (Frequently Asked Questions) from the Society for Human Sexuality explains how the process works in Nevada's legal brothels.

The World Sex Guide

http://www.worldsexguide.com

Free site

Whether you're interested in learning about the availability and legality of prostitution in the United States or elsewhere in the world, check out this site. Much of the information was obtained from postings to the **alt.sex.prostitution** newsgroup.

Escorts Are Available

If you're looking for an escort service in a major city, visit **http://dir.yahoo.com/ Business_and_Economy/Companies/Sex/Adult_Services/Escorts/**, **http://escortsoncall.allthetime.com**, or Sultan's Harem at **http://www. sultans-harem.com**.

The Least You Need to Know

➤ One way to meet people with similar romantic or sexual interests is by placing and responding to personal ads on the Web. Although placing your own ad and browsing the ads of others are usually free, you may be expected to pay for the privilege of responding to ads.

➤ America Online members have access to a great free area for personals called Love@AOL.

➤ If you're yearning for a sensual getaway, the Web can help.

➤ Many sites include information and guides for people interested in exploring "the lifestyle" that some people call *polyamory* and others know as *swinging*.

➤ Clubs that feature exotic dancers are discovering that the Web is an excellent place to advertise. Numerous directories can help you locate and preview clubs near where you live.

➤ A variety of sites and FAQs online explore legal prostitution in Nevada, escort services around North America, and the history and practice of prostitution around the world.

Chapter 23

Information, Please!

In This Chapter

➤ Learning about safe sex practices and sexually transmitted diseases (STDs)

➤ Choosing, using, and buying condoms on the Net

➤ All about oral sex, masturbation, and the G-spot

➤ The art of kissing

➤ General sexual information and techniques

You probably won't be surprised to learn that sex on the Internet isn't limited to looking at pictures of naked people. You can also find a wealth of sexual information online. Read this chapter to learn about safe sex, choosing and using condoms, oral sex, masturbation, the G-spot, kissing, and sexual techniques. It's not only informative...it's fun, too!

Safe Sex Information

Sex with a new partner carries risks that go far beyond wondering whether we will have anything to say to each other the next morning. Fortunately, safe sex information is readily available on the Web. Many of the following sites should be considered required reading. (See Table 23.1 at the end of this section for some additional safe sex sites you can visit.)

Enjoying Safer Sex

http://wso.williams.edu/peerh/sex/

Free site

Williams College in Williamstown, Massachusetts, maintains this site filled with straightforward, easy-to-understand information regarding safer sex and sexuality. It includes birth control methods and their expected success rates, techniques for ensuring the safest sex possible, and diagrams detailing how to use various contraceptives.

Men's Health and Sexual Health

http://www.menshealth.com/

http://www.sexhealth.com

Commercial/Membership sites

Not just sterile text, Men's Health is designed as an illustrated electronic magazine.

These two magazines cover topics relating to health, nutrition, exercise, sex, and relationships. Both entertaining and informative, they deserve a space in your Favorites or Bookmarks.

Safersex.org, an Online Journal of Safe Sexuality

http://www.safersex.org/

Free site

Along with safe sex information, this site offers something more: video clips demonstrating the proper way to put on a condom, cartoons, sex myth debunking, and a visit to a condom factory. Be sure to read the section about safer oral sex. We were very impressed with this site. The Safer Sex Institute should be applauded for its work.

Table 23.1   Additional Safe Sex Sites

Site Name	Address
American Social Health Organization	**http://www.ashastd.org**
The Body	**http://www.thebody.com**
Cafe Herpe	**http://www.cafeherpe.com**
Take Care—Your Guide to Safer Sex	**http://www.takecare.co.uk/**

Condom Sites

Yes, condoms have moved from the corner drugstore to the Web. If you're too embarrassed to buy them from the cute checkout girl, you can order them from many of the sites listed in Table 23.2 at the end of this section. These sites are worth visiting even if you don't intend to place an order. You may learn that your favorite manufacturer has other condom styles that you would like to try, for example.

Splish, Splash

Hal Jackson: "Funny thing, sperm...."

—*Made in America* (1993)

Banana Bob's Jungle Hideaway

http://bananabob.com/

Commercial site

Banana Bob's sells condoms in tropical colors: Banana Yellow, Jungle Green, Red Passion, Sky Blue, and Midnight Black. "If you're going to monkey around, wear a banana!"

The Guide to Love and Sex: Trojan Condoms

http://www.loveandsex.com

Commercial site

Everyone knows about Trojan condoms. They have been making circular imprints in wallets for a long, long time. But did you know that there are 24 different varieties? This site has a chart showing you all the types, sizes, and sensitivities available. You can also play games, send a postcard, and order a free condom from the site.

Choose options from this handy selector to determine the correct style of Trojans to buy.

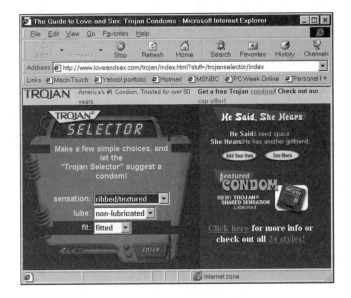

Table 23.2   Additional Condom Sites

Site Name	Address
Condom Country	**http://www.condom.com/**
Condom Sense	**http://www.csense.com/**
Condomania	**http://www.condomania.com/**
Condom Rose	**http://www.condomrose.com**
Condoms Express	**http://www.condomexpress.com/**
Durex World	**http://www.durex.com/**
Lifestyles Condoms	**http://www.lifestyles.com/**
Official Condom Directory	**http://users.deltanet.com/~agkid**

Oral Sex

Whether you're interested in learning about safety procedures or techniques, here are some sites at which you can find some fascinating information about oral sex.

Now Say, "Ahh"

Francis Mahoney: "What's the matter? Did you get your face caught in a zipper?"

—*Why Me?* (1990)

How Safe Is Your Oral Sex?

http://www.gai.com/text/aids22.htm

Free site

The U.S. Centers for Disease Control, the *Journal of the American Dental Association*, The AIDS Commission of Toronto, and several other respected organizations state their opinions here concerning the safety of oral sex.

Safer Sex

http://www.safersex.org/

Free site

To learn about safe oral sex practices, research studies, and the risks of contracting an STD from oral sex, go to **http://www.safersex.org/oral**.

Masturbation

Wanking, jacking off, choking the chicken.... For those who can't keep their hands off themselves—and why would you want to?—here are some sites that explore one of our favorite pastimes. (See Table 23.3 for some additional masturbation sites.)

Flying Solo

"As an amusement it is too fleeting; as a public exhibition there is no money in it."

—Mark Twain on masturbation

Wankers Over 50

http://www.wankers.com/

Membership site

Alternate title: Everything you ever wanted to know about the art of self-stimulation. This site is supposed to be for single men older than 50, but we also found it interesting. It includes a FAQ page, suggested techniques and toys, and a fabulous list of 100 or so euphemisms for masturbation including clearing the snorkel, going on Pee Wee's little adventure, loving the muppet, and the one gun salute.

World Wide Wank—The Stuck-Together Web Pages

http://www.well.com/user/earl/WorldWideWank.html

Free site

'Tis a silly site (to paraphrase *Monty Python*). The thoughtful hosts have everything in nice, big print for those with "masturbation-induced vision impairment." You will find an interview with Larry David (writer of *Seinfeld's* "The Contest"), masturbation-related quotes, masturbation mistakes (ouch!), helpful tips from religious tracts on how to stop, and—if you don't *want* to stop—you can read Bianca's *Good Vibration Masturbation Guide* (**http://bianca.com/shack/goodvibe/masturbate**).

Table 23.3   Additional Masturbation Sites

Site Name	Address
alt.sex.masturbation FAQ	**http://www.masturbationpage.com/ asmfaq.html**
Jackin' World	**http://www.jackinworld.com**
#Masturbation Home Page	**http://www.masturbation.org**

That Hits the Spot (Literally): G-Spot Information

Guys, if you don't know where the G-spot is, you certainly *should*. No more excuses. These sites tell you what you need to know. Your partner will thank you for it, enthusiastically.

If you don't know where the G-spot is located, check this figure from About The G-Spot.

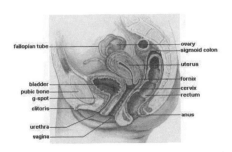

Did You Say Feminine or Feline?

"You made a woman *meow*?"

—*When Harry Met Sally* (1989)

Table 23.4   G-Spot Information

Site Name	Address
About The G-Spot (That Mysterious Pleasure Zone)	**http://minou.com/aboutsex/gspot.htm**
About the G-Spot	**http://www.sexuality.org/mvgstim.html**
G-Spot Play	**http://very-koi.net/gspot.htm**
The G Spot and Female Ejaculation	**http://www.txswingnet.com/art002.html**

Kissing

Kiss. Hello Kiss. Goodbye Kiss. French Kiss. Kiss me, you fool! I Want to Kiss You All Over. Kiss from a Rose. It's In His Kiss. And Then He Kissed Me. Birthday Kiss. I Kissed a Girl. Na Na Hey Hey Kiss Him Goodbye. Kiss Me Quick. Just One Kiss. First Kiss. Howza Bouta Kiss, Babe? Sealed with a Kiss. Kiss Me, Bliss Me. Eso Beso! Kiss Me Like You Mean It. Kisses Sweeter Than Wine. Love & Kisses.

When in Rome

Quentin Hapsburg: "You do speak French don't you?"

Lt. Frank Drebin: "Unfortunately, no...but I do kiss that way."

—*Naked Gun 2 1/2: The Smell of Fear* (1991)

As these song titles attest, kissing is a sweet, lovely thing. If you want to learn more about the how's, why's, and when's, visit the Web sites in Table 23.5.

Table 23.5 Kissing Information and Technique Sites

Site Name	Address
The Art of Kissing Homepage	http://www.kissing.com/
Dr. Date's Guide to Kissing	http://www.doctordate.com/archives/guide58.html
Kissing	http://www.flirts.com/kissing.html

Sexual Information, Techniques, and Assorted Silliness

We were amazed to find so much informative, fun, and sexual material on the Web. Visit the sites in this section to round out your education. You will find a list of additional interesting sites in Table 23.6.

Table 23.6 Other Sexual Information Sites

Site Name	Address
About Anal Sex	http://minou.com/aboutsex/analsex.htm
Billy Wildhack: Swimming with the Sexbots	http://www.billywildhack.com
Erotica's Sex Tutorials	http://www.skinful.com/erotica
Go Ask Alice	http://www.goaskalice.columbia.edu
Kinsey Institute for Research in Sex, Gender, and Reproduction	http://www.indiana.edu/~kinsey/
Michel Foucault's History of Sexuality	http://cgi.student.nada.kth.se/cgi-bin/d95-aeh/get/foucaulteng
My First Time: Erotic Stories of Love and Sex	http://www.myfirsttime.com
Sexual Health Network:	http://www.sexualhealth.com/
Sexual Health Infocenter	http://www.sexhealth.org/infocenter
Sexual Positions	http://www.skinful.com/erotica/positions/positions.htm
Skinful Erotica's Sex Tutorials	http://www.skinful.com/erotica
Ten Rules of Anal Sex	http://www.sexuality.org/l/incoming/analrule.html

The Adult FAQ Website

http://www.adultfaq.com/

Free site

Do you have a question about sex? Better still, do you have an *unusual* question about sex? This is the place to get it answered. You'll find 72 FAQ links that cover vanilla sex and beyond...*way* beyond. (If a little knowledge is dangerous, would a lot prove to be safe?)

Center for Positive Sexuality

http://www.positive.org

Free site

Parents, here's a site for your teenager that has good information about sex. "No preaching. No moralizing. Just the facts." Pamphlets and posters can be ordered from the site for a nominal charge.

Dr. Ruth Online!

http://www.drruth.com

Free site

Good ol' Dr. Ruth. America's most famous sex therapist is not only a best-selling author, lecturer, media personality, and professor, she also has her own Web site filled with FAQs, sex tips, sex polls, desktop goodies, and discussion boards. (And while we're on the subject of sexual advice, let's not forget the Playboy Advisor at **http://www.playboy.com/faq/faq/advisor**.)

Ivillage.com Relationships

http://www.ivillage.com/content/0,1625,2549,00.html

Free site

This page is all about how to "Jump Start Your Sex Life." Not that anyone we know might need to read this (we know *you* certainly don't), but just in case you know some poor souls who might benefit....

Nights Of Passion

http://www.h-studio.com/nights/passion.html

Commercial site

Seduction for Two is a card game for couples to help them rekindle the romance in their relationship. The site also has a great list of ideas to try out at home. Here's an example:

> #32 Improving "Afterplay": Listen to romantic music while cuddling. Saying "I love you" has very special meaning when whispered. Keep refreshments and a towel within reach. Engage in light and fun conversation. Share with your partner what you liked. Stay awake by massaging your partner.

The Pink Kink Catalog

http://www.razberry.com/raz/pink/top.htm

Free site

If you look for something hard enough, you're sure to find it. This site lists examples of "kinky" sex found in mainstream romance novels. Its purpose is to demonstrate that women are every bit as likely as men to be drawn to themes of domination. Here's just one example of what they found:

> On page 116: She is punished by the hero who sexually arouses and then refuses to satisfy her. She issues him a general apology, but he says: "You must be specific, woman; thus you will remember what earned your punishment."

—*Warrior's Woman*, by Johanna Lindsey (Avon Books, 1990)

Sex Laws

http://laws.home.ml.org/

Free site

This is serious stuff—a state-by state listing of sex-related laws. Although most of the laws make perfect sense, you might be surprised to learn what is illegal where you live. Do you know that oral sex is illegal in some states, for instance? It never hurts to be informed.

Sexologist

http://www.sexologist.org/

Free site

The American Board of Sexology sponsors this search site listing board-certified sex therapists, counselors, and educators in every state.

Not Again!

"If sex is such a natural phenomenon, how come there are so many books on how to do it?"

—Bette Midler

Sexuality.org

http://www.sexuality.org

Free site

This is it. The best. No doubts whatsoever. We would type this site name in *neon*, if we could, with big flashing arrows pointing to it. Anything you ever wanted to know about sex and its myriad variations is sure to be covered somewhere in the hundreds of informative articles to be found at Sexuality.org.

The Top Ten Things Men and Women Do Wrong in Bed

http://www.tumyeto.com/tydu/features/meninbed/meninbed.html

http://www.tumyeto.com/tydu/features/meninbed/womeninbed.html

Equal-opportunity kvetching at its finest. (*Note*: Men get *way* more than 10 things to whine about. No fair!!)

The Wet Spot

http://www.arlington.com/~pmouth/wetmain.html

Free site

This is an advice site with smart, friendly answers to questions about sex and relationships.

World Sexual Records

http://www.ece.utexas.edu/~jmeans/Worldsex.html

Free site

They're all here: the biggest, smallest, longest, shortest, most prolific, and the truly astounding. Here's one of our favorites:

Chi Kung is an ancient Taoist art of body control (it dates back to 2700 B.C.) and claims to resist disease, retard aging, prolong virility, and, in general, make one a sexual superstar. What makes this art unique is that one can only achieve this sexual nirvana by strapping weights to his penis and doing repetitive lifts.

Even if the supposed benefits don't materialize, you will at least have a new method of carrying a six-pack in from the car.

The Least You Need to Know

➤ You can learn about safe sex practices from dozens of excellent Web sites. You can also learn how to recognize and deal with sexually transmitted diseases.

➤ If you have any questions about the effectiveness of condoms, as well as how to choose and when to use them, major condom manufacturers' sites will tell you exactly what you need to know. You can even buy them directly from the same Web sites, as well as from the many condom catalogs available online.

➤ Everybody talks about the G-spot, but few men seem to believe that it's real or—if they do—know where it is. Improve your love life by learning that the G-spot is *not* a myth.

➤ Kissing is one of the most pleasurable things we can do with our lips. You can learn all about it from kissing Web sites.

➤ You can learn a lot online to improve your sex life. One of the best things about sex education on the Web is that so much of it is based on people's personal experiences, which they can share anonymously.

Part 3

Chat

This part focuses on chat (the process of interacting in real-time with other people on the Internet by typing to one another) by using audio (microphone), and by using video (desktop video camera). The chapters discuss the process, techniques, etiquette, and dangers of chat, as well as the software you need and where to get it. These chapters also point you to some of the best chat environments available on the Internet.

Chapter 24

An Introduction to Chat

In This Chapter

➤ Preparing for chat by picking a screen name

➤ Learning the special language of chat

➤ The ins and outs of chat relationships

➤ Protecting yourself and your identity

Unless you have been living under a rock, you have already heard about *chat*, the process of having text-, audio-, or video-based conversations with people on the Internet. Recently, chat has been heavily covered by magazines, newspapers, and TV talk shows—concentrating for the most part on the lurid aspects of it, such as the broken marriages, broken hearts, and the occasional murder that results from putting your trust in strangers. Dangers aside, chat is an excellent way to meet new people, make friends, and fall in love (or lust).

Who chats? Everybody! At any given moment on a chat server or dedicated chat program, it's not unusual to find males and females ages 14 to 60, single, married, separated, or divorced, all chatting with friends or trying to be noticed. My mother-in-law bought a computer just so that she can chat! We have met physicians, psychologists, bikers, and deep-sea divers in chat. The *only* thing we can assume that chatters have in common is access to a computer and the Internet.

Where and How Can I Chat?

As recently as a few years ago, participating in chat meant that you logged on to an *IRC* (Internet Relay Chat) server, joined a chat room (sometimes called a *channel*), and started typing. IRC chat rooms often contain 20 or more people, logged on from all over the world. Do not confuse IRC channels with Netcaster channels (part of Netscape's Communicator) or the Microsoft Channel Guide (included with Windows 98), neither of which have anything to do with chat. These channels deliver Web content to your computer. IRC channels differ completely from those.

In the past few years, however, chat has changed from IRC group chats. You can now chat "graphically" on Web pages or run a dedicated chat program that enables you to do any or all of the following:

➤ Have private conversations with another user

➤ Exchange files with users, such as personal pictures

➤ Instantly see when your chat friends are online and exchange messages with them throughout the day

➤ Play sound effects as you chat

➤ Web surf with others, leading them to Web pages that you want them to see

➤ Represent yourself as a character in a 3D world, walking around and *looking* for people to chat with

➤ Use a microphone and/or desktop video camera for audio and video chats

See Chapters 25, 26, and 27 for information about available chat programs, as well as how to obtain and use them.

To give the devil his due, we have to admit that although IRC was the first group chat program, it certainly isn't the one that has attracted all the publicity and attention from the media. Historically, IRC has just been too arcane and difficult to set up and use. When the media talks about chat, they usually refer to America Online, which really popularized the idea of online chat before the big Internet boom in 1995.

For more information about using America Online, see Chapter 9.

Choosing a Screen Name

To chat you must first pick a chat name (also called a *screen name* or *handle*) to identify yourself to others. In some chat environments, you may be able to change names as often as you want. In others, you may be stuck with the name you pick.

One Name, Many Names

You can have a different name in every chat environment or program. In some, you can even have *multiple* names or create a new name every time you log on. If you want chat friends to be able to find you, it's a good idea to find a name that you like and stick with it. When you want to be anonymous or are hiding from certain chatters, use a different name.

Depending on the name chosen, you may find that a lot of people want to talk to you or, conversely, that you're widely shunned. Here are some tips for picking a chat name:

➤ **If possible, try to choose a name that reflects your sex** A gender-neutral name provokes two reactions: (1) Guys will hit on you, assuming that there's at least a 50-50 chance that you're female; and (2) others may not talk to you at all, because no one likes to look foolish by guessing another person's sex incorrectly.

➤ **Interesting spellings are fine, as long as they can easily be typed** To get your attention in a group chat, people will have to address you by your chat name. You want your name to invite people to talk to you, so don't create one that is impossible to spell or contains 50 characters (and, therefore, takes forever to type).

➤ **Clever and witty count—especially in screen names** Until you begin typing, all people can see is your name. Clever names attract conversation.

➤ **Decide the types of people you want to attract** Because screen names are created rather than bestowed on you at birth, people will assume that your name reflects who you are—your profession, location, or interests. (If you want to come off like a warthog, try a name like Asslovr or Big10inch.)

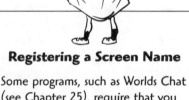

Registering a Screen Name

Some programs, such as Worlds Chat (see Chapter 25), require that you register your screen name. Once registered, the name may be difficult or impossible to change. Before settling on the first one that pops into your head, try it out in another chat program and gauge the reactions it gets.

The Language of Chat

The first time you wander into a chat room and start reading the text as it scrolls up the screen, you may be stunned by what you see. All the spelling, capitalization, and punctuation rules you learned while growing up are out the window!

In chat, expediency is king. Until you get the hang of chat, and learn to type with lightning quickness, get your message across with as little effort as possible. Forget the Shift key—many chatters don't capitalize proper nouns or the first word of a sentence because it's too much work and slows down their typing. (*Aside from James:* In two years of chatting, I have only met one chatter other than myself whose chat conversations read like correspondence—that is, complete sentences with proper capitalization and punctuation.)

To save even more time, commonly used words and phrases are often reduced to abbreviations or acronyms, and emotions or facial expressions are represented by *smileys* or *emoticons*. Read the following sections to learn many of the ways that you can communicate with as few words as possible.

Chat Shorthand

To quickly express a thought, action, or emotion, chatters have concocted hundreds of text abbreviations and acronyms that will initially leave you scratching your head. Table 24.1 lists the ones we have seen used most often. You should be able to safely incorporate them into any chat without leaving others scratching *their* heads.

Table 24.1   Chat Abbreviations

Abbreviation	Meaning
asl or a/s/l	Age, sex, location? (frequently typed in group chats to learn information about others in the room)
bbl	Be back later
bfn	Bye for now
brb	Be right back
btw	By the way
cul8r	See you later
cya	See ya (good-bye)
dl	Download
eg	Evil grin
ggp	Gotta go pee
im	Instant message (AOL term)
imho	In my humble opinion
irl	In real life (as opposed to chat)

Abbreviation	Meaning
k	Okay
lmao	Laughing my ass off
lol	Laughing out load
lpk	Long passionate kiss
msg	Message
pls	Please
ppl	People
r	Are
roflmao	Rolling on floor laughing my ass off
rotfl	Rolling on the floor laughing
tia	Thanks in advance (when requesting a favor)
ttfn	Ta-ta for now
u	You
ur	Your
w/(*some text*)	With (as in, "w/cheese")
wb	Welcome back
y	Why
zzz	Sleeping or bored

During a chat, if you see an abbreviation that you don't understand, don't be afraid to ask what it means. You may mark yourself as a newcomer for *that* chat session, but you will never have to ask again, right?

If you would like to see a *lot* of chat abbreviations—including many obscure ones—pay a visit to Shano's Acronym Database at **http://www.shano.com/acronym/**.

Expressing Actions

To differentiate actions from the surrounding text, it's common practice among chatters to surround the action with asterisks or angle brackets. To send someone a kiss, for instance, you might type ***kiss*** or **\<kiss\>**. Other examples include ***hug*** and **\<hug\>**; ***smile***, **\<smile\>**, and ***s***; and ***grin***, **\<grin\>**, ***g***, and ***eg*** (evil grin).

269

Smileys (Emoticons)

Another way to express emotions in chat (or in email, for that matter) is by typing *smileys*—facial expressions created by combining character symbols.

The common smiley is typed like this:

:-) or **:)**

To see the smiley face, tilt your head to the left (all smileys lie on their side). The ":" represents the eyes, the "-" is the nose, and the ")" is the smile. As you can see, the nose is optional.

Most chatters restrict themselves to a few common smileys, such as these:

;-)   A wink, used to indicate that something clever or suggestive was just said.

:-(A frown or sad face.

:->   A devilish or sarcastic remark has been made.

Frankly, we are too lazy to use (or memorize) most of the thousands of smileys that exist. If you want to use them like a chat pro, visit **http://members.aol.com/ bearpage/smileys.htm** for more info.

Chat Relationships and Romance

As you spend more and more time in particular chat rooms, channels, and dedicated chat programs, you will meet many people who will become friends. The capacity for deeper relationships is there, too—whether it be romance, love, sex, or all of the above that interest you. Many people develop serious relationships on the Net, and the dynamics of chat encourage it in the following ways:

➤ **Net time is compressed, when compared to real time.** A month or two of companionship in chat often seems like 6–12 months of real time. In fact, it's not uncommon for people who have known each other in chat for less than a month to progress to a cross-country or international meeting.

➤ **Being attracted to someone in chat means that you admire his or her mind, not just looks.** When you find yourself attracted to someone in real life, it's often because of the way he or she looks or the sound of his or her voice. In chat, people know you only by what you *say* (reflecting what you *think*). With the physical aspects conveniently out of the way, you will find a lot of people who seem attractive.

➤ **Chat relationships occur because of the amount of time devoted to chat.** Although a few people pop in and out of chat at their convenience, many more treat chat as their new hobby, devoting hours each day to it, seven days a week. A typical chat session may last several hours. When was the last time that you spent several hours talking to your girlfriend, boyfriend, or spouse? Under these circumstances, it's harder to figure out why relationships *don't* occur.

Five Attractive Qualities in a Chatter

If you're looking for a chat relationship, you will find that the qualities others seek in chat partners parallel those attributes they look for in real life.

1. **Intelligence and wit**   Much of group chat—particularly in IRC, AOL chat, and other similar environments—consists largely of inane babble. The witty stand out.

2. **Sense of humor**   Knowing what's funny; knowing when and when not to laugh; and being able to evoke an occasional smile, giggle, or guffaw can score big points.

3. **Honesty and openness**   Nobody likes a liar and—unless you tell the same lies to everyone—it's easy to get caught.

4. **Empathy**   Many people come to chat because they are troubled about something in their lives. Being a good listener is an important attribute to possess.

5. **Reliability**   Treat chat appointments like you would any other appointment. If you're expected at a certain time and program (or chat channel/room) but can't be there, send email or an instant message.

The Progression of a Chat Relationship

Most romantic or sexual chat relationships have a fairly predictable progression.

1. **Initial attraction**   "Gee, she's witty (or sexy or sensuous or flirtatious). Maybe we have things in common."

2. **We meet again ... and again**   The frequency or length of your chat sessions increases. You look forward to seeing her and may find yourself sitting online, waiting for her to appear. Your conversations now involve mild flirting—regardless of whether you are naturally flirtatious.

3. **Planned chat meetings**   You plan your schedules around each other. You may talk at regular times each day.

4. **Aural meetings**   You find yourself dying to hear what the other sounds like, so you agree to meet in a voice chat program (see Chapter 26) or exchange phone numbers.

I Had a Day Like That, Once

"And what's romance? Usually, a nice little tale where you have everything *As You Like It*, where rain never wets your jacket and gnats never bite your nose and it's always daisy-time."

—D. H. Lawrence

5. **Cyberlove and/or cybersex ensues** It appears that you have found a girlfriend, boyfriend, or lover. Because this may well be a long-distance relationship, you strive for the next best thing to being there: cybersex in chat programs or phone sex.

6. **Meeting in real life** This is the big step in any chat relationship—crossing the line between fantasy and reality, and deciding whether to pursue a physical aspect to your relationship. Like blind dates, many chat relationships come to a screeching halt at this stage. Others, however, blossom into a sexual relationship, love, and even marriage.

Exchanging Pictures

You probably noticed that the exchange of pictures wasn't mentioned anywhere in these steps. It wasn't mentioned because when—or *if*—it takes place can vary considerably. Some people *never* exchange pictures—because they haven't had one scanned or have no recent ones; because they don't want their chat partner to know what they look like or are not confident about their looks; or because doing so removes the relationship from the realm of fantasyland, forcing it to cross over into real life (occasionally with a resounding *thunk*).

Those looking for a real relationship rather than just a Net one often insist on seeing a current picture soon after meeting a new person. In fact, doing so on the first meeting may be the only time when such a request isn't treated with suspicion or worry. Waiting until after an attraction has been acknowledged leaves you both in the uncomfortable position of recognizing that the relationship may end after the picture exchange—with hurt feelings on one or both sides.

Reconciling Chat with Real Life

Determining how chat fits into your real life causes extraordinary concern and pain for many chatters. It tends to be most troublesome for those who are already married or in a committed relationship. If this is your situation, the questions that you will have to wrestle with include the following:

➤ **Is this fantasy or reality?**   If you treat chat relationships as harmless fun and have no intention of ever meeting in person, it might not have an impact on your real-life relationship (but don't count on it). Many people rationalize their chat relationships in this manner; some are more successful than others.

➤ **Is a Net relationship or cybersex cheating?**   A better question to ask is this: "Is my cyber relationship interfering with my real one?" If you find your-self spending more time with your cyberlover than your significant other or spouse, consider a request to stop chatting as an intrusion on your cyber romance, or think that sex with your spouse or significant other is cheating on your chat partner, the answer is a big YES!

➤ **What am I seeking in chat?**   Married people in particular should answer this question before venturing into chat. If you're just looking to kill time and perhaps find a few new people with whom to share ideas, chat may be an excellent outlet for you. If you're in a relationship, however, chat can pose serious problems. If you wouldn't want your wife to spend several hours a day talking to strange men, don't be surprised if she feels the same way about you doing so with strange women. And if you don't believe that chat can cause problems in marriage, ask around. You will be astonished at the number of women and men in chat who are in the process of going through a divorce—often triggered by supposedly harmless chat relationships.

Cyber Romance: Stories and Sociology

If you would like to read about some actual cyber relationships (ones that worked and ones that didn't), receive advice on managing them, or learn more about how such relationships work and the issues involved, visit the Web sites in Table 24.2. To learn more about *cybersex* (having virtual sex with an online partner), read Chapter 27.

Table 24.2   Cyber Romance Web Sites

Site Name	Address
Cyber Romance 101	**http://web2.airmail.net/ walraven/romance.htm**
Cybermating and Virtual Romance	**http://www.discovery.com/area/ history/courtship/courtship6.html**

continues

Table 24.2   Cyber Romance Web Sites CONTINUED

Site Name	Address
Cybersociology	**http://members.aol.com/ Cybersoc/is1nikki.html**
Electronic Relationship Advisor	**http://www.pan-arts.com/era/**

Keeping It Safe

We tell our kids not to talk to strangers. But that's exactly what we do in chat. We're talking to people that we have never met in person. It's not unusual to find ourselves opening up to them; telling them secrets about our lives, ambitions, and fantasies.

If you're a newcomer to chat, it's important to remember that chat is filled with the same mix of people that you would find anywhere. Some are nice, and some aren't. In chat, we have seen people who picked fights with others just to provoke a reaction, ones who impersonated us and tried to ruin our reputations, others who made up rumors and spread lies, and a few who have stalked our friends.

Keep in mind that everyone you meet in chat may not be who they seem. It's commonplace for some chatters to experiment with *gender-shifting* (pretending to be female when they're actually male or vice versa), make up things about themselves to liven up the conversation, or just tell outright lies. Women in chat have a common saying that tells the whole story: "There are no short men in cyberspace."

While you are sorting out who to trust in chat and how much personal information you can safely give them, remember these tips. (Some people *never* veer from these rules—even with people they have chatted with for a year or more.)

➤ Keep your last name private. A first name is enough to identify you and avoid the "Hey, you!" syndrome.

➤ When someone asks where you are, your state is sufficient. (If you aren't from the United States, your *country* is enough.) The less detailed information concerning your location that you offer, the less likely someone will be able to find (or stalk) you.

➤ *Never* give out your phone number or address unless you're ready to have that person show up unannounced at your front door.

➤ This isn't a police interrogation. You don't have to give out *any* personal information. Think of it this way: If you wouldn't feel comfortable telling these details about yourself to a stranger you just met in Wal-Mart, don't feel obligated to tell it in chat.

➤ Think twice before accepting programs from other chatters. It's not uncommon for hackers to send viruses or system control programs embedded in what appear to be innocuous programs. After running these programs, you may be opening yourself up to serious security problems. (Our son recently learned this lesson the hard way: He had his hard disk reformatted by a 12-year-old hacker.)

➤ Do not assume that your anonymity is protected by the Internet. Experienced Internet users can track down people through email and other methods.

If your children chat, make sure that they abide by these rules, too. If you're concerned that they might slip up, see Chapter 7 for a discussion of programs you can install to prevent this information from slipping out in chat. And, if at all possible, try to steer them to chat venues designed specifically for kids.

Please don't assume from this that everyone you meet in chat is a liar or potential stalker. But do keep in mind that *some* might be.

Protect Your Identity, but Don't Lie

Occasionally, someone will suggest that the best way to protect yourself in chat is to lie. Even if you can't see them or hear their voices, people in chat will become your friends. How would you feel if it turned out that someone you considered a friend had lied to you about major life details? Never forget that chat is *not* a computer game. Those are thinking, feeling human beings with whom you are conversing.

The Least You Need to Know

➤ Choosing a chat name isn't a trivial decision. Create one that reflects how you want to present yourself to others.

➤ Familiarize yourself with the most popular chat abbreviations, acronyms, and typing conventions. Whether you want to use them is up to you. Because others *will* use them, however, you need to know what they mean to follow the conversation.

➤ Love and sex are readily available in chat. If that's not what you're seeking, it's better to make up your mind before venturing into chat. Regardless of whether you want to participate in a relationship, relationships will find *you*.

➤ Chat relationships have a typical progression, much like relationships in real life.

➤ You can take concrete steps to protect your identity in chat. Think carefully before giving out key information such as your last name, address, or phone number.

Chapter 25

Text Chat

In This Chapter

➤ Exploring text chat in different chat environments (IRC, server-based chats, Web-based chats, and 3D chats)

➤ Learning the basics of cybersex

Text chat refers to any interactive conversation in which the participants type words to express their thoughts. It doesn't matter whether the words appear on a Web page, a dedicated chat program, or an instant messaging program—or even whether the person doing the typing is represented by an icon or a three-dimensional avatar. It's *all* text chat.

We can categorize text chat by the type of environment in which it occurs, and that's how this chapter is divided. This chapter explores the following text chat environments:

➤ IRC (Internet Relay Chat)

➤ Server-based chats

➤ Web-based chats

➤ 3D (avatar) chats

Even if you're convinced that chat has to involve audio or video to be meaningful or interesting, be sure to flip to the end of this chapter and read about *cybersex*. (Yes, it's real and can occur in *all* chat environments.)

An Intro to Text Chat

Regardless of the chat environment you decide to explore, you will find that text chat has several common features. First, after you start the text chat program or Java applet, you are asked to log on. If you're a new user, you are expected to supply a *username* to identify yourself to others. Some chat environments have restrictions on usernames, such as the allowable length and whether it can contain spaces. Also, usernames must generally be unique. If someone else has already registered the name, you are asked to pick another one.

Logging into IRC

In Internet Relay Chat (IRC), you can connect to hundreds of servers around the world. To log on, you must pick an IRC network (such as DalNet or TalkCity) and a server and port number (such as irc.dal.net:6667). IRC programs such as mIRC and PIRCH provide lists of networks and servers from which you can choose. If one network or server won't let you connect, try others.

After completing the logon, you will either be in the main chat area (in Worlds Chat, for example), be asked to choose a room/topic area (IRC, The Palace, and AOL Chat), or your name will be added to the list of online users (LOL Chat, AOL Instant Messenger, ICQ, and Powwow). Where you find yourself depends on the program/ chat environment you're in.

If you're entering a group chat environment, such as Worlds Chat or IRC, you are ready to begin chatting. In one-on-one chat environments, such as LOL Chat, AOL Instant Messenger, ICQ, and Powwow, you must first find someone to chat with— either by sending that person a message through the chat program or by waiting for someone to contact you in the same manner. Most one-on-one programs provide a way for you to send messages to others who are online—to introduce yourself and request a chat.

After you join a group or one-on-one chat, the chat process is pretty similar. You type a message and then do whatever the program requires to send it, such as pressing **Return** or clicking a **Send** button. (In some programs, such as ICQ chat and LOL Chat, your messages are sent as they are typed. There's no need to press **Return** except when you want to start a new paragraph.)

Messages appear in this scrolling window

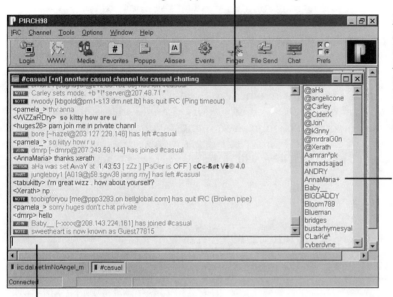

In IRC, messages are sent by typing in the message line and then pressing **Return** *to indicate that the message is finished. This screen shows a private chat session between two people.*

User list

Type your message text here

Group Chat Chaos

In group chats that follow the IRC model, it can take time to get used to the way that the messages chaotically appear onscreen. Basically, there is no order to the messages; no one is required to "take turns." Some people may quickly send half a dozen messages in a row, whereas others may say little or nothing at all. For this reason, some people use the main chat area only to find a willing chat partner, and then quickly retire to private messaging with that person.

IRC

IRC (*Internet Relay Chat*) is not a program or a company. It is a group of linked servers that enable thousands of individuals from around the world to simultaneously participate in group chats. The two most popular Windows programs for IRC chatting are shareware called mIRC (**http://www.mircx.com**) and PIRCH (**http://www. pirch.org**). If you have a Macintosh computer, you can use Snak (**http://www. snak.com**) to chat in IRC. Most IRC programs enable you to participate in multiple chats at the same time, conduct private chats with friends, run scripts, play WAVs, and more.

Although current programs go a long way toward simplifying IRC and extending its capabilities, it is a tough environment in which to learn about chatting. Designed to work with virtually any computer, IRC is command-line based—that is, unless your IRC program has menus to perform common commands, you must learn the IRC language to execute them. For example, you type **/me** before text to express an action (such as, **/me gives Rachel a tiny kiss** will print James gives Rachel a tiny kiss).

Microsoft Chat

http://www.microsoft.com/windows/ie/chat/

Microsoft Chat is an IRC-based chat program with a twist: Everyone is represented as a cartoon character in a comic strip (see the following figure). Text appears in a cartoon balloon above your character's head. You can freely switch between comic and normal IRC chat at any time.

Current users

Microsoft Chat is a radically different environment for IRC fans.

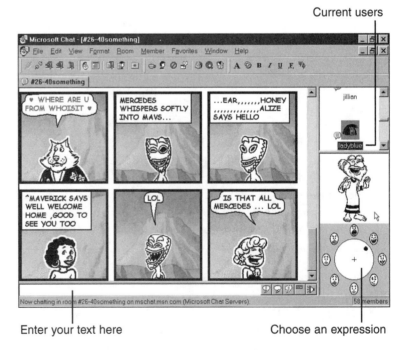

Enter your text here

Choose an expression

Java-Based Chat Sites

If you do much random Web surfing, you are bound to run into Web pages that have Java chat programs embedded in them. In most cases, these are IRC interfaces. (From a software standpoint, you're better off running a standalone IRC program, but accessing IRC from a Web page *is* kind of a kick.) If you'd like to put a Java IRC program (such as the one shown in the following figure) on your own home page, go to **http://www.webchatting.com**.

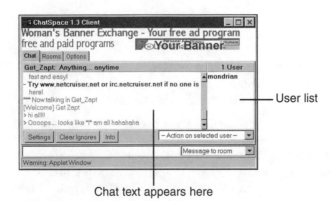

Friends who visit your home page can now chat with you—as long as you're there!

User list

Chat text appears here

Server-Based Text Chats

Following are some of the most popular server-based chat programs (that is, all users are connected to a central server).

LOL Chat

http://www.lolchat.com

Free software

LOL Chat has more features than most people will ever use. It's a real-time chat program in which each person gets a separate section of the chat window. You can exchange files, play sound and music WAVs for each other, and express yourself in a variety of fonts and colors. You can view the user list to see who's logged on and send a message to anyone you choose.

Many people can be in a chat, although one-on-one chats are far more common. You can copy and paste text into the chat window, keep track of your contacts with the Address Manager, Web surf as a couple or group, and launch an attached audio chat program so that you can talk rather than type. Best of all, LOL Chat is free.

The LOL Chat personal information pages are especially helpful. Reading them enables you to learn a bit about the people behind the chat names. Many people have pictures posted on their info pages, so you can also *see* whom you're talking to. (That's the theory, anyway.)

281

And now for the official LOL Chat etiquette directive:

> You can say whatever you want in a chat session with people who agree to that conversation. It is up to you to act like an adult and make sure that you keep it to the chat sessions. As we said above, we don't know what you're chatting about…we don't want to know…as long as you don't harass the other members of the community, you can do what you want in your chat sessions.

We can live with that.

AOL Chat

Many people get their first exposure to chat as AOL members. To reach the Chat area, click any **People Connection** icon or enter the keyword *people*. If you don't care about the topic, click **Chat Now** to join a general chat in the Town Square.

If you're looking for a particular topic, click **Find a Chat**. For sex topics, the best Featured Chat category to start with is **Romance**. Click it (or any other category), and then click the **View** button to see a list of all rooms for that category. To go to one of the listed rooms, double-click it or select it and click **Go Chat**. If the chosen room has fewer than 25 people, you will be added to its participant list and can begin chatting. If it's full, you may be offered the chance to join another room on the same chat topic that isn't full.

Member Chats, created by AOL members, has fewer topic restrictions.

Click to choose Member or Featured chats

Chat categories

Current room list and number of participants

You may also want to check out the Member Chats. These are chat rooms that have been created by AOL members. Because there are fewer topic restrictions, many of the more erotic chats can be found here. You can switch between the Featured and Member Chat lists at any time by clicking the appropriate button.

If you like, you can even start your own chat room. Click **Start Your Own Chat**, choose a category for the chat (such as **Romance**), and enter a title for the room.

After you're in a chat room, you can learn something about whom you're chatting with by double-clicking a person's name, and then clicking **Get Info**. If the person has created a member profile, it will appear onscreen.

AOL Instant Messenger

http://www.aol.com/aim

Free software

One component of the AOL software that users have raved about for years is Instant Messenger, a pop-up window in which AOL users can exchange messages or chat with any other AOL member who is online. Recently, a general version of AOL Instant Messenger was released. It enables Internet users to exchange instant messages or have chats with AOL users. An AOL Instant Messenger button can even be added to Netscape Navigator, so you can launch it without leaving your browser. AOL Instant Messenger is a great one-on-one chat environment and provides a way for non-AOL users to keep in touch with friends who are AOL members.

Searching for a Chat Room by Topic

If you don't see a chat topic that interests you, you can search for one by clicking **Search Featured Chats**, and then typing a keyword such as *kinky*.

ICQ

http://www.icq.com

Free software

The following is a test. You hear a helium-voiced female say "Uh-oh!" If your first impulse is to glance at your monitor so that you can respond to a flashing yellow box (signifying an incoming message), you are dismissed. The rest of you, please read on.

ICQ (as in "I Seek You") is a free multifunction program that lets you know when friends are online. After downloading and registering your copy of ICQ, you get your own ICQ number and the username of your choice.

Now comes the fun part: creating a contact list of friends (who also have the software). An unobtrusive control panel displays your list (see the following figure), showing who is online or offline. You can send messages and files, share URLs, chat in a separate text window, check your email, and launch related software, such as audio chat programs.

To-date, almost 8 million people use ICQ, and with good reason. It's easy to learn, has extensive online documentation, and does what it's supposed to do (most of the time). And, at least for now, it's free.

All message and chat commands originate in the floating ICQ window.

Powwow

http://www.tribal.com

Free software

Powwow offers one-on-one text chats, special areas (called *communities*) in which you can have group chats, and online games. Many of the communities created by the millions of Powwow users are strictly for adults. You can learn more about them at **http://ww2.tribal.com/Communities/adultcomm.cfm**.

Web-Based Chats

You can participate in any of the following text chat programs without leaving your browser by using a plug-in or ActiveX component or by running a Java applet. Some programs such as The Palace are also available as standalone applications.

Chatropolis

http://www.chatropolis.com

Membership site

As far as Web page-based adult chats go, Chatropolis seems to be the place to be. Although it is a membership site, new users can access plenty of free rooms for an introduction to how the site works.

The Palace

http://www.thepalace.com

Free software

The Palace is a two-dimensional chat environment. You are represented by an icon, small picture, or smiley face that you can move around on the screen. As you type, your words appear above your icon in a cartoon balloon. The Palace home page includes a list of sites that use its chat system.

More Web Chat sites

For a list of some sex chat sites, go to **http://webcrawler.com/people_and_chat/chat_by_topic/sex_chat**.

Although you can try out The Palace using any Java-enabled browser (such as Netscape Navigator or Internet Explorer), in the long run you'll prefer to use the dedicated standalone Palace software (to avoid Java-related crashes).

Yahoo! Chat

http://chat.yahoo.com/

Free site

Many search engines are offering new services to attract visitors. And chat—when done well—has the potential to attract a *lot* of users. Yahoo! has implemented an easy-to-use Java chat area. Be sure to wander into some of the adult rooms.

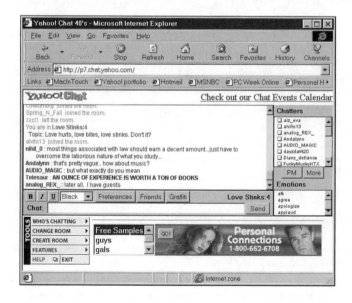

The Yahoo! Chat applet is almost as simple to use and as powerful as many standalone chat applications.

HTML-Based Chat Pages

Unless the chat is irresistible, flee these chat sites. HTML (*Hypertext Markup Language*) is the programming language used to create Web pages. Unfortunately, HTML isn't well suited for creating an interactive chat. One telltale sign of most HTML chats is that you are asked to repeatedly click the browser's **Refresh** or **Reload** button to check for new text. As you can imagine, this is *not* conducive to chat. (On the other hand, HTML won't crash Windows. Java applets can—and, in our case, frequently do.)

3D Chats

The three-dimensional chat programs are as realistic as you can get with a text-based chat program. Although the primary means of communication is still typed text (a few programs also have audio support), you are represented by a 3D character called an *avatar* that you can freely move about in a realistic 3D environment. Any character that you make eye contact with can also see you. When an avatar's back is to you, the person may not even know you are there. In fact, 3D chat programs often make people feel like they're in a computer game—the resemblance is inescapable. (At times, you may yearn for one of *Doom*'s chain guns, just to liven things up a bit when the chat gets boring.)

In any event, because the characters are solid and can be moved, the possibilities for sexual interaction—at least, *fantasy* sexual interaction—are there. Consider 3D chats a visual stimulus for your imagination.

Worlds Chat Gold

http://www.worlds.net

Commercial program

When you first go to Worlds Chat (a PC-only chat environment), you are asked to choose an avatar from their gallery. You'll see just plain folks, vampires, penguins, fish, aliens, and...the dreaded *plaid guy*! Guests have only limited choices in the gallery and are assigned ID numbers (rather than names) each time they enter Worlds Chat. Registered users, on the other hand, have many avatars to choose from and can even create their own. In addition, they have registered names (up to three can be created) rather than numbers.

After choosing an avatar, you enter the Hub (see the following figure). Worlds Chat (WC) is set in a space station; the Hub is a central area for arrivals and hanging out. You can select from six *pods* (theme rooms) by clicking on the map icon: Glee, Sadness, Sky, Desert, Garden, and Gothic. Guests must stay in the main pod areas, but members have a huge, wonderful world to explore. Gardens, orchards, a koi pond (don't step on the cat!), labyrinths, castles, and skywalks are just a few of the places members can visit. Each area has appropriate sound effects and music. It will take you weeks to see all of Worlds Chat, and even longer to learn its many tricks and secrets. You can even learn how to *fly*!

Move in this window

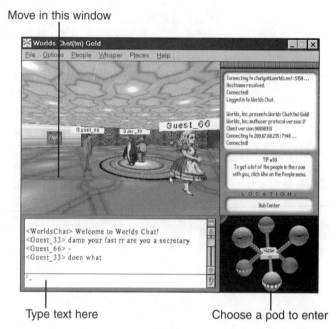

With little Alice and talking bunnies roaming about, Worlds Chat sometimes bears a resemblance to Wonderland.

Type text here

Choose a pod to enter

Worlds Chat has many private areas, and one-on-one conversations are usually respected by anyone who happens to "walk" by. Communication is text based. You can speak aloud to the room or pod, "whisper" to one person, or send a "group whisper" to a few select friends. If you want to know whether a friend is anywhere in Worlds Chat, you can page the person by typing her or his screen name, followed by a colon. Worlds Chat is extremely easy to learn and use.

You can make unlimited visits as a guest. We recommend that you download the guest version of Worlds Chat (**http://www.worlds.net/wc/downloadwc.html**).

You will find that the WC folks are a friendly, helpful bunch. (Just mind your manners.) In time, you'll discover that it's an interesting mix of Mayberry RFD and Melrose Place. As you can tell, we're rather fond of Worlds Chat. Should you decide to pay it a visit, give our regards to the cow. *Moooooo*!

Worlds Chat and Modem Speed

Even though Worlds Chat is a 3D chat program, it works great with even older modems, such as 28.8 and 33.6Kbps models. Because the data for all Worlds Chat rooms and characters resides on your hard disk (rather than on the Worlds server), the only information transmitted during a session are character positions and the chat text.

Microsoft V-Chat

http://www.microsoft.com/windows/ie/chat/

Free software

If you're raring to try out 3D chat, but don't want to invest much money (or *no* money), download a free copy of Microsoft V-Chat. In V-Chat, you connect to an IRC server and are represented as an avatar in a 3D environment. To people who are using text-based IRC programs such as Mirc or Pirch, you will appear as any other user— that is, anything you type will just show up in their text window. In this way, V-Chat works the same as Microsoft Chat.

Roomancer

http://www.moove.com

Commercial program

Roomancer is a 3D program that has been in beta for a *long* time, but it has real potential. The avatars can move in ways that mimic human movements, instead of merely gliding along like the avatars in most 3D chat programs. A single command can instruct your character to dance, give a nearby character a kiss (careful with that feature), or perform one or more exercise movements, for example.

Throughout the beta period, James never ran into more than half a dozen people. Perhaps the readers of this book can help populate Roomancer. You can download the guest version at **http://www.moove.com/visitor_us.htm**.

Cybersex: The Sound of One Hand Typing

Cybersex is sex between two (or more) people using the Internet as the medium. Participants describe what they would like to do (or imagine that they are doing) to each other, how (and what) they are feeling, and so on. Masturbation may or may not be a part of a cybersex session.

Cybersex is the ultimate form of safe sex. You are free from risk of disease because there's no physical contact. The only serious risks are emotional. Determining whether cybersex (or the intense emotions involved in an Internet romance) is real or fantasy is also up to the participants. To many, cybersex is very real. The people involved are interacting directly with each other, and the emotions, arousal, and orgasms experienced are also real. To others, it is merely a harmless form of entertainment, "zipless sex" between strangers, or a game of conquest.

Where does cybersex occur? The obvious place is in dedicated sex chat rooms, such as those found on many Web sites and in IRC channels with names like #sex and #netsex. Cybersex can also be found in almost any chat environment you visit, however. Horny people abound. It's just a matter of finding them...or of them finding you.

If you want some additional perspectives on cybersex and cyber romances, try the following Web pages:

➤ Cyber Romance 101
   http://web2.airmail.net/walraven/romance.htm

➤ Cybermating and Virtual Romance
   http://www.discovery.com/area/history/courtship/courtship6.html

➤ Electronic Relationship Advisor
   http://www.pan-arts.com/era

➤ Internet Dating, Love Online
   http://www.wildxangel.com

How About a Laptop Dance?

"Since we have two hands, what's wrong with having one of them on a mouse?

"I have always said that masturbation is perfectly natural and instrumental in preparing you for enjoying sexual pleasure with another person. The myth that it will make you go blind is only true if you stare at your monitor too long."

—Dr. Ruth Westheimer, "Spanking the Mouse: In Defense of Online Sex," *The Web Magazine* (1996)

The Least You Need to Know

➤ All IRC software (whether a dedicated program or Java applet) connects to the same IRC servers. This enables thousands of users running a variety of different programs to chat with one another.

➤ The Microsoft Chat and V-Chat programs add special features to IRC that are only visible to other people running the same program.

➤ Many chats are now implemented as Java applets that are part of some of the Web pages you can visit.

➤ In server-based chats, such as LOL Chat, all users generally connect to a single server, making it very easy to tell when your friends are online.

➤ In 3D environments, you are represented by an avatar and can freely walk around in three-dimensional rooms, changing your orientation to meet (or avoid) people.

➤ Cybersex can be a wonderful, emotional, and stimulating experience.

Chapter 26

Audio Chat

In This Chapter

➤ System requirements for audio chatting over the Internet

➤ Limitations of audio chat technology

➤ Using Freetel and Mplayer for audio chats

Whether you're just dying to hear a chat partner's voice for the first time or want to take cybersex to a new level, audio chat may be for you. With just a microphone and a free or inexpensive audio chat program, you're on your way.

Many audio chat programs are available, and many are free. This chapter shows you how several of them work.

Audio Chat 101

Audio chat (also known as *Internet telephony*) enables you to talk to other people over the Internet. Participants use their existing Internet connections to speak to one another instead of making long-distance calls. No charges accrue when talking on the Net, other than your normal ISP or information service fees. You can use audio chat programs to talk for free to people anywhere in the world.

Identifying Yourself to Others

When registering for most chat programs, there is generally no requirement that you use your real name or your real email address (unless the software company intends to email you some sort of confirmation). For privacy reasons, you may not want to provide either. In fact, most chat programs will accept *any* name or email address, as long as it looks real (such as zorro@elsewhere.com).

Audio chat has some limitations:

➤ It is *not* like using the telephone. The quality is seldom as good as a phone conversation, and it can include delays, lost speech segments, and echo.

➤ If you both speak at the same time, you invariably step on each other—that is, you may miss all or part of what the other says.

➤ You both must be on the Internet and running the software at the same time. (You may have to prearrange your calls.)

➤ You both may have to use the same program. Although some audio chat programs allow callers to use *other* chat software, many don't.

As you can see, Internet telephony is not a substitute for the telephone. But it is a fun way to talk for free with chat partners, while maintaining your anonymity. (Neither of you have to reveal any phone numbers.) Audio chat capabilities can be inexpensively added to most computers. All you need is a decent sound card (or a computer with built-in audio capabilities), an inexpensive microphone (typically costing between $10 and $30), a set of speakers or headphones, and an audio chat program. Most new PCs and Macintosh computers come with everything you need except the microphone and chat software.

Audio Chat Software

So that you have an idea of how audio chat software works, the following sections describe two popular products: Freetel and Mplayer. (Note that typical *video* chat programs, such as Microsoft NetMeeting, may also offer audio chat. See Chapter 27 for details.)

Half- Versus Full-Duplex Audio

Depending on the audio capabilities built in to your system (or those of a sound card that's installed) and the audio drivers you're using, you will be capable of transmitting either half- or full-duplex audio. *Half-duplex* audio means that sound can be transmitted in only one direction at a time—either incoming or outgoing. *Full-duplex* audio means that sound can simultaneously be sent and received.

The implication is that when both people have full-duplex audio capabilities, the conversation should be similar to talking on the telephone. In practice, however, this isn't the case. Unless you take turns talking and listening, you will miss much of what the other person says. (Full-duplex *is* better than half-duplex, but not significantly better.)

I Hear an Echo

Although many audio chat programs attempt to filter out background noises, you may occasionally notice that you hear an unsettling echo—that is, in addition to the other person's voice, you can hear your own. The usual cause for this is that the other person has his/her microphone too close to the speakers. To avoid this problem, users can increase the distance between microphone and speakers or buy a headset. (A headset with both speakers and microphone ensures greater privacy, too.)

Freetel

http://www.freetel.com

Commercial site

Freetel is a PC-only, advertisement-supported audio chat program. You can download and use Freetel as often and for as long as you wish, for free. If you decide to register your copy (for $29.95 or $39.95, depending on the additional features and capabilities you want), you get priority access to the Freetel audio server and the option to remove the advertisements from the program window.

As soon as you launch Freetel, it attempts to connect to its server, adds your name and personal comments to the directory of users who are currently online, and then displays the user directory. You have three ways to call another user:

➤ You can connect to anyone listed in the directory by double-clicking her/his name.

➤ If you have spoken to a person before, her/his name appears in the drop-down list on the left side of the Freetel window. Double-click the name to attempt to connect with that person again.

➤ If you can't remember a person's screen name, you can type part of it into the text box (at the top of the name list) and click Find. All matching names will be shown in the directory window.

Picking a Chat Name for Freetel

If you're into random chats and want to improve your visibility in the user directory, give yourself a last name that begins with an unusual character, such as a tilde (~). Because the directory is sorted alphabetically by last name, your name is more likely to be seen by others if it appears near the beginning or end of the directory. (Special characters cause this to happen.)

Speaker controls   Current username

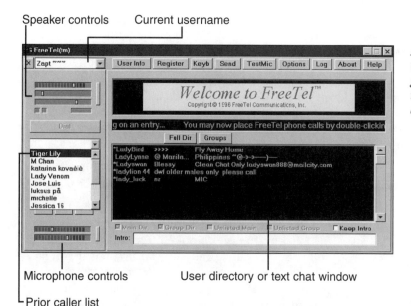

After a call is in progress, the Freetel window can generally be ignored—unless you need to make audio adjustments.

Microphone controls   User directory or text chat window

Prior caller list

Audio quality in Freetel varies from crystal-clear to mediocre, depending on the participants' computer hardware, audio server traffic, Internet traffic, the phase of the moon, and color of underwear you happen to be wearing (at least it sometimes seems this way to us). The same can be said for virtually any audio chat program, however. If the audio quality is bad, you can use the Boost option to improve it—at the cost of a greater audio delay.

During conversations, you can type messages in a chat window. This is especially useful when you need to correct communication problems. Freetel also allows file transfers between users. They occur in the background and are not supposed to interfere with the audio.

Calling from Text Chat Programs

LOL Chat (a text chat program discussed in Chapter 25) can be configured to launch Freetel at the click of a button, automatically attempting to initiate a voice call between you and the person with whom you are currently chatting.

Mplayer

http://www.mplayer.com

Membership site

How about a nice game of backgammon or Hearts? Mplayer combines Internet game-playing with chat. You can use Mplayer for straight chatting (text or audio), chatting while playing a game ("Ooooo … Nice move, sexy!"), or just playing games while keeping your comments to yourself.

Basic membership in Mplayer is free, but you can only chat and play certain games. Paying members can play additional games, including head-to-head commercial ones, such as Quake.

Private Chats

If you want to be alone with someone in Mplayer, you can start your own room. Click the Create Room button, add a password to the room, and then let your chat partner know the room's name and password. Everyone else is locked out.

After logging on and reaching the main menu, click the Chat button or, if you're up for it, click Games and choose a game that you want to play. If you pick Chat, you are shown a list of the chat areas. If sex or love is what you're looking for today, try the Romance area.

Next, you are transported to the Chat Lobby for the chosen area. You can type to others that you see here, joining in the group discussion. To find out more about someone in the Lobby, right-click the person's name and choose View User's Member Profile. To move to any of the existing chat rooms (where you can talk to fewer people and use audio), double-click the room name or select it and click the Enter Room button. After you're in a room, all you have to do to talk is click and hold down the Talk button, and then speak into your microphone.

Other Internet Telephony Programs

The particular audio chat program you select will depend on many factors, including the following:

➤ The amount of money you're willing to spend

➤ Whether you have a PC or a Macintosh (not all programs are available for both platforms)

➤ The particular program(s) your chat partners use

➤ Whether you also want or need video chat capabilities (see Chapter 27)

Table 26.1 lists several additional audio chat programs you may want to consider.

Table 26.1 Other Internet Phone Programs

Site Name	Address
GatherTalk	**http://www.cixt.cuhk.edu.hk/gtalk/**
Net2Phone	**http://ww.net2phone.com/**
PhoneFree	**http://www.phonefree.com/**
Speak Freely	**http://www.fourmilab.ch/netfone/windows/ speak_freely.html**
VocalTec Internet Phone	**http://www.vocaltec.com**
VoxPhone Pro	**http://www.etech-canada.com/world.htm**

The Least You Need to Know

➤ With the addition of an inexpensive microphone and an audio chat program, most Internet-connected computers are ready for audio chatting. Computer-to-computer chatting carries no additional charges beyond what you already pay your ISP or information service (such as America Online).

➤ Audio chat is not as clear, convenient, or echo-free as a telephone call.

➤ Video chat programs often support audio chat, too.

Chapter 27

Video Chat

In This Chapter

➤ Group video chatting with CU-SeeMe

➤ Video chat etiquette

➤ Using one-on-one video chat software

If text and audio are good, then video chat is better. You don't have to type smiley faces or *hahaha* to show that you're smiling or laughing. The other person can see (and, optionally, hear) *exactly* what you're doing.

Like other types of chats, there are only two basic kinds of video chats: group and one-on-one. In group video chats (popularized by a program named CU-SeeMe), anywhere from two to two dozen people may be transmitting and sending video simultaneously. One-on-one chats are equally popular and can be very conducive to video sex. Although many of the one-on-one programs (such as Connectix Videophone) are commercial, Microsoft NetMeeting (a free program) has made this type of chatting readily available to all.

Except on an Airplane

"Never do anything standing that you can do sitting, or anything sitting that you can do lying down."

—Chinese proverb

Group Chats with CU-SeeMe

Developed at Cornell University as a free program and also available as a commercial program from White Pine Software, CU-SeeMe is the premier program for group video chats. Perhaps the best way to imagine what CU-SeeMe is like is to imagine a text-based chat session with live video.

Cheap Video Cameras

The QuickCam (**http://www. logitech.com/Cameras**) represents one of the cheapest entries into the world of video chat. Current color models can be purchased for around $100.

Free Phonebook

Streak's Reflector Scanner provides a downloadable reflector list that you can import into your CU-SeeMe phonebook. This is an excellent way to get started with CU-SeeMe without having to hunt for working reflectors.

Chat participants all connect to the same server (called a *reflector*), and everyone transmits video of themselves at the same time. Because most reflectors can support between 8 and 25 users, you decide how many video windows will be open and which participants you will view. As in text chats, members are identified by a handle or nickname rather than by their real names. CU-SeeMe also has a text chat window in which you can enter or view comments.

To participate in CU-SeeMe chats, you need only two things: the CU-SeeMe software and a desktop video camera (or an ordinary video camera connected to a video capture card).

CU-SeeMe (**http://www.wpine.com/software**) is considerably easier to use and has a superior interface to the free Cornell software (available from **http://www.cu-central.com/CUv1.htm**). You can download an evaluation copy of the program from the White Pine site. The only restriction when running the evaluation copy of the program is that your video chat connections will automatically disconnect after 15 minutes.

Using CU-SeeMe

CU-SeeMe does not have a central server to which you connect as you do in some chat programs, such as LOL Chat and Worlds Chat. Instead, you choose the particular reflector you want to visit (much like choosing a chat room in IRC or a Web page with your browser) by entering its *IP* (Internet Protocol) address in CU-SeeMe. For a list of reflector addresses, go to Cammunity (**http://www.cammunity.com**), CU-SeeMe Reflector Lists (**http://www.rocketcharged.com/cu-seeme**), and Streak's Reflector Scanner (**http://scanner.cuseeme.net**).

Conference IDs Are Important, Too

Some reflectors support multiple chat rooms (called *conferences*). Some conferences may be for adults only, others for couples only, and so on. By default, when you connect to a reflector, CU-SeeMe assumes that the conference ID is 0 (zero)—usually a general room. If the reflector has other areas, you must know their specific conference IDs. (You can usually find out about the conference IDs by reading the reflector's home page on the Web or the CU-SeeMe connection screen that appears when you connect to conference 0.)

To set a conference ID for a reflector using White Pine's CU-SeeMe, right-click the reflector name in CU-SeeMe's Contact list, choose **Properties**, and click the **Connection** tab. If you are manually dialing the reflector, click the **Conference** tab. If you are using the free Cornell version of CU-SeeMe, you set a conference ID by opening the phonebook, selecting a reflector, and then typing the conference ID in the box provided.

The best way to determine whether it is worth creating a contact card for a reflector (using the White Pines software)—so that you can easily visit it again—is to make your initial visit using the Manual Dial feature. Follow these steps:

1. Click the **Manual Dial** button.
2. Type or paste the reflector's address (such as 207.155.127.16) in the Internet Address box.
3. Click the **Conference** tab to set the conference ID (if it is any number other than 0).
4. Click **Manual Dial**.

If the connection goes through and you enjoy your visit, you can create a contact card for the reflector by clicking the **New Card** button. After a reflector has a contact card, you can connect to it any time you like by double-clicking the reflector's name in the Contact Cards list.

Gone with the Wind

Like personal Web pages, reflectors come and go. They may also change IP addresses or add new conference IDs. If a reflector has a Web page, be sure to bookmark it to avoid forever losing a favorite reflector.

Of course, the majority of your CU-SeeMe sessions will involve reflectors that are in your Contact Cards list or phonebook. You can visit any reflector by just double-clicking its name.

After the connection to a reflector is made, windows will automatically open to display the video of other connected participants. To close any user's video window, double-click it (White Pines) or click the close **X** (Cornell). Similarly, to view the video of a different person, double-click her/his name in the Participant list. If you want to chat (as well as see and be seen), type your comments into the chat box and press **Return** to send them. When you want to leave the reflector, click **Hang Up** (White Pines) or **Disconnect** (Cornell).

Turn Off Your Microphone, Bunky

Because video is the point of CU-SeeMe, you'll find that most reflectors do not want users to transmit audio as well—it wastes bandwidth and competes with the video transmissions.

CU-SeeMe Etiquette

The following few tips will keep you from incurring the wrath of the reflector owners (*refmons*) and other users:

➤ **Check your send and receive settings**.

Each reflector has preferred settings. If yours are set too high, it creates problems for other participants. (Try 15–25 frames per second for both the maximum send and receive settings, and 1–5 frames per second for the minimums.) If you are unsure what the proper settings for a given reflector should be, just ask the question in the chat window.

➤ **Obey the site restrictions**.

Many sites—both general and adult—have rules governing what is and is not proper behavior. Violations may result in your ejection from the reflector. Begging women to put on a show is usually a no-no, for example, as is similar rude behavior. (The philosophy is that if someone wants to show off, she or he will.) Appropriate appreciative comments when it *does* happen, however, are always welcome. If a single person attempts to enter a couples-only site, he/she will usually be disconnected.

Similarly, don't assume that all reflectors are for adults. In fact, the majority of reflectors are not adults-only. Colleges and businesses set up many reflectors. Transmitting nude video of yourself or discussing sex on these reflectors will invoke the same reactions you would get if you stripped in front of the neighborhood supermarket.

➤ **No lurkers are allowed**.

Most sites do not allow *lurkers* (people who do not transmit video) or they limit them to a few people. If you do not have a camera or do have one but don't have CU-SeeMe set to transmit video, you may find that you won't be allowed to connect to some reflectors or—after being connected—are quickly disconnected.

➤ **No direct connections without an invitation**.

Sending private messages to participants (*geeking*) or attempting a direct one-on-one connection is considered rude at best and a serious reflector infraction that will get you banned at worst. Always ask first or wait for an invitation.

➤ **No video captures**.

Although some people freely expose themselves in adult CU-SeeMe sessions, few of them want the pictures saved for posterity. Refrain from capturing the images.

Like a Frat Party

"In a typical CU-SeeMe session, what you have is a bunch of horny guys trying to coax one woman out of her clothing."

—Steve, an East Coast refmon

Membership Reflectors and Conferences

Like sex sites, some reflectors and conferences are set up as money-making ventures. Strip clubs and sex-related Web sites sometimes run reflectors as an added attraction, for example. And an adult-oriented reflector can have better control of the action if it is a members-only site.

These sites may just bar all nonmembers from entering, place a limit on the number of nonmembers who can connect at any given moment, or limit nonmembers' connect time. If any restrictions apply, they will normally appear on the reflector's initial connection screen.

Note that many reflectors have their own home page on the Web, so you can read about membership requirements as well as any restrictions that guests have imposed on them. Visit CU-Central (**http://www.cu-central.com**) for an example of a typical membership reflector's Web site or SINamaXXX (**http://www.sinamaxxx. com**) for info on several free adult reflectors.

Get CUnnected!

http://www.mindspring.com/~uh-oh/cunnect.htm

Commercial site

If you're tired of repeatedly trying to connect to busy reflectors, the CUnnect auto-dialer program can help. As the site advertises:

> "CUnnect is a utility program designed to automate CU-SeeMe connections. Once activated, it will relentlessly attempt to connect to even the busiest reflectors. With features like Multi-dial, CUnnect can cycle through a list of your favorite reflectors and notify you of a CUnnection by playing your favorite .wav file. It keeps track of your time online and even avoids long lock out periods by automatically reCUnnecting you just before your time limit is up. It can even translate phone books between different versions of CU-SeeMe."

One-on-One Video Chat Software

One-on-one video chat software is also very popular among the romantically and sexually inclined. Unlike CU-SeeMe, one-on-one programs normally rely on one or a mere handful of dedicated servers. This usually means that you can easily find your friends, because you are always connecting to the same server.

Microsoft NetMeeting

http://www.microsoft.com/netmeeting

Because it is free and widely available, Microsoft NetMeeting is quickly becoming to one-on-one chats what CU-SeeMe is to group chats. And unlike CU-SeeMe, there are no NetMeeting lurkers. Although NetMeeting is well known as a video chat program, you are not *required* to transmit video. Many users are perfectly happy sticking with NetMeeting's audio and text chat components. NetMeeting is also well suited to one-on-one business conferences because it includes features such as a shared "whiteboard" (a drawing area in which both participants can simultaneously draw and write), a text chat window, and the capability to transfer files and share computer programs.

When you start NetMeeting, it attempts to connect to one of nine servers. Once connected, your name is added to the list of online users for that particular server. You can chat with any user on any server, however. To view the directory for a server, choose its name from the Directory or Server drop-down menu. To call a person, double-click his or her directory entry. If the person accepts your call, you can begin chatting immediately—using video, microphones, or the text chat window.

Speed Dialing

If a chat is one that you might like to repeat, you can add the caller to your Speed Dial list. Each time you log on to NetMeeting, the program checks all servers to see whether any of the people on your Speed Dial list are online. You can then call them by double-clicking their entry. This saves you the hassle of trying to find them when you don't know what server they are logged on to.

An icon here shows that the
user has a video camera

To see a different server's
directory, select it here

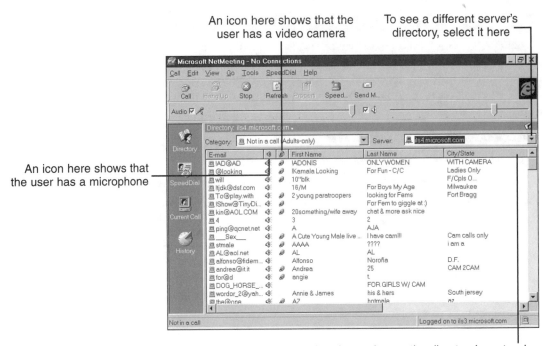

An icon here shows that
the user has a microphone

Click a column header to change the directory's sort order

Other One-on-One Video Chat Programs

A wide range of one-on-one video chat programs are available (see Table 27.1), and
some of the major programs, such as Microsoft NetMeeting are free or offer free trial
versions. Some one-on-one programs can also be used for group video chats.

Table 27.1   One-on-One Video Chat Programs

Product Name	Address
CineVideo/Direct	**http://www.cinecom.com**
Clearphone	**http://www.clearphone.com**
I Visit	**http://www.ivisit.com**
Intel Video Phone	**http://www.connectedpc.com/cpc/videophone**
WebPhone	**http://www.halcyon.com/welcome/webphone.htm**

The Least You Need to Know

➤ To experience video chat, you need a desktop video camera (available for as little as $100) and a video chat program. A microphone is optional, but occasionally can be used with one-on-one video chat programs.

➤ The most popular software for group video chats is CU-SeeMe. You can connect to free CU-SeeMe reflectors all over the Net. Some reflectors, however, require a membership.

➤ CU-SeeMe reflectors are identified by unique IP addresses, in the same manner as Web sites.

➤ If you don't like group chats, you may want to try one of the many one-on-one video chat programs, such as Microsoft NetMeeting.

Glossary

When you read an Internet, computer, or sexual term that is unfamiliar to you, turn to this section for a definition.

ActiveX component Add-on software (especially for Microsoft Internet Explorer) that provides your browser with new features, such as the capability to play particular types of multimedia files or handle streaming video. ActiveX components, or objects, can be automatically downloaded and installed for you.

adult verification system or **age verification system** A password system (such as Adult Check) that verifies that you are an adult and can legally enter some sexually oriented Web sites. An annual or monthly fee applies for most adult verification systems. You should note that many such systems exist, and each Web site will specify the ones they accept.

address, site See *URL*.

address book An email program feature or a related utility that you use to record individuals' and companies' email addresses. These programs often offer facilities to record other useful information for each address, such as a mailing address, phone numbers, Web URL, and so on.

address box The box in a browser window where you can type or paste the address (or URL) of the Web page you wish to visit.

amateur site A Web site that features pictures of women and men who are not professional models.

anime A Japanese cartoon art style, frequently featuring characters with large, round eyes. *Manga* is the family-oriented version; *Hentai* is the adult version.

AOL Abbreviation for *America Online*, a popular information service and Internet service provider.

aphrodisiac Traditionally a food, scent, or substance that arouses the sexual senses.

application A computer program; software that you run to accomplish a particular computing task, such as word processing, Web browsing, or reading and sending electronic mail. The terms *application* and *program* are used interchangeably.

archive One or more files compressed (reduced in size) into a single file.

attachment A file sent along with an email message.

avatar A three-dimensional, movable character used to represent you in some chat programs, such as Worlds Chat.

AVI A movie clip stored in the Microsoft Windows Audio/Video Interleave format. AVI files may or may not be able to be displayed on your computer, depending on the compressor that was used to create them.

banner A clickable advertisement found on many Web pages. When you click a banner, it takes you to a different Internet site.

BBS Abbreviation for *bulletin board system*. A local, national, or international computer service where you can dial in through your modem to exchange messages with other users and—in most cases—download files of various types. Many software and hardware companies maintain bulletin board systems to provide an additional way for their end users to contact them. Privately run BBSs have all but disappeared in today's Internet environment.

BCC Abbreviation for *blind carbon copy*. In an email message, persons listed in the BCC line receive a copy of the message, but their names are not visible to other recipients (those in the To or CC lines).

BD/SM or **BDSM** Abbreviation for bondage and discipline/sadomasochism.

BinHex An encoding scheme used to send Macintosh files over the Internet (as email attachments or downloadable files, for instance).

bookmarks Within your browser, a list of favorite Web pages and sites. By choosing a bookmark from a menu or separate window, you can easily return to the site. (Netscape Navigator calls them *bookmarks*; Internet Explorer calls them *favorites*.)

bps Abbreviation for bits per second. Refers to the connection speed of your modem to the Internet. A 33.6Kbps modem, for example, means that the modem's top speed is 33600bps. (When a modem uses one of the many common data-compression routines, the *actual* speed or throughput can be as much as 400% faster.)

browser   A computer program used to view content on the part of the Internet known as the World Wide Web.

browser cache   A portion of your hard disk set aside by your browser to temporarily store graphics and other material that has been downloaded by your browser from the Web pages you have visited. When you visit a page that hasn't recently changed, the browser loads as much of the material from the cache as it can, instead of downloading everything from the Internet again.

CC   Abbreviation for carbon copy or courtesy copy. In an email message header, entering a person's email address in the CC line results in that person receiving a copy of the message as well as those whose names appear in the TO line.

channel   An IRC chat room on a particular topic, or a special preconfigured topic area for Internet Explorer that can lead to Web pages.

chat   Conversing with one or more people on the Internet in real-time by typing messages, using microphones, or using a desktop video camera.

chat room   A discrete area of a chat server or program, usually dedicated to a particular topic, such as "Married and Flirting."

click-through   Clicking a banner in one site to go to another, which generates a record of the identity of the referring site and may result in a small cash payment to the referring site's owner.

Close box   The tiny box (Macintosh) or X (Windows) in a window or dialog box that, when clicked, closes the window or dialog box.

commercial site   A Web site that generates income by selling items or services, such as calendars, T-shirts, or phone sex. See also *free site* and *membership site*.

Control Panel   A Windows or Macintosh system software utility, usually used to control hardware (such as the display) or to provide systemwide software features.

CU-SeeMe   A popular program for group video chats, available from Cornell University (free) and White Pines Software (commercial).

cybersex   A shared sexual experience during a text, audio, or video chat session.

demo   A demonstration version of a commercial software program that has limited features or stops functioning after a specified time period. Manufacturers often provide free demo versions online so that users can determine whether they would like to buy the full working version of the program.

dental dam   An implement, often fashioned from a piece of a condom, used to prevent the oral spread of sexually transmitted diseases (STDs) during cunnilingus.

desktop video camera A camera connected directly to your computer that is capable of transmitting live images in real-time.

dialer A program used to connect the computer to the Internet, such as Dial-Up Networking (Windows) or PPP and FreePPP (Macintosh).

dialog box A small window that appears in response to some user action, usually to prompt the user to do something, enter some information, or make a choice.

disclaimer The legal notice you have to read and agree to before entering an adult site.

domain name The registered name of an Internet service provider, government unit, educational unit, or commercial company, such as AOL.com, Worldnet.net, and so on. The domain name is the last segment of every email address (such as spiffy.net in **bob276@spiffy.net**) and is often a portion of Web addresses (such as **http://www.intel.com**).

download To electronically receive a file (a program or image, for example).

electronic greeting card A greeting card that you design on the Web by choosing a picture, the text of the greeting, and optional elements such as music and animation. A pickup number is then emailed to the recipient, notifying her or him that a card is waiting at the Web site.

email (sometimes **e-mail**) Abbreviation for *electronic mail*; text and other documents exchanged between users over the Internet.

email address The unique name that identifies an Internet account, composed of a username, the @ symbol, and the domain name where the account resides (such as **zippie@gogomedia.net** or **kbbaby35@aol.com**).

encryption Encrypting a file scrambles its contents, making it unreadable by others unless they know the password/keyword to unscramble it.

Favorite Places Similar to browser Favorites and Bookmarks, the Favorite Places list in the America Online software enables users to record their favorite areas of AOL and favorite Web pages, and then revisit them at any time by just choosing them from the list.

Favorites See *bookmarks*.

fetish A sexual preoccupation with a particular type of object (such as panties, leather, or latex), body part (such as feet or breasts), or sexual activity (such as spanking or bondage).

Forward When referring to email, forwarding a received message causes a copy of it to be sent to a new recipient. It's a common practice for many people to forward great jokes that they received as email, for example.

free site A Web site that anyone can enter and fully explore without being asked to provide a credit card number or any other form of payment.

freeware Free-for-use computer programs.

FTP File Transfer Protocol, the protocol used to move data to and from FTP sites (file repositories on the Internet).

geeking Sending uninvited, private messages to another user in a CU-SeeMe chat.

gender bender An individual in chat who poses as a member of the opposite sex.

GIF files GIF is a file format (Graphic Interchange Format) popularized by CompuServe, one of the larger information services. GIF and JPEG (Joint Photographic Experts Group) are the two graphic file formats that can appear on Web pages. GIF files are normally used for drawings; JPEGs are popular for photos.

guest Anyone who is using a membership Web site without having paid a subscription fee. Guest privileges at the site are normally time-limited or have other restrictions.

history A list of recently visited Web pages automatically created by your browser. Clicking entries in your History list or folder is one way to revisit Web pages that you did not store as Favorites or Bookmarks.

home page A Web site's main or starting page.

HTTP Hypertext Transfer Protocol, the protocol used to transfer data over the World Wide Web.

HTTPS Secure Hypertext Transfer Protocol, the HTTP protocol encapsulated in a Secure Socket Layer connection to make it difficult for anyone to see the information being transferred. Frequently used for credit card transactions on the Internet.

Inbox The area of an email program where all incoming/new messages appear.

Information service A commercial online content provider, such as America Online and CompuServe.

installer A program used to install another program and related files. Usually the term *installer* is reserved for Macintosh programs. Windows installers are generally called *setup programs*.

Internet A network of millions of computers around the globe, all connected via telephone lines, cables, and wires, enabling connected users to view and exchange data in the form of Web pages (HTTP), email, and files (FTP).

Internet service provider (ISP) A company that provides Internet access for end users. When accessing the Internet, you instruct your computer to dial a telephone number that connects you to a computer at the ISP's office.

IRC (Internet Relay Chat)   A text-based group chat environment. Some IRC servers are designed to handle thousands of chat participants at the same time, divided into hundreds or thousands of chat areas called *channels*.

ISP   See *Internet service provider*.

Java applet   A program written in the Java language, normally displayed running in a browser window. Browser-based chat is often implemented in Java, for example. While loading, you can usually recognize a Java applet by the conspicuously empty gray box it displays in the browser window.

JPEG file   A file format used to transfer photos and other graphics in a highly compressed form. Developed by the Joint Photographic Experts Group. Also see *GIF files*.

keyword   A one-word text string, such as *elephant*, *redhead*, or *sex*, that you enter as a search criteria. Most search engines enable you to enter multiple keywords or phrases, in addition to performing single-keyword searches.

link   Text or graphic embedded in a Web page, email message, or newsgroup post that, when clicked, displays a different Web page—either in the same or a different Web site. A Web site creator can also use links to display a different area of the current page, instruct your browser to download a file, or create a blank email message with the To: address already filled in.

lurker   An individual in a CU-SeeMe chat who is not transmitting video of herself/himself. Many reflector sites limit the number of permitted lurkers.

mailing list   An email list to which you can subscribe, guaranteeing regular deliveries of a particular type of material, such as dirty jokes. Depending on how the list was designed, the material may all come from a single source or it may consist entirely of messages from the list participants (much like a newsgroup).

member   When referring to a sexual Web site, a member is an individual who has joined the site, normally by paying a subscription fee.

membership site   A Web site that charges a fee—usually based on a period of time, such as a week or month—to permit people to view the material contained in the site.

minimize   To shrink a window so that it can only be seen in and accessed from the Windows taskbar.

modem   A hardware device (either inside your computer or outside of it) that enables computers to connect to the Internet or to another computer over a standard telephone line.

MOV files   Movie clips that are in QuickTime (Apple Computer) format. Other popular formats for movie clips are AVI and MPEG. See also *movie clip*.

movie clip   Any downloadable movie file. See also *MOV files* and *streaming audio and video.*

MPEG   Movie clips compressed in the MPEG format. The Motion Picture Experts Group developed the MPEG format.

newsgroup   A set of Usenet messages on a particular topic, such as **alt.sex. binaries.erotica.spanking**.

newsgroup reader   A program used to read, send, and manage newsgroup posts and subscriptions.

parental controls   Software or a software option that enables parents to limit what their children can do on the Internet, such as accessing sex sites, giving out their real names and addresses in chat, and so on.

plug-in   A browser add-on used by Netscape Navigator that provides new capabilities, such as the capability to play certain types of sound or video files.

polyamory   Loving more than one person. Known in some quarters as "swinging" or "the lifestyle."

pop-up consoles   When you visit or click certain links in some sexually oriented Web sites, additional browser windows automatically open. Although these windows occasionally serve as navigation consoles for the site (enabling you to easily jump from section to section), more frequently they are just advertisements for other services or other sites. To many users, pop-up consoles are extremely annoying and sites that employ them are to be avoided.

post   (n.): A newsgroup message. (v.): To send a message to a newsgroup.

RSACi   Abbreviation for Recreational Software Advisory Council on the Internet; sponsors one of the major Web page content rating systems. The RSACi system is implemented in Internet Explorer.

real-time   Occurring now. For example, most chats occur interactively in real time.

Reflector   A CU-SeeMe server to which users connect, identified by a numeric address such as **250.222.16.30**.

Refmon   Abbreviation for reflector monitor; the individual who runs a given reflector site.

refresh   To reload the current Web page from the Internet.

screen saver   A program or utility that displays a moving pattern or series of pictures after a predetermined time of computer inactivity (5 minutes, for example) has elapsed.

scrollbar   A gray bar at the right side or bottom of a document window that, when clicked in, changes your view of the current page, scrolling it up and down or left and right. You can also click the arrow at either end of a scrollbar to make the document scroll.

search engine   A Web page (or component on a Web page) that enables you to search for information on a Web site, across the entire Web, or in newsgroup messages. To use a search engine (AltaVista, for instance), you enter keywords that describe what you are seeking, such as *polyamory* or *sex toys*.

Secure Socket Layer (**SSL**)   An encryption mechanism used by the Secure Hypertext Transfer Protocol, and other protocols, to ensure that the transmission isn't intelligible to anyone other than the party for whom the information is intended.

server   A computer dedicated to managing Internet network traffic, such as validating user logons, handling incoming and outgoing email, and managing access to files, for example.

setup program   See *installer*.

shareware   Computer programs that you can "try before you buy." If you like the program, you are required to send its author the requested fee.

spam   Unwanted, unsolicited advertisements, usually in the form of email or newsgroup posts.

Status area   A portion of a window or its frame where messages are relayed to the user. In most browsers, for example, the status area is in the lower-left gray area of the browser window and is used to show that particular materials are being downloaded from the Web, the identity of the URL for the link the cursor is currently over, and so on.

STD   Abbreviation for sexually transmitted disease.

streaming audio and video   Audio or video files that play as they are downloaded to your computer. The most popular streaming audio format is RealAudio. Popular streaming video formats include RealVideo and Vivo.

StuffIt Deluxe   A Macintosh utility used to create and open file archives. If your only interest is extracting files from downloaded archives, a utility called StuffIt Extractor is all you need. See also *ZIP file*.

subscribe   When referring to newsgroups, this indicates that you have instructed your newsgroup reader to follow a particular newsgroup by recording its name and periodically downloading new posts. You can also subscribe to email *mailing lists*.

surfing (also **Web surfing**)   A colloquial term for using a browser to visit pages on the World Wide Web.

taskbar The bar normally found at the bottom of the Windows desktop that shows the names of all programs currently running.

Terms of service The restrictions and privileges that a subscriber is granted for a particular service, such as an ISP, America Online, chat sites, and Web sites.

thumbnail A tiny graphic representation of an image (a photograph or drawing) that, when clicked, displays the image at full size.

URL (Uniform Resource Locator) The address on the Internet of a particular Web page, such as **http://www.yahoo.com**.

Usenet See *newsgroup*.

username The name or "handle" that you use to identify yourself to other chat program participants, such as SexyGrrl or roadrunner25.

wallpaper An image displayed as the Windows desktop.

WAV A common Windows audio file format; frequently used to record sound effects, speeches, and music. Other popular formats for audio files include AU, AIFF (Macintosh), MP3 (music with vocals), and MIDI (instrumental music).

Web browser See *browser*.

Web page One page of a Web site.

Web site A collection of linked, related Web pages created by a person or company.

Web surfing See *surfing*.

World Wide Web The graphic- and multimedia-rich portion of the Internet; frequently referred to just as the Web.

ZIP file A Windows/PC archive consisting of one or several compressed files. ZIP archives are commonly used on the Internet to package related files together and to shorten transmission times. To create an archive or to extract its contents, you must have a special program, such as WinZip. See also *StuffIt Deluxe*.

Index

321

T

Taskbar Properties dialog box, 96
tattoos, 156-157
    see also body modifications
telephones (Internet), 291
text
    chat
        3D, 286-290
        AOL Chat, 282
        AOL Instant Messenger, 283
        ICQ, 283
        IRC, 279-280
        Java-based, 281
        LOL Chat, 281-282
        Microsoft Chat, 280
        navigating, 278
        Powwow, 284
        server-based, 281
        Web-based, 284-285
    saving, 24
    software, 23-24
therapists (sexologists), 258-262
Throbnet Websites, Inc., 186
thumbnail graphics, 37-38
toys (sex), 213-216
    advanced, 217
    erotic food, 219-220
    jewelry, 215
transvestites, *see* cross-dressing
travel and erotic vacations, 243-245
trials (free), Web sites, 108
Trojans, *see* condoms
troubleshooting platforms, 41
Turbo Browser
    installing, 74
    keyboard shortcuts, 75
    starting, 74-75
    viewing graphics, 73
    Web site, 73
typing URLs, 33

U

uncompressing files, 77-79
    StuffIt Expander, 78-79
    WinZip, 77-78
Uniform Resource Locators, *see* URLs
unsending email, 121
unstuffing files, 19-20

URLs (Uniform Resource Locators)
    AltaVista, 24
    Amsterdam Tonight, 46
    Angelfire, 67
    copying, 33
    DejaNews, 24
    Erotic Postcards, 176
    Free Agent, 17
    Gay Sex from Amsterdam, 188
    Hardchannels, 184
    Hotmail, 67
    Hotpants Asia, 184
    iname, 67
    Kim's Page, 185
    Live Sex from Amsterdam, 187
    Lycos, 24
    Microsoft, 14
    Netscape, 14
    Paint Shop Pro, 18
    Persion Kitty's Adult Links, 83
    RChat, 28-30
    searching, 28
    Sexside.com, 189
    Sizzle, 185
    Smut Archives, 186
    Space Amazones, 188
    StuffIt, 19
    Throbnet Websites, Inc., 186
    Turbo Browser, 73
    WinZip, 19, 77
    Yahoo!, 67
    zdnet.com, 19
    zdnetmail, 67
Usenet newsgroups, 24, 60
utilities
    downloading, 38
    encryption, 100
    hiding files, 99
    picture viewers, 71
        file compressors, 76-79
        Quick Vue Plus, 75-76
        Turbo Browser, 73
        Web browsers, 73
    StuffIt Expander, 78-79
    WinZip, 77-78

V

vacations (erotic), 243-245
Victorian vices, *see* BD/SM
video, 24-25
    cameras, 12
    chat, 29, 299
        conference/reflector memberships, 304
        creating contact cards, 301
        group (CU-SeeMe), 300-303
        lurkers, 303
        Microsoft NetMeeting, 305
        one-on-one software, 305-307
        reflector addresses, 300
    formats, 41
    interactive, 187, 190-192
        executing, 45
        Gay Sex from Amsterdam, 188
        Live Sex from Amsterdam, 187
        Sexside.com, 189
        Space Amazones, 188
    Kim's Page, 185
    live
        searching, 26
        software, 26
    pay Web sites, 109
    Scour.net, 185
    searching, 25
    Sizzle, 185
    Smut Archives, 186
    streaming, 184
        executing, 42-44
        freeware, 44
        Hardcore channels, 184
        Hotpants Asia, 184
        Throbnet Websites, Inc., 186
View menu commands
    Arrange Icons, 73
    Folder Options, 98
    Internet Options, 90
    Refresh, 98
View Pro, 18
viewers (graphics)
    Internet software, 18-19
    Word 97, downloading, 23
viewing
    adult material, restricting children, 94
    email (AOL), 118

327